Better than Alphα

Better than Alpha

THREE STEPS TO CAPTURING EXCESS RETURNS IN A CHANGING WORLD

CHRISTOPHER M. SCHELLING

New York   Chicago   San Francisco   Athens   London
Madrid   Mexico City   Milan   New Delhi
Singapore   Sydney   Toronto

1 2 3 4 5 6 7 8 9   LCR   26 25 24 23 22 21

ISBN   978-1-264-25765-2
MHID   1-264-25765-1

e-ISBN   978-1-264-25766-9
e-MHID   1-264-25766-X

This publication is designed to provide accurate and authoritative information in regard to the subject matter covered. It is sold with the understanding that neither the author nor the publisher is engaged in rendering legal, accounting, securities trading, or other professional services. If legal advice or other expert assistance is required, the services of a competent professional person should be sought.
                —*From a Declaration of Principles Jointly Adopted by a Committee of the*
                American Bar Association and a Committee of Publishers and Associations

McGraw Hill books are available at special quantity discounts to use as premiums and sales promotions or for use in corporate training programs. To contact a representative, please visit the Contact Us pages at www.mhprofessional.com.

Contents

PART III
Evolving Alpha

9   Process Alpha—Smart Habits 195

10   Organizational Alpha—Smart Governance 221

11   The Future of Alpha 259

       References and Suggested Reading 267

       Index 283

Acknowledgments

During my career, I have worked with some fantastic investors, mentors, and colleagues, all of whom together are too numerous to list. But I would be remiss if I didn't explicitly thank Keith Black and TJ Carlson. No one has been more instrumental in my approach to research and investing than Keith, nor anyone so influential to my thoughts on management and governance as TJ. I am indebted to both.

Of course, I must thank my editor Stephen Isaacs and the rest of the team at McGraw Hill for shepherding an entirely unprepared new author through the publishing process. His patience and counsel have been much appreciated. I have also been fortunate enough to profit from the confidence placed in me as a writer and the generous benefit of helpful edits over the years by my colleagues at *Institutional Investor,* namely Mimi Chiahemen for her tireless support, Amanda Cantrell for her unerring improvements to my work, and of course Leanna Orr and Kip McDaniel for their leadership. I would not be an author without them.

This book was also immeasurably improved by the input of several friends who generously gave of their time to read drafts of the manuscript and make helpful suggestions along the way, including Brian Portnoy, Gailen Krug, Bruce Cundick, Ben Happ, and last but most emphatically not least Tom Masthay. I greatly appreciate their insights.

Lastly, to my readers: Writing a book on investments is an act of hubris, insanity, or most likely some combination of the two. I'll leave it to you to decide which relative proportions apply in this case, but I'm incredibly grateful for your attention nonetheless. I can say with absolute certainty I have learned far more from writing this than you will from reading it, so thank you for indulging me.

1
What Is Alpha?

Tactics without strategy is the noise before defeat.
—SUN TZU

Introduction

Whether you are a young employee entering the workforce and beginning to save for retirement, a middle-aged executive putting money aside for college tuition for your kids, or a pension plan manager investing billions to generate the income that retired pensioners will use to pay for their groceries and mortgages, we all need to invest. But figuring out how isn't so easy.

One of the challenges consumers of financial products face, individuals and institutions alike, is deciphering the seemingly unending stream of acronyms, buzzwords, and professional jargon created by this increasingly specialized and technical industry. Too often, the point is not to move toward clarity for clients, but rather to create confusion and opacity by drowning them in interminable verbosity.

After all, an uninformed and confused client makes for a more profitable counterparty, just like the easy mark at the poker table. If people don't fully understand what they are buying, and can't assess the relevant risk and potential conflicts of interest, they certainly won't be able to appropriately price the asset or service.

Complexity is beguiling. It could be the synthetic collateralized debt obligations that were marketed and sold by investment banks during the global financial crisis as high-quality bonds despite being made up of credit default swaps, which themselves were derivatives of other underlying shaky loans. Or it might be a relative-value hedge fund with thousands of line items across dozens of strategies and little transparency other than the impressive math credentials of the founders and some aggregated risk statistics. But as a result of this complexity, the Street usually gets the investor to overpay.

You may ask yourself what's all this got to do with alpha? Well, alpha is another technical term with a mathematical definition that can be used to mislead. Even when not intentionally misused, it can still create unnecessary confusion where simpler, clearer language might better serve clients' needs. And just possibly, alpha has never really existed at all.

I've spent the past 15 years at various institutions trying to identify investment firms that actually do "generate alpha," and the simple truth is that the vast majority of them do not, despite the fact that nearly all of them pretend to. (Even many of the ones that sell beta claim to do it better than their peers!) At times, I've been beguiled by the alpha mirage and have hired investment shops in the mistaken belief that they will beat a market. Sometimes they have, but often I've discovered that it was actually just luck, or worse, simply unappreciated risk. I've even seen a hedge fund refer to its historical returns as "100% Pure Alpha" in its pitchbook, only to witness that same hedge fund implode and shut its doors a few years later.

Soon individual investors will likely face some of these same challenges. The so-called democratization of alternatives is increasingly allowing retail investors to access alternative investments like private equity and hedge funds, which have historically only been available to institutions. This inexorable development is the result of competitive pressure not only from the industry as firms look to find creative ways to sell products like liquid alternatives through retail distribution channels, but also from regulatory changes designed to permit and even encourage individual investors to participate in these markets directly.

After hearing about the strong performance of the hedge fund masters of the universe for decades, aggressive retail investors have been clamoring to get in on the hedge fund action that previously only accredited investors had access to. Never one to forgo latent demand, Wall Street created products intended to replicate or mimic the return streams of average hedge funds. So-called liquid alternatives have grown substantially, from an estimate of less than $100 billion in assets industrywide in 2008 to $350 billion by 2018. However, since these liquid products were packaged into SEC-registered investment vehicles, such as mutual funds or exchange-traded funds, they were prevented from actually implementing the same strategies utilized by hedge funds. Although assets under management have surged, returns have disappointed.

Recently, there has even been talk about permitting more investors into private vehicles. The JOBS Act of 2012 was a first meaningful salvo in the regulatory battle. This law was intended to encourage the funding of small businesses, but by increasing the permitted number of shareholders of record in private companies from 500 to 2,000 and removing some restrictions around marketing, it also allowed hedge funds and private equity funds, which are structured as limited partnerships, to do the same thing. And many took advantage of this fact, aggressively peddling their wares to high-net-worth and mass affluent investors. In fact, sales of true private alternative partnerships through investment advisors surged 149% in 2018 to $19.2 billion,[1] largely from the distribution of nontraded real estate investment trusts, interval funds, and private business development companies.

Recently SEC chairman Jay Clayton said he wants a complete overhaul of all regulations regarding private placements to make them more accessible to individual investors. Indeed, in a press release in December 2019, the SEC issued a proposal essentially making it easier for more people to qualify.[2]

It is more important than ever to arm investors with the tools to better understand what they are really buying, because chances are it isn't alpha. The goal of this book is to pass on some of the lessons I have learned—to provide some thoughts on what alpha is and isn't, where it comes from, how to identify it (or at least know when it's not there so you don't pay for it), and what we should be focusing on instead. Maybe a bit of clarity can help prevent others from making some of the mistakes I've observed (and yes, sometimes committed), like overpaying for unappreciated risk or mistaking beta for alpha.

The Definition of Alpha

We may have gotten a bit ahead of ourselves. Time for a little level setting. Let's provide more background on alpha for those readers less familiar with the concept. Those not in need of a refresher should feel free to skip the technical discussion on alpha versus beta.

Put simply, alpha is a quantitative metric that's intended to measure an investor's ability to beat the market. It represents an active return, where a manager selects securities that differ from the market to outperform it. Alpha is excess returns, positive or negative, versus what the market generated on average. Sometimes this ability is also described as an "edge," a competitive advantage that ostensibly results in consistent superior performance.

But alpha is more than just higher returns. Often managers simply take more risk or a different risk to generate higher returns than their benchmark. Although that's not really alpha, they all sell it as if it were. Put another way, all alpha should be excess return relative to the risk taken, but not all excess return is really alpha. Figuring out which is which is precisely the trick.

Here is the technical definition of alpha taken from Investopedia:

Alpha is used in finance as a measure of performance, indicating when a strategy, trader, or portfolio manager has managed to beat the market return over some period. Alpha, often considered the active return on an investment, gauges the performance of an investment against a market index or benchmark that is considered to represent the market's movement as a whole. The excess return of an investment relative to the return of a benchmark index is the investment's alpha. Alpha may be positive or negative and is the result of active investing. Beta, on the other hand, can be earned through passive index investing.[3]

This definition of alpha contains the important related concept of beta. Beta is simply the return that would have been generated by passively owning all the securities in a particular market. It's an index return. For example, in large-capitalization long-only US public equities, beta would be the return of the S&P 500 index. An investor could buy an index mutual fund, or alternatively purchase all 500 stocks directly in the proportions determined by the index, and that investor would achieve beta returns.

If, however, an investor selected a subset of equities—say, 50 individual stocks—and this basket meaningfully underperformed or outperformed the market with similar risk, the difference between the two returns would be alpha. But to measure the presence and magnitude of alpha, you first have to accurately account for the effect of beta. So here comes the uncomfortable part: a little math. It's important to note again that alpha can be positive or negative. Mathematically speaking, alpha is a residual, what's left over from a regression equation. This regression equation is not that different from the standard slope-intercept form (Equation 1.1) that we all learned in school. Remember it? You may have last seen it in high school algebra.

$$y = mx + b \qquad\qquad (1.1)$$

where m represents the slope of the line; x is the input variable; b is the intercept, a fixed constant; and y is the output of the equation. For the slope intercept equation in Figure 1.1, the equation is $y = 2x + 3$. Hence, the slope m of this line is 2. Recall that slope equals "rise over run," which for a slope of 2 means that the y-axis point increases by 2 for each single-point increase in the x variable. Finally, this equation has an intercept constant of 3, which I picked randomly, and shifts the line upward on the y axis. So if x is 0, then y equals 3. If x is 1, then y equals 5. And so on to plot the entire line, as long as you know the slope m and intercept b.

In a financial equation known as Jensen's alpha (see Equation 1.2 below), alpha is denoted by the Greek letter α and corresponds to the intercept constant b from the slope intercept form. Beta is characterized by the Greek β, and it replaces m as the slope of the line.

The returns (R) to an individual investment manager or individual security are like the y output, and the market returns equate to the x input.

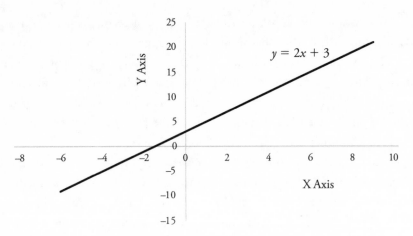

FIGURE 1.1   Slope intercept graph

Unlike the slope intercept form, however, the returns are known, and the residual is the unknown. So we'll start with the equation in the same form as above and move it around to solve for the unknown.

Equation 1.2 may look daunting, but it simply states that the returns to a specific manager must be equal to the beta of the manager with the market multiplied by the excess return of the market, or the market return above the risk-free rate (which is essentially cash), plus the risk-free rate (which everyone can earn), plus the specific alpha. In plain English, an individual manager earns the market return relative to his (or her) slope with the market, plus cash, plus (or minus) alpha.

$$R_{manager} = [\beta_{manager} \times (R_{market} - R_{risk\,free})] + R_{risk\,free} + \alpha \qquad (1.2)$$

We can then reorganize this to solve for alpha, which is the unknown variable, by subtracting the risk-free return and market components from both sides. When we do this, we are left with

$$\alpha = R_{manager} - [\beta_{manager} \times (R_{market} - R_{risk\,free})] - R_{risk\,free} \qquad (1.3)$$

This equation shows us that to calculate the alpha of a manager, we first begin with that manager's total return. Then we deduct the return that the manager would have gotten for simply investing in the market. This market component is itself made up of three separate underlying pieces: (1) the manager's beta to the market, (2) the market return, and (3) the risk-free rate of return.

Let's discuss the risk-free rate of return, because that's the easiest. This is basically the return on very short-dated Treasury bills, or essentially cash. When this return is very low, as it has been for quite some time, it is not very meaningful in terms of affecting the calculation. For the sake of a few examples below, we'll just assume it is zero (so we can ignore it). When the risk-free rate is zero, the market component simplifies to beta times the market return.

The actual market return should be easy to understand but sometimes hard to know. In our initial public equity example, it would be the total return for the S&P 500 index. It's important to pick the right market benchmark; otherwise, any alpha is merely a mirage.

Finally, that leaves us with beta. Beta is a complicated formula calculated by comparing the manager's return to the market, and it adjusts the market return to account for the manager's co-movement with the market.[4] It combines into one number a measurement of the risk of a manager's return relative to the market's risk and correlation to the market. If a manager is highly correlated and higher risk, the beta can be higher than 1, unlike correlation, which is mathematically bounded between 1 and −1. If a manager is equal risk but lowly correlated or moderately correlated but much less volatile than the market, then the beta will be lower.

At the extreme, if beta is zero (and the risk-free rate is still ignored), 100% of the manager's return stream can be attributable to alpha, as the hedge fund manager claimed above! Of course, a beta of zero almost assuredly means you have just selected an inappropriate market benchmark, as investors in that hedge fund later came to discover.

Perhaps a few more examples will help clarify this. Let's assume we have identified a manager with a return of 10% and a market index return of 10%. If we continue to ignore the marginal effect of cash, it would appear that this manager generated no alpha. Once we account for a range of potential betas, a much different story emerges, as shown in Table 1.1.

TABLE 1.1   Impact of Beta on Alpha

Manager Return	Beta	Market Return	Beta Component	Alpha
10.0%	0.6	10.0%	6.0%	4.0%
10.0%	0.8	10.0%	8.0%	2.0%
10.0%	**1.0**	**10.0%**	**10.0%**	**0.0%**
10.0%	1.2	10.0%	12.0%	−2.0%
10.0%	1.4	10.0%	14.0%	−4.0%

We can see how important the manager's beta is in determining whether alpha was generated or not. If the manager was perfectly correlated with the market, then alpha would be zero. Even though the total returns remain identical, if the manager had a beta of only 0.6, then in that scenario 40% of the total return, or 4.0%, would be alpha. This manager took significantly less return than the market and managed to keep pace with it. On the other hand, if the manager's beta was actually 1.4, then they should have made 14% for the amount of risk they took, and their alpha is −4.0%.

While the calculation for beta is too complex for these pages, beta itself is an output that is heavily dependent upon the selection of the market. So what happens if managers get to pick their own index?

Let's imagine that manager above who generated 10% did in fact have a beta of 1.0 to the market, which also returned 10.0%. This manager's alpha is zero, as shown. What if, however, there was another similar index that returned 9.5% for the year—fairly close to the other index? And the manager had a beta of 0.95 to that market—still fairly correlated—a scenario depicted in Table 1.2.

Voilà! The manager transformed a purely market-driven return into a positive albeit small alpha, just like magic. It's certainly easier to do that than actually generating alpha, and since investors are willing to pay more for alpha, it's also more profitable than selling the return as beta, which it truly is. It sure looks like it's alpha in the second row of the table, and the only way to prove it isn't is if you can find the right index and show it is actually only beta. So the index derives beta, and beta determines the alpha. It should be apparent how important it is to pick the correct index. Though as we'll see, it turns out that's not necessarily so easy.

TABLE 1.2 Alpha Example

Manager Return	Beta 1	Market 1 Return	Beta Component	Alpha
10.0%	1.0	10.0%	10.0%	0.0%
Manager Return	**Beta 2**	**Market 2 Return**	**Beta Component**	**Alpha**
10.0%	0.95	9.5%	9.0%	1.0%

So you made it through the math, and it wasn't so bad, was it? Now you know what alpha is. And as you've seen, it's easy to manipulate alpha by gaming the choice of beta. If you can't beat the index, just pick a different one that you did beat in hindsight. Obviously, if stock pickers try to use a bond index as their beta, that is transparently self-serving and a glaring risk mismatch. However, it can be a lot more difficult where managers can tilt their portfolio toward select characteristics of the underlying assets that do in fact differ from common benchmarks, or worse, where managers can change exposures and move across asset classes over time. So the question is, how do you select an appropriate benchmark?

Thankfully, organizations such as the CFA Institute and CAIA Association have written extensively on what makes an effective benchmark. While there are some differences in the lists that various institutions use, I've distilled them down to what I believe are five critical characteristics to look for when deciding which benchmark to use for a given manager.

Five Critical Characteristics of an Effective Benchmark

1. **Specified in advance.** Although this may not always be the case, investors should try to select whichever benchmark they choose prior to funding the investment allocation. If you cherry-pick the benchmark afterward, you are opening yourself up to hindsight bias. However, like most things in life, this rule can sometimes be broken, particularly if the manager strays from what he or she was supposed to do. Then, using a different benchmark to analyze returns will allow an investor to gain a better understanding of how the manager generated those returns, and thus make a more informed decision going forward whether to terminate or retain the manager and/or renegotiate fees.

2. **Relevant and appropriate.** Investors should ensure that the benchmark they select accurately reflects the investment mandate, objective, or strategy. This means that not only should the benchmark contain underlying assets that are highly similar to the account, such as an index of large-cap US equities for a large-cap US equity account; it also means that the index return itself should be matched on risk characteristics. For instance, the volatility, leverage, and liquidity profile of both must be similar. Using a broad equity index as a benchmark for an industry-focused fund or using a long-only index for a long-short strategy would violate this principle.

3. **Measurable and transparent.** An effective benchmark must be quantifiable. But more important, the constituents of the index universe should be clearly identified and their performance easily calculated. This may seem common sense, but many indexes are proprietary and do not disclose what the components of the return stream are. This makes it impossible for an investor to independently verify and understand what is in it. An ideal benchmark is one that is transparent and can be recalculated by hand by market participants.

4. **Investable.** An appropriate benchmark should also be accessible via a passive investment vehicle in which investors could put new dollars to work. If the index is purely theoretical and not investable, it fails to meet this requirement. For instance, investors may require a return of cash plus 3% for an investment. While that is fine for determining a cost of capital or a hurdle rate, it is not a benchmark. No one can purchase a passive, low-cost fund to generate that return profile; otherwise, that's what the risk-free rate (cash) would be! A good benchmark must actually be available as an actionable investment opportunity.

5. **Comprehensive.** The benchmark should provide broad coverage of the market or asset class in which the allocator is investing. An index can have all the characteristics above, but if it is simply too limited or concentrated, it loses its effectiveness. For example, an index purporting to be a total stock market index would not be very comprehensive if it merely covered 40 out of the roughly 4,000 publicly listed stocks in the United States. This concentration introduces confounding risks that reduce the effectiveness of the index. A good benchmark should take advantage of the law of large numbers.

If managers are using a benchmark that doesn't meet these criteria, no matter what excess return they are able to show you, the chances are it isn't alpha. They've probably just cherry-picked an easy-to-beat beta.

The last mathematical point about alpha is that it is a zero-sum game. The total net alpha in the equity market is zero, because the average return equals the benchmark return, by definition. For every manager that has a 2% alpha, someone else has to have a −2% alpha for the index return to equal itself. So for something to truly be durable alpha, there has to be a reason why a specific manager or strategy can continue to extract excess returns from the other side of a trade. That's easier said than done.

With these points in mind, investors may be better armed to separate alpha from beta. However, even picking the right benchmark is still not enough to ensure excess return is truly alpha. Managers can still game the calculation after the fact by making slight changes to their portfolio. For example, a bond manager may purchase some bonds that have more credit risk or longer duration than the index that the bonds are benchmarked against. This will give them a higher yield, and probably higher return, but it still won't be alpha—and it might be hard to catch. Or a large-cap equity fund could buy a few small-capitalization stocks that go on to demonstrate strong growth and outperform. Well, if the small-cap index itself beats the large-cap one, that's not truly alpha either.

My hope is you can start to see why alpha is easy to disprove—but virtually impossible to prove. To be sure, an investor has to have a deep understanding of the attribution of the manager's returns.

Now that you know what alpha is, theoretically at least, we'll turn to understanding where it came from before we can figure out where it is going. The remainder of this book is laid out into three main sections. The next section, Part I, chronicles the history of alpha, where it has appeared and subsequently disappeared across financial markets. Part II then describes a framework for thinking about investing as a spectrum of skills instead of a binary mathematical division between alpha and beta. This section will also help better frame our understanding of how alpha evolves. Then Part III describes some ways to improve our approach to thinking about alpha, which will aid us in our often unproductive efforts to find it. There's a better way to go about building portfolios, one not predicated on this old version of alpha at all. In fact, a new paradigm for alpha will help investors achieve better outcomes going forward.

And finally, I'll end with some concluding thoughts about what I believe the future holds. But first, let's turn to public markets and look at the history of active equity management, because that's where the concept of alpha was born.

Notes

1. https://www.fundfire.com/c/2639173/318743/alts_product_sales_advisors_jump?referrer_module=emailffalts&module_order=0&code=WTNOamFHV nNiR2x1WjBCMGJYSnpMbU52YlN3Z05ETXdPRFl5TXl3Z05UWTNO akEzTVRBMg.
2. SEC (2019).
3. Chen (2020).
4. Beta is technically defined as the covariance of a manager (or an asset) with the market divided by the variance of the market. In addition to being highly dependent upon the index selection, the periodicity selected for the calculation is very important as well. For instance, the beta of the daily returns of Exxon Mobil stock (XOM) with the S&P 500 from February 2018 to February 2019 was 0.86. However, the beta of monthly returns for XOM with the S&P from February 2014 to February 2019 was just 0.39, a quite substantial difference.

PART I
Chronicling Alpha

2
Public Markets— Figuring Out Factors

Don't look for the needle in the haystack. Just buy the haystack.
—JACK BOGLE

The History of Active Equity Investing

A comprehensive history of public equity markets is not the intention of this chapter, but in our quest to explore the nature of alpha, a brief discussion is certainly in order. Today the market capitalization of publicly traded US stocks is roughly $35 trillion. It is a marketplace dominated by giant investment management firms such as BlackRock, with $7.4 trillion in assets under management, and the Vanguard Group, with $5.3 trillion. However, this industry was not always so institutional.

While mutual funds can be traced back to the Netherlands in the late 1700s,[1] the mutual fund industry as we know it today was created by an unassuming but ambitious young man from Alabama named Jonathan Bell

Lovelace. Born in Brewton, Alabama, in 1895, Lovelace, or JBL as he came
to be known, was a math whiz with a taste for adventure. Upon graduating
with a bachelor's degree in architecture and a master's in mathematics in only
three years from the Alabama Polytechnic Institute, later renamed Auburn
University, JBL decided to join the army to fight in World War I.

His high math scores on the entry vocational aptitude test saw him
assigned to the artillery, where JBL discovered that his uncanny arithmetic
abilities allowed him to rapidly calculate in his head the trajectories necessary for antiaircraft artillery fire to hit fast-moving targets. And according to
historical accounts, his artillery unit was the first in France to shoot down a
German plane.[2] In large part owing to these skills, he had risen to the rank
of captain by the time he ended his service to his country.

After serving out his tour of duty and returning home, the young man
decided to move to Detroit in 1919 to join up with one of his army bud-
dies, Eddie MacCrone, who had founded a small investment brokerage. JBL
threw himself into the statistical research of stocks, and he quickly become a
favorite of the firm's important clients—clients such as Walter Chrysler and
C. S. Mott, the founder of General Motors. JBL enjoyed picking stocks so
much that he tried to persuade MacCrone to launch a trust to pool investments in what would have been the first mutual fund. MacCrone, however, wanted his brilliant employee to focus exclusively on underwriting new
equity issuances, a highly profitable business for the firm.

The two came to a compromise, with JBL continuing to help price new
issues while MacCrone helped him establish a closed-end investment company called the Investment Company of America. Unlike an open-end fund,
this company charged high fees—50% of the profits above a 6% rate of
return—and made extensive use of leverage to amplify performance. Within
five years, JBL's successful stock picking had made him a partner in the brokerage firm E.E. MacCrone.

However, over the course of the next several years, JBL found himself
increasingly confused, as the prices of publicly traded equities had seemingly become disconnected from the factors that he had used so successfully
to predict prices. Fundamental financial metrics of the businesses, such as
revenue and profit margins, were no longer statistically associated with the

subsequent price performance of the stock, and he couldn't figure out why. Valuations just made no sense to him anymore.

By September 1929, Lovelace had seen enough, and he cashed out all his personal stock positions. Unsuccessful in his attempts to convince MacCrone to become more conservative in the management of the business and the trust, JBL decided to leave the firm and sell his ownership stake. True to his adventurous nature, JBL was on a train bound for California when the stock market crashed in October 1929. In just three days, stocks had fallen by nearly 35%. Despite recovering a bit by the end of that year, the sell-off would not stop, and equities would not find a bottom until 1932, after losing 86% cumulatively.

Although he had accumulated enough personal wealth to be retired at the ripe old age of 34, within a few years, the stock-picking itch had returned; and in 1931, he founded an investment firm named Lovelace, Dennis & Renfrew, which would ultimately go on to become Capital Research and Management Company. Today Capital Group, as it is formally called, has just over $2 trillion in assets under management, including approximately $93 billion in the Investment Company of America, of which it took over management from the failing brokerage firm E.E. MacCrone in 1933.[3] MacCrone had fallen into debt to the tune of more than a million dollars— nearly $20 million in today's money—and the sale of this business line to his old friend helped him remain solvent for a few more years.

Capital Group grew into one of the behemoths of the industry, with leadership handed down first to JBL's son Jon and then to Jon's son Rob, who is chairman of the firm today. For generations, the bedrock principle of the firm has been that fundamental research—evaluating the financial performance of a business's operations—is the critical basis for forming a view about the direction of the price of a stock. All else being equal, businesses that have more assets, more sales, and more profits relative to their stock price should outperform. This fundamental research has resulted in substantial outperformance for their clients.

From 1934 until the end of 2019, a dollar invested in the Investment Company of America would have grown into $16,550 versus just $7,602 for the S&P 500, a whopping annualized net return of 12.0% for the mutual fund[4] as compared with the 10.9% return of the index. And the volatility of the fund has been slightly lower than the index, too, resulting in an average annualized Jensen's alpha of around 1.4%. Perhaps even more impressive, although the Investment Company of America beat the S&P 500 52% of the time, it did even better in down years. For the 21 times the S&P had a negative annual calendar return over this entire period, the fund beat it 15 times, a full 71% of those down years!

This consistent, repeatable excess return is precisely the holy grail type of alpha that investors search for. Now, the Lovelace family has built the Capital Group into a great company to be sure, but it is certainly not alone. Similar processes have long been used by so-called value investors in the mold of Benjamin Graham and his protégé Warren Buffett to consistently generate alpha over long periods of time. Benjamin Graham, the father of value investing, authored what are often considered to be two of the best investment books ever written: *Security Analysis* (1934) with David Dodd and *The Intelligent Investor* (1949). Using his approach, which focused on equities in businesses with a low price relative to earnings and a high book value of assets relative to price, the Graham-Newman partnership returned about 20% per year from its founding in 1936 until 1956, a period during which the stock market averaged around 12%.[5]

Many fundamental investors have used similar valuation-based approaches to generate strong returns over long careers. Portfolio managers like John Neff or Sir John Templeton, and firms like Dodge and Cox, which also dates back to the 1930s, are just a few examples of other investors that long implemented valuation-based stock-picking methods to consistently outperform broad market indexes.

However, this type of persistent alpha seemed to run completely contrary to the work of most financial economists of the time, who believed it was impossible to consistently beat markets. Nobel Prize–winning economists Harry Markowitz and William Sharpe pioneered asset risk and asset pricing models in the 1950s and 1960s that made use of a single factor, or risk premium, to predict asset returns, namely the market. In fact, they laid the theoretical foundation for Jensen's alpha we discussued in Chapter 1.

Other academics in the sixties and seventies like Burton Malkiel and Eugene Fama used these pricing models to show that any excess return from a diversified pool of stocks versus the market factor was likely luck, since it did not seem to persist over time. Both Malkiel and Fama published influential research during this time showing that stock returns were essentially random and investors weren't able to consistently beat the market.[6]

Their argument basically went like this: Sure, anybody could beat the market with a few stocks. But since a concentrated portfolio upped the chances of both significant underperformance and outperformance, it statistically looked like luck. And for those investors that constructed a big enough portfolio of stocks, essentially diversifying away any of this so-called idiosyncratic risk, the vast majority of them would pace the market. A few could outperform for short periods before mean-reverting back to average. And with enough people participating in markets, a few would even be able to outperform for longer periods simply due to random chance. But no one should be able to consistently and predictably generate repeatable alpha that could be identified ahead of time.

Thus the efficient market theory came to dominate financial economics, and it made sense. Stock market returns were unpredictable. And the more people learned about investing, the more money poured into stock markets, which meant the harder it should be to outperform. Nevertheless, over time, a growing body of research began to show that excess returns were not completely unpredictable, either.

Ironically, the very father of efficient markets himself, Professor Fama, is credited with the discovery of the first of these market anomalies, or factors that had explanatory power over returns. In one of the most heavily cited financial articles of all time published in the *Journal of Financial Economics* in 1993,[7] Fama and his colleague Kenneth French introduced three common factors that were predictive of stock returns along with two for bonds. The coauthors were able to show that in addition to the overall stock market effect, the size of the company's market capitalization and the ratio of book value of shareholders equity to share price were strongly predictive of subsequent returns. Over the period 1963 to 1990, smaller-cap companies consistently outperformed larger ones, and businesses whose market price was lower relative to the book value of their equity outperformed more expensive ones. Value had been validated!

This research was considered groundbreaking and led to a wave of academic and practitioner exploration looking into other factors to bet on, and more factors were indeed found. In 1997 Mark Carhart, one of Fama's pupils, empirically proved the existence of price momentum.[8] This effect showed that those stocks whose prices had risen recently tended to continue outperforming, and vice versa. Even later research showed the presence of a volatility anomaly.[9] Low-volatility stocks were shown to outperform high-volatility stocks, which is the opposite of what the classical belief about the risk-return relationship predicted. Higher return should compensate higher risk, but that's not what the risk premium research proved.

The result of this research has been the development of increasingly complex multifactor models that describe equity returns. Instead of alpha being calculated above a single market risk premium, more comprehensive models incorporated these new factors into the formula for alpha. As the Fama-French three-factor model (Equation 2.1) shows, there was now a beta to a size factor and a beta to the value factor in addition to the market return:

$$R_{manager} = [\beta_1 \times (R_{market} - R_{risk\ free})] + R_{risk\ free} + \beta_2$$

$$\times\ size + \beta_3 \times value + \alpha \qquad\qquad (2.1)$$

Since the models were able to explain more of the returns, alpha—by definition a residual—went down.

These factors worked so well that they came to define how investors think about stock markets. Morningstar created its eponymous equity style boxes to incorporate this research. No longer did allocators simply hire active managers or purchase an index. Instead, now they needed to decide whether they should hire an active small-cap value manager, buy a mid-cap growth fund, or allocate to a simple large-cap blend portfolio.

Equity managers were required to outperform relative to whatever box they were participating in, as opposed to a simple overall equity index. And if they couldn't beat the factor, why not just buy the factor? But first, let's go

back to the development of another branch of the equity investment industry, namely indexing.

Rise of Passive Investing

Meanwhile, a young man from New Jersey, John Clifton Bogle, nicknamed
Jack, was determined to create a better mutual fund option for the masses.
Heavily influenced by the writings of yet another Nobel Prize–winning efficient market proponent, the economist Paul Samuelson, Bogle decided to write
his senior dissertation at Princeton on mutual funds. Impressed by the 130-
page opus titled "The Economic Role of the Investment Company," another
Princeton alumnus, Walter Morgan, the founder of Wellington Fund, decided
to give the driven young graduate a job. Immediately after graduating magna
cum laude in 1951, Bogle moved to Boston, the mutual fund hub of America,
to join Wellington. At the time, 46% of total industrywide mutual fund assets
were managed by firms headquartered in Boston,[10] and it was the perfect place
for someone with ambitions to change the industry to begin his career.

Bogle quickly rose through the ranks, becoming the heir apparent to
Morgan. In 1965, he was tapped to run the firm, and Jack Bogle was now
in a position to enact his audacious plans. Wellington Fund was a balanced
fund, diversified across stocks and bonds, and this conservative style was not
really in favor during what was a go-go era for stocks. Seeking to strengthen
his firm's competitive position, Bogle wanted to find a strategic partner. His
first attempt at initiating a merger with industry leader Capital Group, then
called American Funds, failed, as the Lovelaces were entirely uninterested in
a potential tie-up.

Pivoting to a different firm, Bogle spearheaded the acquisition of a tiny
Boston business called Thorndike, Doran, Paine & Lewis. With just $17
million in a very aggressive growth stock portfolio, the firm appeared to be
an odd fit for the much larger, more staid Wellington. And the timing could
not have been much worse, as the early 1970s saw equities enter into a correction that did not bottom until October 1974. Several of the funds created
by the new aggressive partners wound up being liquidated. And even worse,
the new portfolio managers had positioned the historically conservatively

managed Wellington Fund much more aggressively, with more exposure to riskier stocks and more equities overall. Wellington didn't hold up as well as expected during the bear market, and the firm was struggling to retain assets.

A decade after taking over the firm, Wellington had shrunk from a $2.2 billion firm to just $1.5 billion in assets under management.[11] His signature management move a complete failure, Bogle was unceremoniously dismissed from the only firm he had ever worked at.

Not one to take his termination lying down, Bogle, still chairman of the advisory board for all of the underlying Wellington funds, proposed a revolutionary motion at the next fund meeting: that the independent board of advisors for each fund terminate Wellington as the manager and mutualize. What this meant was that the shareholders for each fund would in essence own the management firm. Not only was the battle between an investment fund and its management company entirely unusual, but the suggestion that mutual funds should be owned by their investors instead of being managed for the profit of an investment company was—and remains today—unprecedented. The idea of essentially a nonprofit investment management firm? *Heresy!*

Presented with the two unsavory options of either firing Wellington as the manager of the funds with no viable replacement or voting against Bogle's clearly investor-friendly recommendation, the board did what any sensible decision-making body would do—it compromised. After much negotiation, Vanguard was born. Naming the new mutual company after HMS *Vanguard*, Lord Nelson's flagship at the great British victory over Napoleon's fleet at the Battle of the Nile in 1798, Bogle said he wanted the new firm to send a message to the fund industry, that Vanguard would be at the forefront of a movement.

The new entity would be the asset management firm, owned by the shareholders of the funds and run for their benefit, and it would be responsible for administration of the business. Bogle would run Vanguard. As a compromise, Wellington would be retained as an external vendor, subadvising the funds as a third-party asset management firm. Bogle, back in the driver's seat, immediately set out to negotiate fee breaks for his funds from Wellington.

However, Bogle's legacy would rest on his next achievement, the creation of the world's first index fund. Having become disillusioned with the failures of active management and attempting to beat the market, Bogle decided to try to create a product that was broadly accessible to average investors with low minimum investment requirements, low cost, and low turnover and that would simply keep pace with the S&P 500. His old professor Paul Samuelson was a vocal supporter of the novel concept, and in 1976, Vanguard launched its first product not managed by Wellington, the First Index Investment Trust.

However, this innovation was again met with derision for being "unmanaged," a portfolio of stocks composed seemingly indiscriminately. Many brokers and financial advisors refused to pitch the product to their clients, as it clearly implied that the effort of picking individual stocks was a fool's game. Some competitors went so far as to call it socialist and inherently un-American. One firm actually flooded the market with flyers depicting an angry Uncle Sam imploring investors to "Help Stamp Out Index Funds!"[12]

Thankfully for retail investors everywhere, Bogle remained undeterred by the critics. If anything, criticism only seemed to encourage and motivate him! For the next 20 years, Bogle piloted Vanguard to become another giant of the industry, before formally retiring in 1996. However, Bogle remained involved with Vanguard first as chairman and then finally chairman emeritus until his passing in 2019. An outspoken critic of abusive practices across the investment industry and a proponent of indexing, Jack Bogle will be forever linked with the firm he built.

Today indexers have taken over the asset management game, with the two largest firms in the industry—BlackRock and Vanguard—among them. Vanguard's 500 Index Fund, the successor to the First Index Investment Trust, has half a trillion dollars in it alone.

According to research from Morningstar, assets in passively managed equity funds now exceed those of active management, with equity indexers holding $4.27 trillion compared with the $4.24 trillion managed by stock pickers.[13] While just a slim majority, this represents a profound transformation from years past. For example, in 1987, active managers had 6½ times the amount of assets index funds had! And still in 2007, active funds retained nearly 80% of market share. However, active mutual funds have experienced outflows every single year since 2006 as investors have pivoted aggressively away from them in favor of the cheaper passive approach. But what happened to drive clients away from active management so suddenly and so completely?

Failure of Active Management

In hindsight, the reason for this wholesale revolt by investors is apparent. Roughly 65% of active large-cap mutual funds trailed their benchmark in 2018,[14] which represented the ninth year in a row that simple indexing beat the majority of stock pickers. Many active managers argue this is cyclical, and a reversion to the mean is likely to come as their investment style comes back into favor. But trends have just been getting worse for the stock pickers. While nearly two-thirds of active managers trailed their bogey over a 1-year period, over the trailing 10 years, fully 85% failed to beat the index. And over the last 15 years, more than 9 out of every 10 actively managed large-cap stock funds have underperformed the S&P 500.

It's just getting harder and harder for high-powered, professional portfolio managers to beat the stock market. And considering the average active mutual fund charges a 1.0% management fee versus the 0.25% charged for the typical passive product, the decline of active management and the rise of passive seem all the more inevitable.

In fact, if we go back to our earlier story about the long-term outperformance of the Investment Company of America, the story repeats itself. From inception in 1934 through the 1980s, the flagship fund of Capital Group beat the S&P 500 index net of fees nearly 60% of the time, 33 out of these 56 years. This is a truly impressive accomplishment that probably is not mere chance. However, since then, the Investment Company of America has not fared nearly as well, outperforming only 12 years in the three subsequent decades, just 40% of the time. This is almost the mirror image of its prior dominance—for 56 years the active fund won 60% of the time, and for the next three decades, the index won 60% of the time.

What has happened that has made it so hard to beat the index? Let's spend a minute discussing market efficiency.

Market Efficiency

Market efficiency is generally described as the degree to which all publicly available information is already reflected in the clearing price of a security. In theory, the more efficient a given market is, the harder it is to outperform a simple passive basket of all the securities in it. When prices reflect value, there is no opportunity for alpha. This is what Eugene Fama and Burton Malkiel preached as creators of the efficient market theory. Doubtless, it is largely true. Although many markets are highly efficient, none are perfectly efficient. Information is reflected in prices as long as that information is widely available and easily digestible. If information is asymmetric—that is, if some market participants have more information than others—then markets will be less efficient.

Capital markets are not homogenous things, nor are market participants. Some markets are more opaque; some are more transparent. Some are more regulated, and others less so. Some markets have far more knowledgeable participants all vying for returns, which means more and more informed people engaged in price discovery. Market participants learn over time. As a result, efficiency varies dramatically both across markets and over time. But large-cap US equities in particular have become incredibly efficient. As an example, let's look at an analysis comparing this sector with emerging market equities, which are pretty widely regarded as less liquid, less regulated, and less well capitalized, and hence should be less efficient.

Using data from eVestment, I analyzed the distribution of the performance of equity managers in both markets. First, I looked at the rolling three-year average return of managers in each market from 2007 until 2015. Then, I removed the top 10% of managers from the distribution each year and recalculated an average return for the bottom 90% of managers. Finally, I compared the excess return of the average manager of the full distribution with the average of the bottom 90% as a means of investigating how much excess return the top 10% were able to extract from each market as a rough proxy for efficiency. The less efficient, the greater should be the expected outperformance, and vice versa. The resulting series is presented in Figure 2.1.

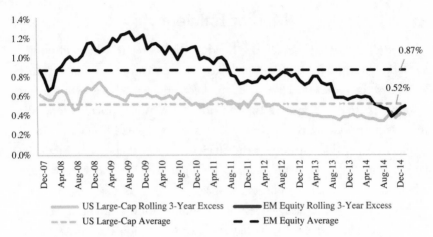

FIGURE 2.1   Contribution to the average return of the top 10% of managers

The first thing this analysis tells us is that large-cap US equities are in fact more efficient than emerging markets. Over this admittedly small period, the top decile of managers in US equities increased the average return versus the manager sample without them by 52 basis points per year. The same effect in emerging markets was 0.87%. However, it's interesting to note this effect is dwindling across both markets, making it harder to outperform, but the shrinkage is even more pronounced in the emerging markets. Over these seven years, it has fallen by half, suggesting emerging markets are notably more efficient today than in years past. This should of course impact an investor's belief in the availability of, and his or her ability to access, alpha.

It's clear that equity markets are highly efficient and are only becoming more so. Charles Ellis, founder of Greenwich Associates and vocal advocate for indexing, has estimated that over the past 50 years, the number of investment professionals actively engaged in price discovery has risen from around 5,000 to well over 1 million today.

Looking at the market structure itself, things have also changed dramatically over the past several decades. In 1996, there were approximately 9,000 publicly listed stocks in the United States. Pursuing these opportunities were about 6,500 mutual funds and 500 hedge funds. Fast-forward to 2019, and there are now less than 4,000 public stocks traded to select from, and there are many more investors going after them. Using recent estimates from various sources, there are approximately 9,700 mutual funds, about 5,000 exchange-traded products, and nearly 10,000 hedge funds fighting for excess returns in a shrinking market.

In effect, the needle is getting smaller while the haystack keeps getting bigger. Which brings us to the paradox of market efficiency. I once had a supremely confident hedge fund manager tell me without equivocation, "Chris, I am market efficiency." While his delivery was off-putting, in many ways he was right.

The more investors seek to exploit inefficiencies present in a given market, the more efficient such a market becomes as those opportunities are priced away. Conversely, the more investors become convinced of the infallibility of a market's efficiency, the more inefficient that market will become as less participants engage in active price discovery.

There are of course other ways one can measure the efficiency of a market, such as falling commissions, shrinking bid-ask spreads, improving market depth, and increasing liquidity and volume. However, no matter how we measure it, equity markets are more efficient than ever, as you can see in Table 2.1. The value proposition of being a "free rider," or passively participating in the beta, has never been more attractive. Following the advice of Jack Bogle, more and more market participants are simply buying the haystack.

TABLE 2.1   Increasing Equity Market Efficiency

	2001	2019
Average daily NYSE dollar volume	$30.1 billion	$178.6 billion
Fidelity online stock commission	$14.00	$0
Average bid-ask spread in SPX (as % of midpoint)	2.2%	0.7%

But this isn't the end of the story, either. As we will see, alpha and beta are not entirely separate entities; rather they are two ends of an investment spectrum. Intertwined with the fall of active and the rise of indexing has been the growth of factor investing.

Factor Investing

Although Fama and French ultimately won the Nobel Prize for their work on factors related to stock returns, it was several relatively unheralded academics that effectively commercialized these insights.

After achieving his bachelor's degree in physics from Tufts University, Richard Grinold took a break from his studies to join the US Navy and serve his country during the Vietnam War. After putting in his four years as a navigator on a destroyer, and with the casualties from the war beginning to climb, he decided to return to more scholarly endeavors and pursue a doctorate in operations research at the University of California, Berkeley. Upon graduating, Grinold stayed on at the university as a full professor, but he moved over to the then wildly fashionable field of finance in the early 1970s.

It was in the Berkeley finance department where Grinold began to collaborate with an ambitious economist by the name of Barr Rosenberg. Rosenberg had set up a consulting firm aptly named Barr Rosenberg Associates, or BARRA as it came to be known, in part to help Wells Fargo Asset Management design its approach to index investing through sophisticated beta modeling. By incorporating prior work on efficient markets and factors and adding data about individual companies' liabilities, earnings, and industry sector, Rosenberg was soon hawking his "Barr's better betas" to the investment industry, at a time when passive investing was still in its infancy.[15]

Due to strong demand for his research, by 1979, Rosenberg decided to bring his friend Grinold on board full-time, who would become BARRA's director of research and later president. Soon BARRA wasn't just measuring beta with the firm's models, but also designing stock portfolios, essentially creating custom indexes. However, the collaboration didn't last forever, and in 1985 Barr Rosenberg, who seemed to suffer from a perpetual case of professional wanderlust, left to once again start his own eponymous firm, this time an asset management business called Rosenberg Institutional Equity Management.[16]

At the same time, Wells Fargo Investment Advisors launched a series of strategies that were managed using Grinold's research at BARRA. And in 1987, needing help on the research side, Grinold hired a brilliant postdoctoral student who had come to Berkeley to study the extinction of the dinosaurs. With a PhD in physics from Harvard, Ronald Kahn soon turned his curious scientific mind to investigating drivers of stock returns. Eventually, the folks at Wells Fargo decided to hire Grinold directly to manage funds for them, and later Kahn was hired back by his former boss at the successor firm, Barclays Global Investors, or BGI.[17]

The funds that BGI managed based upon this research were called Alpha Tilts, and instead of building a stock portfolio to simply match an index, or a concentrated active portfolio of stocks selected based upon detailed financial research, BARRA sort of split the difference, using computers to analyze reams of data across thousands of stocks and select broad portfolios in weights based upon certain characteristics. These characteristics will sound very familiar—the models looked at price to book, price to earnings, price to sales, earnings quality (which selects businesses with conservative accounting practices and avoids those with aggressive ones), and even two kinds of momentum, earnings and price momentum—factors that academic research had shown to predict higher returns. Alpha Tilts bought diversified pools of stocks, but slightly "tilted" the portfolio toward these risk premia—buying a little more value, a little more earnings, etc., than what the index owned.

In essence, these Alpha Tilt funds also bought a haystack instead of trying to find the needle buried in it, much like indexing, but they did it a little smarter. As opposed to blindly buying one bale of hay randomly, factors allowed an investor to quickly compare several different haystacks and pick the best deal among them. For example, let's picture a row of 4-foot x 5-foot haystacks weighing 800 pounds on average and priced at a fixed $50 per bale. If the farmer had a scale, the buyer would be able to select the haystack that actually weighs 810 pounds and get a bargain for his 50 bucks.[18] Factors were the scales that gave the Alpha Tilt strategies that edge.

And what an edge it was. As of June 2003, the Barclays Global Alpha Tilt Large Cap Stock Fund had solidly beaten the S&P 500 fourteen out of its first seventeen years in existence.[19] In fact, in the early 2000s, BGI had products across most equity markets—across various equity markets, including small capitalization stocks as well as geographically focusd products like the United Kingdom, Europe, Australia, Canada, and the Far East—all of which consistently trounced their respective benchmarks since inception. Just as the research had predicted, these underlying factor exposures were able to generate consistently higher returns than the basic index did.

Other practitioners jumped on the factor bandwagon with similar products. Specialist firms like Dimensional Funds Advisors, Research Affiliates, AQR, Scientific Beta, and Wisdom Tree, as well as many of the massive index shops like Northern Trust Asset Management and State Street Global Advisors, all spun out competing offerings. Whether they were called fundamental indexes or smart beta, they all did basically the same thing—construct diversified portfolios of stocks based upon proven research into risk premia intended to slightly and consistently outperform the traditional capitalization-weighted indexes, like the S&P 500.

And for a long time these risk factors worked. Research published in the *Journal of Portfolio Management* looked at 40 years' worth of stock returns.[20] By sorting stocks into quintiles based upon four well-known factors—market capitalization, book to market, momentum, and volatility—the authors were able to isolate the effects of these individual characteristics.

As opposed to merely tilting a diversified portfolio of long stocks in the direction of a factor—like purchasing a bit more value on average, as the fundamental index and smart beta providers did—these authors created pure risk premium exposure. Basically, they sorted stocks into quintiles depending upon how the stocks ranked in each of the various factors, and then bought the most attractive 20% while short-selling[21] the least attractive fifth against them.

For instance, by purchasing the smallest 20% of the stock market and selling the largest fifth of stocks against it, an investor could collect nearly 5% per annum. Even better, buying the cheapest fifth of the market each year and short-selling the most expensive quintile against it would have earned an investor 11.6% annualized (see Table 2.2).

Each factor the authors researched generated consistent pure excess returns over the period 1972 until 2012 and that is even accounting for conservative assumptions for trading costs. But the fact that this pure risk premium exposure—not merely the moves of the underlying stock market—was able to generate such strong returns for over four decades suggests the stock pickers who had essentially done the same thing years earlier, like Lovelace, Graham,

TABLE 2.2 Factor Performance from 1972 to 2012

Quintile	Market Capitalization	Book to Market	Momentum	Volatility
Top	9.74%	19.67%	15.19%	10.21%
2nd	10.92%	13.78%	13.43%	12.31%
3rd	13.23%	12.07%	14.01%	12.17%
4th	12.14%	9.99%	11.99%	12.97%
Bottom	14.71%	8.05%	9.64%	12.44%
Top–Bottom	−4.97%	11.62%	5.55%	−2.23%

and Buffett, maybe never really had the magic alpha touch to begin with. Perhaps they just had found a better beta.

Indeed, subsequent research has shown that after controlling for exposures to known factors, such as those above, no mutual fund managers have ever generated persistent, repeatable alpha.[22] All predictable excess returns have instead come from these underlying fundamental characteristics that drive returns.

But perhaps this has been isolated to just the equity market. The stock market is heavily invested and widely followed, and maybe this contributes to greater efficiency than that of other markets. It may be a fair point that alpha can be found in other segments of the capital markets, just not equities. To address this, let's first take a look at the bond markets.

The Bond King Loses His Crown

In 1965, on his way to fetch doughnuts for the incoming Phi Kappa Psi pledge class at Duke University, Bill Gross was in a hurry. Ignoring the rainy conditions, the wiry senior floored the gas pedal in his Nash Rambler in the hopes of making it a quick trip. Unfortunately, he lost control of the car and crashed into oncoming traffic.[23]

Gross's injuries were substantial, and he spent a good portion of his final college year in the hospital convalescing. During his stay, the psychology major picked up a copy of *Beat the Dealer* by Ed Thorpe to pass the time.

Thorpe was a mathematician and later a very successful hedge fund manager in his own right, but he is probably best known for this book. In it, he detailed methodical ways gamblers could keep track of the odds present in a deck of cards and actually overcome the house's edge when playing blackjack. Thorpe is often called the godfather of card counting as a result.

Fascinated, recovered from his injuries, and with no real direction aside from his upcoming enlistment in the navy, the young man decided to head to Las Vegas after graduation. With nothing more than $200 in his pocket, a hefty dose of resolve, and an uncanny ability to focus for hours on end, Gross was determined to put Thorpe's teaching to good use. Although his parents teased him that they would surely see him again in a few short days, Gross played the blackjack tables on the strip 16 hours a day, 7 days a week, for 4 months straight, unerringly counting cards. By the time he reported for duty at the naval base in Pensacola, Florida, Gross had turned that $200 pot into a cool 10 grand.

And thus was born his love of investing. After completing his tour in Vietnam, Gross returned to the states to pursue an MBA at the University of California at Los Angeles. It was during his studies here that he read Thorpe's second book, *Beat the Market*. Thorpe again explored a systematic mathematical framework for evaluating odds, this time showing that mispricing of warrants on equities could be exploited for consistent gains. Gross used this research to write his master's thesis on convertible bonds, which combine options on stocks with fixed-income instruments.

Gross set out to find a job on Wall Street, preferably in the exciting world of equities. However, such opportunities were harder to come by on the West Coast, where Gross wanted to remain for lifestyle reasons. After reluctantly responding to a job opening for a junior credit analyst at the staid Pacific Mutual Life Insurance Company, Gross began a career as one of the greatest bond investors of all time.

Almost immediately upon starting at his new firm, Gross impressed his supervisors with his investment acumen. The premiums from the insurance company had historically been invested almost exclusively in bonds, mortgages, and loans, and Gross was quick to figure out ways to add some excess return to the otherwise sleepy portfolio. In a few short years, Gross and two of his upstart compatriots were able to convince the senior executives at the conservative firm to let them take over effective control of the firm's investment subsidiary, the Pacific Investment Management Company, or PIMCO. Although this business had been set up to initially manage the insurance company's portfolio, the aggressive younger executives were soon managing money for outside clients as well.

Gross and his colleagues built PIMCO into a fixed-income powerhouse, and Gross managed the firm's flagship PIMCO Total Return Fund himself until his departure at the end of 2014 following a messy dispute with the new parent company, Allianz. At its peak, PIMCO managed nearly $2 trillion in assets, with roughly $250 billion of that in Gross's fund alone.

During this time, Gross's returns—as well as the size of his impact on the market—earned him the moniker the bond king. Over the period from 1987 until his exodus in 2014, Gross's portfolio outperformed the Barclays US Credit Bond Index by 1.33% per year,[24] an impressive track record by any measure. However, since his departure from PIMCO, Gross was never able to replicate the successes of his prior track record at his new employer, Janus. And ultimately Bill Gross retired in 2019, and today ETF provider BlackRock is the king of the block in bonds. However, Gross did show us, and other research has confirmed,[25] that it is possible to identify consistent drivers of return in fixed income. Gross was a prolific writer as well, and he offered his thoughts on what factors led to this track record. According to Gross, he was able to consistently add excess returns to fixed-income benchmarks by employing three main tilts in his portfolio—by having more credit risk and shorter duration than the benchmark and by having greater exposure to negative convexity via mortgages and other similar securities.[26] Subsequent research has shown that these factors do account for a significant portion of Gross's excess returns.[27] Without getting into unnecessary details about these technical drivers of return in fixed-income markets, they can be summarized as different types of yield, such as interest rates, credit spreads, or roll yield. But essentially, if you add a little more yield to your portfolio, you can consistently outperform an index.

The simplest way to demonstrate this is to compare the investment-grade Barclays Aggregate Bond Index versus a portfolio of 80% Barclays Agg and

20% High Yield (Figure 2.2). This slight credit risk tilt adds a mere 0.03% to the volatility of the portfolio, but it increases average annualized returns from 5.23 to 5.68%. A single-factor model would call this alpha, but it doesn't make it so—despite what many bond managers would have you believe.

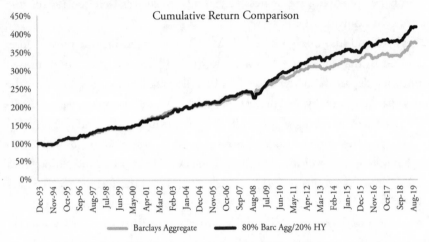

FIGURE 2.2   The outperformance of a yield tilt

Making Commodities Conservative

Commodities markets predate modern capitalism. Trading in physical agricultural commodities is as old as human civilization itself, going back 7,000 years as ancient Sumerians exchanged goats and pigs for goods and services. Futures markets on various commodities have also existed for hundreds of years. Of course, perhaps the most famous historical example was futures on tulip bulbs in Holland during the early 1600s. In what has become commonly known as the first instance of a financial bubble, speculators driven by the frenzied demand for these exotic imported flowers drove prices for futures on certain types of tulip bulbs up to hundreds of thousands of dollars in today's terms. Unfortunately, many speculators were left with huge losses after the fad had passed.

By 1864, futures on wheat, corn, cattle, and pigs became tradable using standard instruments listed on the Chicago Board of Trade, or CBOT. But for a long time, conventional theory held that participating in commodities futures was purely a speculative enterprise. Since supply and demand for the physical commodities are driven by industrial participants, purely financial players in the futures market should not be able to have any informational edge. Gains were thought to be due largely to luck, and most could expect to lose their shirts to more informed market players. As an old Wall Street saying goes, "The fastest way to become a millionaire trading commodities is to start as a billionaire."

However, this didn't stop Bob Greer, the man often credited with creating the first investable commodity index. After graduating from business school at Stanford in the early 1970s, Greer found himself scrolling through rolls of microfilm in the basement of a public library.[28] When studying the performance of physical commodities, Greer had come to realize that without the leverage of futures—which could run up to 10 or 20 times—the typical commodity was no more risky than the average stock. And even better, a diversified portfolio of commodities, like an index, demonstrated similar volatility to a stock index. The only problem with the existing commodity indexes at the time was that they involved the spot prices for the physical asset, which meant they were not investable for almost any investor. Not too many market participants have the logistic capabilities to own and store bushels of corn and barrels of oil.

But Greer had grasped that the liquid futures market that the CBOT had created over a hundred years prior meant an investable portfolio could be constructed using futures; and again, if they were fully cash-collateralized—that is, if they were not levered at all—they would be no more risky as an asset class than equities. However, no real academic work had yet tied the prices of the futures contracts to the underlying physical commodity. That's what Greer was trying to do as he dug through old copies of the *Wall Street Journal* and jotted down the prices of various futures contracts over time into his notepad.

Using these figures, Greer constructed an index that would buy futures on commodities according to their relative importance in global trade. His rules-based approach would also purchase these contracts at a certain point in the calendar and then sell them as they got closer to expiration. And the excess collateral—the cash above the exchange margin requirements—would be invested in 90-day Treasury securities.

This approach to building a commodity index was published in the *Journal of Portfolio Management* in an article titled "Conservative Commodities: A Key Inflation Hedge,"[29] but unfortunately for Greer, it did not get a lot of traction from institutional investors at that time. Commodities just weren't treated like an asset class when constructing portfolios.

Eventually, Greer went on to other things, but then in 1991, Goldman Sachs launched the first investment product to actually track an investable index, the Goldman Sachs Commodity Index. Bolstered by the success of this product, Greer returned to his earlier research, successfully launching competing commodity index strategies, first with Daiwa Securities and later with the bond king at PIMCO. And today, investable commodities products have somewhere around $300 billion to $350 billion in assets under management collectively. Not only have commodities finally found a place in the asset allocation discussion; many of these products have also historically generated consistent albeit modest outperformance relative to the commodity indexes.

Just like they had for stocks and bonds, academics turned to researching to determine which predictable risk premia were correlated with subsequent returns in commodities futures. Although this time these factors were slightly different, the researchers nevertheless were able to identify a handful of key return drivers for fully collateralized commodities futures.[30] While the underlying spot price was a part of the return, the collateral yield—or the income you were able to generate on the fixed-income assets in which the excess margin cash was invested—was also a big part of it. But perhaps the most important factor is what is called the roll yield.

Futures represent the obligation to purchase (or sell, if you have shorted them) an asset at a specific date in the future (hence the name!). Thus, there are multiple futures open for any given asset, creating a forward calendar. These future prices represent the cost of the futures contract itself, and they typically differ from the spot prices, creating a futures curve. A market where the futures are more expensive than the spot price of the physical commodity is said to be in contango; a futures market is in backwardation when the forward curve is trading below the spot price. (See Figure 2.3.)

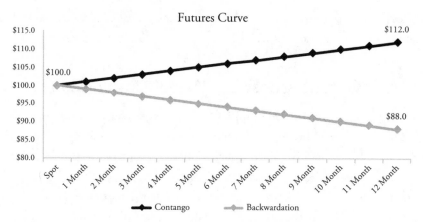

FIGURE 2.3   Backwardation versus contango

Roll yield can be positive or negative depending upon which market structure is in place for a given future. For example, in Figure 2.3, if an investor were to purchase the one-year backwardated future for $88 and hold to expiration, assuming the spot price did not change, that investor would collect $12 for rolling up the curve. Conversely, paying the $112 for the back-end contract in the contangoed market would result in a loss of $12 if spot remained unchanged.

Although spot rarely remains unchanged—it is also subject to price momentum, like equities—the roll yield is the factor most highly predictive of returns in futures contracts. Contracts bought in backwardated markets are more likely to outperform, whereas paying up for a contangoed market is more likely to result in underperformance. Buying $100 for $88 sure looks like value.

To find the commodities futures return, use Equation 2.2:

Futures return = change in spot price + collateral yield + roll yield

$$(2.2)$$

So the total return to commodity futures comes from changes in spot price plus collateral yield plus or minus the roll yield.

It sure appears that momentum, income, and value exist in commodity futures as well. Although the technical metrics are different, it's the same underlying factors appearing again and again, masquerading as alpha. Let's take a look at one last market, this time currencies, to see if we can spot the same patterns one more time.

Getting Conscious About Currencies

Although not as old as commodities, currencies have also existed for thousands of years, well before stocks and bonds. As early as the eighth century BC, the Chinese had begun to utilize miniature bronze castings of weapons and tools as a medium of exchange, as opposed to actually trading the real things. However, this meant that each trade left the parties exposed to the counterparty risk of the other. A miniature replica of a sword was only as good as the word of the man who traded with you. It wasn't until about a hundred years later that the first official currency was minted and backed by a central government.

King Alyattes of Lydia, in what is now part of modern-day Turkey, minted the first true currency, a stamped alloy of gold and silver called a trite. These coins carried the symbol of a lion, the crest of King Alyattes, and this standardized currency allowed for the efficient trade of goods and services. On the back of this financial innovation, Lydia became a trading dynamo and a very wealthy nation. Croesus, of "richer than Croesus" fame, was the son of Alyattes, and he led the kingdom after his father's death.

Alas, the wealth of the Lydians was not enough to protect them from the scimitars of the advancing Persian Empire. However, from the Roman denarius, to Spanish doubloons, Dutch guilders, British pounds, and today US dollars, currencies backed by powerful central governments have facilitated efficient global trade ever since. Today trading of one currency versus another, also called foreign exchange, or forex for short, is the most liquid and active financial market in the world. Global foreign exchange now typically sees average trading volumes on the order of $6 trillion to $7 trillion each day, dwarfing most other capital markets.

For many years, experienced forex traders such as George Soros, Bill Lipschutz, John Taylor, and Sandy Grossman were able to generate consistent outsized returns with repeatable strategies based on a few different styles. While certainly all somewhat unique in their implementation, currency strategies were typically categorized into a few main groupings: trend followers, carry traders, and those employing fundamental valuation methods, such as purchasing power parity.

By now, these factors should look all too familiar to the reader. Trend following is the same as a momentum strategy—buying what is going up and selling what is going down. A currency carry trade is one where an investor attempts to arbitrage interest rate differentials in two different currencies. In practice it works like this: a carry trader borrows in the low interest rate currency, called the funding currency, and uses the proceeds to purchase the higher-yielding currency. It's a yield play, provided of course the exchange rates don't change too much.

And finally, purchasing power parity is a macroeconomic measure that compares the price of a basket of goods in one country with the price of the same basket of goods in another country. If the prices of the goods are equivalent once adjusted for the exchange rate, the currencies are said to be at parity. If the basket of goods is cheaper in one currency, then that currency is undervalued with respect to the other. So it bears a lot of similarity to the value factor in stocks.

All these style factors have generated an average positive rate of return over long periods of time, despite being largely uncorrelated with one another. But once again, academics were able to show that once the return of the risk premia were accounted for, few managers were able to generate excess returns. In fact, using a database of daily returns for active currency managers, research was able to show that roughly three-quarters of managers underperformed systematic, indexlike approaches to implementing strategies in these styles.[31] Even worse, those managers that did outperform in one year were no more likely to outperform the next year than a flip of the coin, but their correlation to these factors—their beta—remained consistent. It turns out, factors work in currency markets, too.

Factor Zoo

With all the success that factors had demonstrated, other academics joined the research trend, looking for new and unique risk premia to write about.

And unsurprisingly they found what they were so urgently looking for. Research published in 2019 documented that since the discovery of the value effect, financial academia has published research papers on roughly 400 discrete factors![32] Figure 2.4. depicts the findings by year. At some point, the addition of an incremental factor adds no more value—pun intended—to a return model.

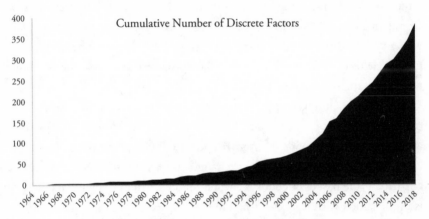

FIGURE 2.4   Rise of the factor zoo

Defining Factors

At this point, it's probably time to discuss what a factor actually is. At its most basic core, a risk premium is just a characteristic that drives investment returns. Think of factors as the building blocks of returns, like atoms are for molecules. Fundamentally, there are only two ways to make money with any investment: to collect income while you own the investment or to sell the investment for more than you paid for it. In other words, income and capital appreciation—there is just no other way possible mathematically. A risk premium is something that drives those returns, not just something that is merely correlated with them. But with all of this statistical research showing hundreds of factors, how can one distinguish between a "true" factor, or a fundamental driver of returns, and a mere anomaly, or a statistical artifact? Which ones are durable, and which ones are the result of data mining or short-term dislocations?

I believe there are four critical characteristics that separate a true factor from these other more numerous pseudo-factors. To be a true, durable risk premium, a factor must meet the following criteria:

1. The factor must persist within a market across time periods.
2. The factor must exist across various markets and asset classes.
3. There must be a fundamental reason why the factor should drive returns.
4. The factor must work at both underwriting individual assets and generating asset class return assumptions.

Does the Factor Persist Within a Market Across Time Periods?

To be durable, a factor must generate excess returns across long time periods, such as 30 or 40 years—ideally even more. If instead the effect was short and fleeting, if say it worked over one decade but never again, then it most likely represented some temporary phenomenon, such as changing regulations, market dislocations, or the shifting preferences of market participants. It's harder to get conviction that such an effect will persist. If, however, something has worked for a century, then it seems a safer bet that some real investment factor underlies it. Some research on stock and bond premiums shows that these have worked going back even longer, hundreds of years in fact.

However, it is important to note that implementation is key. Implementation, or the specific metric used to measure the factor, may change over time, but this doesn't mean the factor stopped working. For instance, let's imagine that book to market no longer works in predicting excess returns for value stocks. Perhaps this could mean that the market has adapted to this particular metric—maybe CEOs are managing asset values to alter the book-to-price ratio because they receive equity compensation and know that this risk premium results in higher stock returns, or maybe quantitative investment managers have updated their valuation models with new metrics, possibly another statistic that has begun to work better, like say price to sales. None of these changes in implementation mean that value isn't a durable factor. It just means that how you measure it may have to change.

In fact, models that use multiple metrics to proxy for a single factor have been shown to generate more consistent returns over time.[33]

Does the Factor Exist Across Various Markets and Asset Classes?

If a factor only works in one select asset class or geography but cannot be found in other asset classes, then perhaps it is not a real phenomenon. It may simply be an anomaly present in that specific market, such as the small-capitalization risk premium. Obviously, small cap is not an effect found in currencies or commodities, which suggests it may not be a fundamental driver of returns. The fact that value, momentum, and yield are not only durable across time, but present in virtually every asset class for which return indexes exist over reasonably long periods,[34] strongly points to a fundamental relationship between these factors and returns. The prevalence of a factor suggests it is an essential element of investments.

Is There a Fundamental Reason Why the Factor Should Be Predictive of Returns?

While persistence of excess returns for a factor over time and across asset classes is empirical evidence ex post that the factor actually drives returns, it does not answer how. For value and yield, the answer to that is simple. As noted earlier, income and capital appreciation are the only two ways to make money, and both of these factors measure those characteristics explicitly ex ante. Buying an asset with a 10% yield means 10% returns are fairly likely, and buying a dollar for 80 cents means a 20% cumulative return is a pretty good assumption.

Clearly, value and yield are real factors, and the answer to the above question is straightforward. However, the fundamental reason why certain other factors work isn't always quite as clear. And sometimes it's altogether murky. For instance, why does momentum work? Is momentum a true risk premium, or is it a semipredictable characteristic of market participant behavior? Just because people do predictably tend to pay more for an asset that has been appreciating recently does not mean it has to continue.

A comprehensive answer to this puzzle is beyond the scope of this section, especially since this question is often the hardest to answer. There are few clear yeses, many obvious noes, and a lot of things that fall into the gray area in between. Momentum may not quite meet this hurdle, since it is more about participant behavior than a true characteristic inherent in the investment, although perhaps it could be argued that momentum is a singular fundamental trait intrinsic to all investments. Small cap, on the other hand, is an example of a clear no. How does a smaller capitalization explicitly lead to higher returns? The answer is it does not, although it may be correlated with them. This suggests other underlying factors correlated with, and potentially causing, both.

Hence, readily identifiable characteristics predictive of returns may be persistent phenomenon, but that doesn't necessarily make them factors per se. Generally speaking, a true risk premium must be an inherent characteristic of the asset that clearly leads to future returns. That is, there must be a causal argument.

Does the Factor Work at Underwriting Individual Assets as Well as Capital Market Assumptions for the Asset Class?

Following up on the prior point, a true factor must fundamentally drive future returns, not merely be correlated with them. Moreover, this relationship should result in the ability to set reasonable return assumptions using the risk premium as an input. It's important to stress this does not mean factors can truly predict returns, but they certainly can be used to help establish realistic parameters around expectations. Once again, yield is the easiest factor to understand. If you buy an asset with an 8% yield, then 8% should be the return assumption, all else being equal. And the same holds for bonds as an asset class. The single most highly correlated variable with future 10-year returns in the Barclays Aggregate Bond Index is the index yield at purchase. This is clear and intuitive.

Conversely, how would one go about modeling the returns to small-capitalization stocks as an asset class? What would be the specific small-cap input into a return model? Well, an analyst would immediately turn to other underlying factors, including the price-to-earnings ratio, book-to-ratio, and the dividend yield to set forward-looking return projections for a single stock. Small capitalization on its own doesn't enter into the equation. Continuing to pick on the small-cap effect, more recent research does show that such third-factor variables, like lower liquidity in the trading of such small securities, explain almost all of this statistical effect.[35]

However, the liquidity premium too is a naïve concept. One does not make money from liquidity. Lower liquidity results in wider spreads, which is just another way of saying larger discounts and higher yields. Often the assumptions for private equity asset class returns are set using public equity returns plus a simplistic liquidity premium. Unfortunately, this gets it backward. No investment generates excess returns because of the illiquidity itself. Any excess returns attributable to differences in liquidity will result from differences in valuation, growth rates, and yield. If the risk factor cannot really be used to set capital markets assumptions, then it's not a true return factor.

We will return to all these concepts in greater detail later. For now, it's just important to understand that to determine that something truly is a factor, it must drive returns for stocks, equity indexes, bonds, and bond markets consistently over time and geography.

So where does it all end? Well, I certainly won't lay claim to a complete knowledge of everything factor-related. Nor is the debate settled. Our understanding of factors will continue to change as the research around them grows. Right on cue, a recent study by Cam Harvey and Yan Liu took a more critical look at just how valid these factors actually are, using multiple techniques to correct for the statistical significance of them.[36] Again, small capitalization failed all their corrected measures, whereas value and momentum comfortably passed every test. So it is probably safe to say that the true number of factors lies somewhere between 2 and 300. Value, momentum, and yield have very strong arguments for being critical components of investment returns.

But don't let them fool you; they were never alpha to begin with no matter how early some of the greatest investors ever discovered them. If you are the first to find them, your returns will look like alpha, but what investors have actually bought was just hidden beta. Undoubtedly, it does take skill to be the first to find a given risk premium. But once others have found it, it doesn't take much skill to replicate it, pick an easy-to-beat benchmark, and sell that return as alpha, although many managers do. It's important for investors to realize there is an adverse selection bias in hiring managers based on their track record of alpha generation; you're probably getting someone who is simply good at hiding beta!

In the next chapter we will discuss hedge funds and their claims to alpha.

Notes

1. According to K. Geert Rouwenhorst (2004), mutual funds actually originated in the Netherlands in the late eighteenth century. An innovative Dutch merchant and trader named Abraham van Ketwich created a trust named Eendragt Maakt Magt, or Unity Creates Strength, which is also the maxim of the Dutch Republic, in order to pool investments from individual investors and diversify across colonial holdings in Austria, Denmark, Germany, and Sweden, among other places. At the time, more than 100 individual securities were traded on the Amsterdam exchange, and this vehicle was the first of its kind to allow small investors to diversify their risk across many of these individual assets. Additionally, there were in fact mutual funds that beat the Investment Company of America to market, namely the Massachusetts Investors Trust. Established on March 21, 1924, this trust was truly the first open-ended mutual fund in America, and it is still in existence today, managed by MFS Investment Management. But Lovelace gets credit in my book for pioneering the industry as we now know it.
2. Ellis (2011).
3. Securities and Exchange Commission (1939), pp. 1241–1247. And JBL got the better of his old pal MacCrone in the deal. The details are a fascinating read.
4. According to information from Capital Group's website and adjusted for average fees and a 5.75% sales load in year 1.
5. Chapman (2019). However, analysis indicates that Graham's investment of $700,000 into GEICO in 1948 eventually grew into a position worth nearly half a billion dollars, contributing more to his returns than all his other investments combined. This raises the question if it was really a repeatable process at all or a singular bet. More on persistence later!
6. See Fama (1965) and Malkiel (1973).
7. Fama and French (1993) got all the coverage, but the duo had actually already introduced size and value a year earlier; see Fama and French (1992). Additionally, both effects had been documented by prior researchers. Banz (1981) had already covered the size effect, and Stattman (1980) demonstrated that the book-to-price factor was predictive of returns. Alas, their names didn't come to be associated with the three-factor model popularized by Fama and French.

8. Although the Fama-French student Carhart got the accolades, Jegadeesh and Titman (1993) had earlier proved the existence of momentum.
9. Ang et al. (2009).
10. See Bogle (2019), p. 13.
11. Ibid., p. 17.
12. Ibid., p. 47.
13. McDevitt and Schramm (2019).
14. https://www.cnbc.com/2019/03/15/active-fund-managers-trail-the-sp-500 -for-the-ninth-year-in-a-row-in-triumph-for-indexing.html.
15. Wells Fargo's indexing efforts predated the Vanguard First Index Investment Trust, but Wells Fargo didn't launch a mutual offering at that time.
16. His firm was very successful for many years. In 1998, he sold a controlling stake to AXA Investment Managers, which renamed the firm AXA Rosenberg. Unfortunately, a coding error in the firm's computer models led to notable client losses in 2009, and Rosenberg failed to notify clients until nearly a year later. Investors were forced to find out the reasons for their underperformance only after the SEC was informed. As an institutional client of the firm, we determined AXA Rosenberg's response and handling of the error to be unacceptable and, along with many other investors, decided to withdraw our assets. Barr Rosenberg was eventually banned from the investment industry by the SEC, and he can now be found teaching classes at the Nyingma Institute, a Tibetan Buddhist center of learning in Berkeley. AXA restructured the business and eventually renamed it Rosenberg Equities under new management and with far lower AUM.
17. Wells Fargo's indexing unit was sold to British bank Barclays in 1995 and was renamed Barclays Global Investors. Eventually, BlackRock acquired the BGI business for $13.5 billion in June 2009, as the British lender was struggling in the aftermath of the Global Financial Crisis and needed to raise cash. This transaction laid the groundwork for BlackRock to become a behemoth outside of just bonds.
18. Which is obviously why hay is actually sold by the pound not the bale, but I needed to continue the analogy.
19. Fox (2003).
20. Amenc et al. (2014).
21. Short selling involves selling an asset without owning it. An investor must first locate and borrow the asset he or she wishes to sell before actually selling. Once the security is sold, or shorted, the investor delivers the borrowed asset to the buyer and collects the cash, which is held as collateral by the asset lender. The investor must then repurchase an identical asset in the future—the hope is, after the price has fallen—and then return it to the lender. If indeed the price has fallen, the investor makes a profit. If the price has risen, the investor would be required to pay the difference. We will talk more about short selling in the next chapter.
22. See Carhart (1997) and Detzel and Weingard (1998).
23. Middleton (2004), pp. 13–16.
24. Dewey and Brown (2019).

25. For instance, see Litterman and Scheinkman (1991), Fama and French (1993), and Brooks and Moskowitz (2017).
26. Gross (2005).
27. Dewey and Brown (2019).
28. Greer et al. (2013), p. 7.
29. Greer (1978).
30. The articles by Gorton and Rouwenhorst (2006) and Erb and Harvey (2006) are perhaps the two most well known, although Till (2006) was published at the same time.
31. Pojarliev and Levich (2008).
32. Harvey and Liu (2019).
33. Amenc et al. (2014).
34. Baltussen et al. (2019).
35. Horowitz et al. (2000). It's also worth noting that the small-capitalization effect has not been as pronounced in the last 20 years, nor is it as prevalent in international equity markets.
36. Harvey and Liu (2019).

3
Hedge Funds— the Incredible Shrinking Alpha

Rule No. 1: Never lose money.
Rule No. 2: Never forget rule No. 1.
—WARREN BUFFETT

The History of Hedge Funds

During the late 1940s, an Australian journalist working for *Fortune* magazine began some research into the investment methodologies of several famous traders of the time for a series of articles he was writing. By the end of 1949, that journalist, Alfred Winslow Jones, had decided to try his hand at actual investing, employing combinations of the strategies he had researched, such as the use of leverage and short selling. A.W. Jones & Co. was created as an investment partnership with an initial investment of $100,000 to do just that. With a first-year return of 17.3%, the world's first hedge fund was off and running.

After years of successfully and secretively investing, in 1966 an article titled "The Jones Nobody Keeps Up With" by Carol Loomis (coincidentally also in *Fortune*),[1] drew broader attention to the successful model Jones had built. According to the article, Jones had beaten the best equity mutual fund over the previous five years by 44% cumulatively, and the top mutual fund over the previous decade, the Dreyfus Fund, by a whopping 87%!

Such success drew numerous imitators, including hedge fund notables such as Warren Buffett, Barton Biggs, Michael Steinhardt, and Julian Robertson. To a lesser extent, others like Ed Thorpe and George Soros adapted the hedge fund model to their own approaches with similar success.

The hedge fund industry of today, a cottage industry during that early period, was built on the success of these first-generation luminaries who had one notable thing in common: returns that dominated the equity markets. Using various sources for estimates of the annualized return of these legendary traders during their heydays paints a picture of a sector that handily beat public equities, as these early investors more than doubled market returns and averaged nearly 22% returns over investing careers that spanned nearly three decades on average (see Table 3.1).[2]

TABLE 3.1   Estimated First-Generation Hedge Fund Returns

Manager	Years	Estimated Returns	S&P 500
A.W. Jones & Co.	1949–1984	16.7%	6.9%
Warren Buffett (Buffett LP/Berkshire)	1965–2015	20.0%	6.6%
Barton Biggs (Fairfield)	1965–1985	15.0%	4.7%
Steinhardt Partners	1967–1995	24.5%	7.5%
George Soros (Quantum)	1969–2000	30.0%	8.5%
Ed Thorpe (Princeton Newport)	1974–1998	20.0%	11.1%
Julian Robertson (Tiger)	1980–2000	26.0%	13.3%
Average	1969–1998	21.7%	8.4%

The second generation of superstars opened shop in the late eighties and early nineties on the back of such track records, obtaining capital from high-net-worth individuals (in some cases, from those listed in the table), family offices, funds of funds, and some leading endowments. A similarly star-studded group of younger investors, including the likes of Andreas Halverson of Viking, David Tepper at Appaloosa, Ken Griffin of Citadel, Dan Loeb from Third Point, James Simons from Renaissance, John Tudor Jones, and Steve Cohen of now-defunct SAC, would have in aggregate averaged almost exactly 20% returns over 20-year track records. Slightly below the returns of the prior generation of masters of the universe, but still doubling the market returns during their tenures. The goal for most of those who invested in hedge funds in these early years was to beat the equity market, full stop.

How did these so-called masters of the universe generate such strong returns? This first requires a brief discussion about what hedge funds are. Hedge funds have a reputation for being universally risky, totally unregulated, highly secretive investment structures that all do very similar things and are exclusively the playground of Wall Street fat cats and the ultrawealthy. They are often portrayed as playing fast and loose with ethical rules. And while it's true that hedge funds do things quite differently from the typical mutual fund strategies we saw in the last chapter, it hardly means they are excessively risky. In fact, today the bigger problem might be that they aren't risky enough.

It's also a myth that hedge funds are unregulated. They are highly regulated in many ways. They have to comply with all federal and state laws on trading, accounting, taxes, etc. They are subject to all the rules and regulations of any exchange that they trade on, such as the SEC rules for owning and trading equities, or the Commodities Futures Trading Commission regulations if they are trading futures, including prohibitions against insider trading, front-running, fraud, market manipulation, exchange margin requirements, and futures position limits. There's really only one rule they are exempt from, the 1940 Investment Company Act that created mutual funds. As long as they abide by certain requirements, such as limiting the amount of accredited investors they have, they are afforded the latitude to invest in ways mutual funds cannot. Furthermore, the JOBS Act of 2012 significantly increased this limit from 500 to 2,000, allowing hedge funds today to raise more money from smaller investors.

Unlike mutual funds, hedge funds have a performance fee. Like private equity funds, hedge funds charge a fixed management fee based on assets, 1 or 2% similar to a mutual fund, but they also collect 20% of profits, something the 1940 act explicitly prohibits for registered funds. Some argue this is nothing more than a free option that incentivizes excessive risk taking, but others argue that it's the carrot that helped drive those strong hedge fund returns in the early years of the industry. There is certainly a greater incentive to generate strong returns when you get paid for performance.

Basically, a hedge fund is a private investment partnership that uses investment strategies typically unavailable to mutual funds, such as utilizing leverage, selling short, and employing futures and derivatives. But this masks the truth that hedge funds are a very heterogeneous group of investment strategies, of which some are low risk, some are high risk, some use little to no leverage, and some use very high leverage. They can trade virtually any asset class. So let's look at what these strategies entail.

Hedge Fund Alpha

The basic investment architecture shared by most hedge funds is called arbitrage, or relative value. Arbitrage simply means the (nearly) simultaneous buying of an asset in one market and selling of a quasi-identical asset in another market. Perfect arbitrage, a scenario that almost never exists in the real world, would occur if for instance a trader were to purchase shares of a company, such as Apple, for $245 in one exchange and instantaneously sell it for $250 in another exchange, realizing a completely risk-free gain of $5.

However, that's a scenario that for all intents and purposes never occurs. Most of what hedge funds do isn't pure arbitrage. For example, a hedge fund might buy a security, like Apple, in one market and sell another similar asset short in a different market. Perhaps the fund would buy Apple and short-sell Microsoft against it, hoping that Apple outperforms its competitor during the investment period. This strategy where an investor buys a stock that appears cheap on certain metrics while selling a related more expensive one against it is often referred to as "pairs trading" specifically or as "long-short equity" more broadly. Clearly, these are similar but not identical assets, and there's no guarantee that their returns will actually be linked, making it riskier than the instantaneous windfall above. That's the difference between true arbitrage and relative value—the degree of dissimilarity between the assets on the long and short side of the portfolio. The more closely linked the assets, the less the risk; the more disparate the assets or the longer the hold period, the greater the risk. It's not truly an arbitrage; it's a hedge—hence the name.

Merger arbitrage, also called risk arbitrage, is a classic example. Risk arbitrage is a trading strategy whereby an investor purchases shares in the stock of a public business being acquired by another public company. The simplest scenario is where Company A announces an intention to buy Company B for $40 per share. If the stock was trading at $30 before the announcement, the $10 difference represents the deal premium. Typically the market will push the new price of the stock up very close to the bid—perhaps it will trade up to $38.50—with the remaining premium reflecting the market's perception of the risk that the deal collapses, or "breaks." Slightly more complicated are stock deals, where the acquiring company exchanges its own stock for shares of the target. This requires the trader to buy the target and short a certain amount of the acquirer. In both transactions, success requires the investor to pick the deals that consummate, at which point you collect the premium, and avoid the deals that break, because the price of the target stock generally plunges once the market sees a deal isn't going through.

Other types of strategies may involve buying debt in a company and shorting the stock against it (capital structure or convertible arbitrage), or trading derivatives such as options or futures against the underlying stocks (index arbitrage or volatility arbitrage), or buying one particular issue of Treasury bonds and selling a different maturity, either shorter or longer, against it (fixed-income arbitrage).

While all these strategies involve some amount of mismatch between the securities on the long and short side of the trade, there is still an economic reason for the two securities to be linked. For instance, equities and debt in one company are both influenced by the financial performance of that same company, just as two companies operating in the same sector will undoubtedly have very similar underlying drivers of demand and production costs, which impact their stock prices. Similarly, derivatives such as options and futures are explicitly priced based upon the value of an underlying asset; hence, their returns are mathematically and inextricably linked, although they can deviate over short periods.

Although it's certainly an oversimplification to suggest that this is the only thing they did, it is true that the first two generations of hedge funds were able to execute on strategies that were largely unknown outside of a few other hedge funds and the proprietary trading desks of the large investment banks. This involved research that allowed them to identify and accurately price seemingly unrelated securities more quickly and efficiently than other market participants, giving them an informational and process advantage that they profitably exploited. The industry forefathers largely initiated such strategies, and the second generation refined them, but by the time the third generation rolled around, the game was already a lot more competitive.

Returning to our merger arbitrage example, Goldman Sachs practically created the strategy in the 1940s when senior partner Gustave Levy ran the firm's one-man trading desk. Noticing how most merger deals ultimately wound up closing, Gus began to capture that spread for Goldman's balance sheet, christening the strategy "risk arbitrage." In 1966, the Robert Rubin (who later became US Secretary of the Treasury) joined the risk arb desk, growing it in scale and prominence within the firm, which he also would go on to run before retiring to public service. During his tenure, Rubin served as a mentor to a host of risk arbitrageurs that were trained in the Goldman way, all of whom eventually went on to launch their own hedge funds. These acolytes included Thomas Steyer (who founded Farallon Capital in 1986), Richard Perry (who launched Perry Capital in 1988), Eddie Lampert (who established ESL Investments also in 1988), and Daniel Och (founded Och-Ziff in 1994).

Obviously, the 1990s saw an enormous increase in the number of competitors in merger arb. Most multistrategy funds and diversified relative value funds, like Long Term Capital Management, began to dabble in it, and corporate raiders and high-profile independent traders like Ivan Boesky migrated into the space as well. This glut of capital resulted in most target stock being pushed right up to the announced bid, shrinking the premium to the point that it hardly compensated for the risk of the deal breaking anymore. Not surprisingly, all these merger-focused pioneers evolved to include various other event-driven trading strategies in their funds.

Such increased competition meant more players jockeying for the same exposure, and this story was replicated across all the traditional hedge fund strategies, one after another. Firms continued to adapt, but hedge fund returns across the industry fell sharply. To look more fully at the history of hedge fund performance, let's turn to some simple index comparisons, using the HFRI Fund Weighted Composite[3] and the S&P 500 Total Return Index to represent hedge funds and equities, respectively. Figure 3.1 charts the comparison.

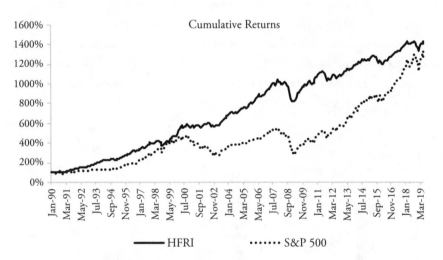

FIGURE 3.1 Cumulative index returns comparison

In looking at the figure, we can see at first glance that the net returns for the "average" hedge fund have been quite competitive with equities over longer time periods. Going back to the beginning of the HFRI index in 1990, hedge funds have compounded at roughly 9.5% after fees while the stock market has generated a total return of 9.2%. Not bad, although questions about the accuracy of the hedge fund index limit some of the conclusions we can draw from this data.[4] Even accounting for some of the potential biases, it still appears reasonable to conclude that returns were at least competitive with those of public markets.

The Decline of Alpha . . .

However, what should also be apparent is the dramatic degradation of returns to hedge funds over the second half of the sample in Figure 3.1. If we simply break the data set into two roughly equal 15-year periods, a dramatic disparity emerges, shown in Figure 3.2. As you can see, from 1990 until about 2004, hedge funds continued their dominant performance versus public stocks, beating the market at 14.4% per annum to 9.9%—less alpha than the first generations were able to crank out, but still quite respectable. However, since 2005, hedge funds have lost their magic touch, trailing a simple public equity index by nearly 50%. Over the last decade and half, an investment into the hedge fund index returned 4.5% per year, while stocks chugged along with their typical 8.5% gains. Something has gone very wrong with the performance of these supposed alpha rock stars.

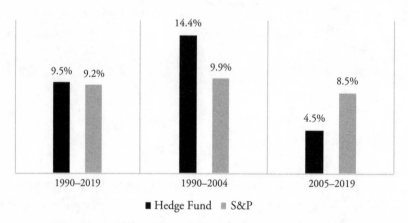

FIGURE 3.2   Hedge fund periodic return comparison with equities

Many articles have placed the blame for this erosion of returns squarely on the shoulders of large institutional allocators that have committed trillions of dollars to the asset class over the last 20 years, causing the industry to exceed its carrying capacity and arbitraging away potential alpha in the process.

Interestingly, early in my career, a research team at JP Morgan predicted just such a thing, calling the inflection point nearly perfectly. In a paper titled "Have Hedge Funds Eroded Market Opportunities?," the authors noted that "hedge funds, with almost $1 trillion under management before leverage, have become a dominant force in market trading. As they grow larger, they will eventually erode the same market opportunities and mispricings they have relied on to create their superior returns. Opportunities are disappearing fastest where hedge funds are very active . . . *and where the same trading rules* have been used for some time" (emphasis mine).[5]

. . . And the Rise of the Institutional Investor

These researchers were eerily prescient. Even by 2006, hedge funds were still largely the purview of the ultrarich, as well as private banks and funds of funds, which catered mostly to those same clients. Research from Barclays Capital showed that institutional investors—like pension funds, insurance companies, foundations, endowments, and sovereign wealth funds—only accounted for a total of about 16% of the aggregated assets under management across the entire hedge fund sector.[6] However, as Figure 3.3 shows, a mere six years later, institutions had single-handedly replaced funds of funds as the biggest group of allocators in hedge funds, jumping to nearly half of the industry assets, as pensions and insurance companies piled into the asset class in scale.

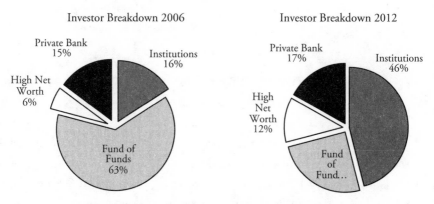

FIGURE 3.3 Hedge fund investor breakdowns (*Barclays*)

During this time, institutions pumped nearly a trillion dollars of new money into these legacy strategies, and in response, the industry grew to accommodate them. According to information from HFR and BarclayHedge, since the beginning of the nineties, the hedge fund industry has exploded from a mere 1,250 funds managing a combined $25 billion in assets to just under 10,000 funds and nearly $3 trillion in assets as of the end of 2018, as shown in Figure 3.4. It's also important to note that this asset growth is even bigger than it looks. All hedge fund strategies use leverage to some extent, some more than others. Gross leverage of 3 to 1 is very common, and for certain strategies like volatility arbitrage, fixed-income arbitrage, and currency trading, the notional assets traded can easily be 10 times equity or more. Such significant leverage amplifies the market impact of these assets, and the high turnover nature of these strategies does even more. This means hedge fund managers today with $3 trillion in fund investments can easily control $10 trillion notional worth of market assets, a huge market footprint compared with that of prior days.

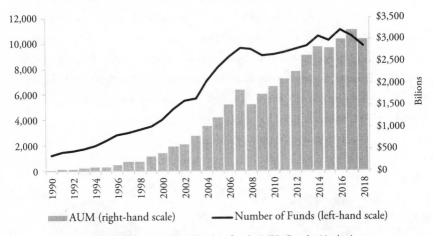

FIGURE 3.4 Growth of hedge funds (*HFR, BarclayHedge*)

And the assets from these large allocators also disproportionately flowed to the largest hedge funds out there. Preqin estimated that at the end of 2014, approximately 11% of the hedge fund firms controlled 92% of the assets in the industry, leaving 89% of the funds out there to fight for the last 8% scraps of the sector's assets under management.[7]

This significant asset concentration comes despite the vast preponderance of research that shows that smaller and younger hedge funds tend to outperform their older, larger brethren. In a research paper from 2009, Melvyn Teo, a professor of finance from Singapore Management University, investigated the performance of over 5,000 unique hedge funds over a 15-year period.[8] His work documented a strong negative convex relationship between hedge fund size and future risk-adjusted returns, and he estimated that smaller funds outperform larger ones on the order of 3.65% per annum after adjusting for risk. Other research has confirmed the same thing—smaller funds tend to outperform, both on nominal and on risk-adjusted bases.[9]

Some of this can be attributed to the impact of more dollars in a given fund chasing the same opportunity set. Another group of academics investigated the impact of asset flows on performance, utilizing an extensive data set of funds of hedge funds.[10] The authors found that among funds of funds that did generate alpha historically, those that experienced significant ensuing capital inflows suffered reduced future alpha levels compared with those that did not. More money chasing the same strategies resulted in lower returns.

Another factor related to size is age. Generally speaking, a bigger fund is also an older one since it takes time to raise assets. You can't launch a $10 billion hedge fund overnight. But research has been effective at disentangling the effects of both size and age and highlighting the impact of each on subsequent returns. One particular paper found that even when controlling for size, each additional year of fund life resulted in an average decline of performance by 48 basis points per annum.[11] This article also showed that as funds grew larger, the effect became even more pronounced, so the effects compounded each other, but both traits were independently deleterious on returns.

To summarize all the research, all else being equal, older, bigger funds generate weaker returns than smaller, newer funds. Despite all the evidence for these conclusions, institutions piled into the big, established shops. Of course, you never get fired for hiring IBM, and when you are committing billions, often in $100 million chunks, you need funds able to take large checks.

While institutional investors pushed aside funds of funds, obviating the need for these intermediaries in the quest to go direct, the industry did not do much to accommodate this massive infusion of capital. Instead, hedge fund managers simply absorbed the capital, growing in both size and number and funneling the money right into the same old well-trodden strategies, which then subsequently declined in alpha production. Why did institutions permit this to happen? Well, simply put, their expectations changed.

Changing Cost of Capital

Broadly speaking, hedge funds can serve one of two roles in a portfolio, that of a return enhancer or that of a portfolio diversifier.[12] Return enhancers tend to have higher-return–higher-risk profiles, but more importantly they tend to have a higher correlation with the traditional drivers of return we observed in the last chapter, such as stocks and bonds. Portfolio diversifiers, on the other hand, offer lower returns and lower risk, but importantly have little to no (and in some cases negative) correlation with equities. However, this is not a binary characteristic, but rather a spectrum, with different strategies falling at different points along the continuum.

Typically hedge funds that trade equity and credit instruments, such as long-short equity funds, distressed credit funds, and some event-driven funds, fall into the return enhancer bucket because they have higher expected returns and higher correlations with traditional stock and bond indexes. On the other hand, strategies like macro funds, managed futures, and more pure arbitrage strategies, as well as exotic strategies like catastrophe bond trading and life settlements, have far lower correlations with traditional markets and can be categorized as portfolio diversifiers. Of course, these binary classifications miss a lot of the gray areas, and many multistrategy funds and relative-value strategies could often be put into either group.

The bigger point is that hedge funds aren't really one thing; they aren't an asset class per se. They are a legal structure, and they can be any asset class, long or short. However, they have to serve a purpose in a portfolio context, like any other investment. The first generation of hedge funds grew on the back of a simple objective, to flat-out beat the equity markets, which they did. As the early-adopter institutional investors began to enter the asset class in the early nineties, for these sophisticated forward-thinking allocators like large US university endowments and the biggest family offices, return enhancement was still the primary role that hedge funds served. And by and large, investors still got what they were paying for.

As you can see in Table 3.2, over the period 1990 to 2004, hedge fund volatility was 6.9%, and the correlation to the equity market was 0.7, which resulted in a beta-to-equity market of 0.33. This is a pretty low beta, and as we learned before, a low beta with high returns means really high alpha. During this second generation of hedge funds, investors got double-digit nominal returns, low absolute risk, and massive alpha—relative to equity markets—of 8.7%. This was a fantastic time to be a hedge fund investor.

TABLE 3.2 Hedge Fund Periodic Statistical Comparison*

	1990–2019	1990–2004	2005–2019
HF returns	9.5%	14.4%	4.5%
HF volatility	6.5%	6.9%	5.8%
HF correlations	0.74	0.70	**0.83**
HF beta to equities	0.34	0.33	0.35
Alpha over equities	4.9%	8.7%	**0.8%**

*Assumes an annualized risk-free rate of 2.30% from 1990 to 2019, 3.68% between 1990 and 2004, and 1.17% over the 2005-to-2019 period based upon one-month T-bills.

However, as the larger and slower-moving institutions piled into the sector, the rationale for the allocation to hedge funds began to change. Realizing that expectations for 20%—or even 15%—compound returns were no longer realistic, hedge fund investors began to underwrite to "equitylike returns with bondlike risk," which is sales-speak for 9%-ish returns with 6%-ish volatility. And since this is what the hedge fund index has done since inception, it certainly seems realistic.

Unfortunately, from 2005 until 2019, the correlation between hedge funds and stocks jumped to 0.83, in no small part because of the concentration of assets that had flowed into the industry. To keep that beta to equities down, managers were forced to reduce volatility to under 6%, managing exposures tightly. Lower exposure to heavily eroded opportunities saw returns plummet. Higher correlation and far lower returns, even with volatility ticking down a touch, mean that alpha has all but disappeared. With nominal returns falling to 4.5% per annum, equitylike no longer works either.

Now the current third-generation justification for a hedge fund or abso-lute return allocation for many institutional investors is that of a pure fixed-income substitute. Unfortunately, as many investors have discovered, no line item should be added to a portfolio just because you want to fill a bucket or simply because it promises diversification. Adding a strategy to your port-folio solely for diversification is like going to Vegas just for the free food. If that's the whole reason, it will certainly cost a lot more than it's worth. Such a clear diminution in the required cost of capital—or a change in the thesis for an investment after the fact to justify lowered returns—has often ended badly. And instead of equitylike returns for bondlike risk, many institutions have found themselves with bondlike returns for highly correlated risk.

A quick look at the returns over the same period, this time including bonds, yields a comparison that doesn't flatter those proponents of this new mandate. While hedge fund returns have eked out modest outperfor-mance versus bonds since 2005, with the Barclays Aggregate Bond Index annualizing at just 4.1%, they have contributed far more risk to the port-folio. Despite the volatility of hedge funds dropping substantially during this period, it was still nearly double that of bonds, as Table 3.3 highlights. However, more striking is the correlation profile. With a correlation of 0.83 to equities, hedge funds don't diversify equity risk away at all. Bonds, on the other hand, exhibited a correlation of 0.00 to the stock market.

TABLE 3.3   Periodic Statistical Comparison with Bonds

2005–2019	Hedge Funds	Bonds
Returns	4.5%	4.1%
Volatility	5.8%	3.2%
Correlation to Equities	**0.83**	0.00

While hedge funds may very well outperform bonds going forward, and may do so with only moderate volatility, they do not play the same role that fixed income plays in a portfolio. Nor should they be expected to. The histori-cal correlation and relatively low volatility of hedge funds were never the main objective of hedge fund managers; rather they were a by-product of differenti-ated processes. Hedge funds, while admittedly not a homogenous group, exist primarily because the investors that ran them were trying to produce strong returns via uncorrelated processes, not simply uncorrelated returns.

It's worth reiterating that the low volatility and moderate to high correlation were never really the objectives. Hedge funds were able to generate solid returns with those risk characteristics by *not* being constrained by the "Morningstar Style Box" approach to investing. They were able to rationally price risk and return across diverse assets, seeking opportunities where other more constrained investors would typically not participate, utilizing leverage and derivatives both long and short to generate strong nominal and risk-adjusted returns. In short, they did things other people weren't doing to generate alpha.

Rethinking the Role of Hedge Funds

Unfortunately, many institutional investors that demanded hedge funds shoehorn themselves into a low-volatility, uncorrelated style box that they weren't really engineered for in the first place have come to regret that decision. For instance, large public pensions like the California Public Employees' Retirement System and the New York City Employees' Retirement System decided to pull the plug on their hedge fund allocations entirely.[13] With their limited transparency and liquidity, inability to scale the asset class, high expenses, and weak returns, hedge funds simply didn't make sense in the asset allocation of these massive investors. They couldn't get enough money into strategies that made enough money, and so quite rationally they exited the asset class.

Even smaller plans have decided to move away from the objective of naïve diversification altogether. In the clearest example of this, the $3 billion Seattle City Employees' Retirement System recently adopted a new asset allocation that removed the plan's 5% target to "diversifying strategies" and instead increased core fixed income by 2% and private equity by the remaining 3%.[14] The retirement system added some actual diversification and actual return enhancement in place of a little bit of neither.

It should come as no surprise that against this backdrop, the industry has witnessed a massive wave of hedge fund closures, including some of the

industries' titans. Goldman Sachs risk arb veteran Richard Perry shut down
his eponymous Perry Capital in 2016 after a near 30-year run, despite evolving beyond pure merger arbitrage. Another Goldman risk arb alum Eric
Mindich, founder of Eton Park, closed shop in 2017. This uncomfortable
reality has not been constrained to event-driven funds, as luminaries across
other strategies, like Leon Cooperman, founder of the long-short equity
firm Omega Advisors, and Louis Bacon, of macro fund Moore Capital, also
closed their doors to external capital due to changing market conditions and
an inability to continue to generate the returns they had grown accustomed
to over three decades. In fact, as shown in Figure 3.5, over the last five years,
the number of hedge funds winding down has exceeded the number of new
hedge fund launches every single year, as the industry retrenches and tries to
find new sources of alpha.

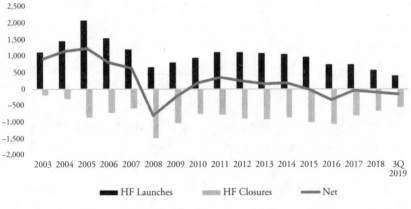

FIGURE 3.5   Hedge fund launches and closures (*HFR*)

The Future of Hedge Funds

The real question is, just where exactly will this alpha come from, because the
old sources just aren't working anymore. Hedge fund alpha has now moved
into negative territory consistently; this is clearly evident in Figure 3.6.

One area that appears to be performing fairly well is quantitative strategies. Index provider Eurekahedge tracks the performance of a set of hedge
funds that incorporate artificial intelligence, or AI, at least in some part into

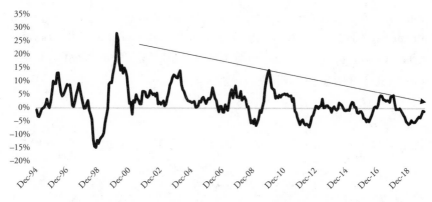

FIGURE 3.6 Hedge fund alpha decline (*HFR, Bloomberg*)

its investment strategy. While AI and machine learning have become nearly ubiquitous buzzwords in the investment world, much of that is more hype than substance. However, this index, an equal-weighted index of 24 underlying funds, is as representative of those quantitative hedge funds that use sophisticated models as possible. Many of these funds use advanced algorithms to scour public market securities for information around valuations, sentiment, price, volume, market depth, and often other alternative data, such as satellite imagery and mobile device data in real time. These computers are basically mining and implementing new and undiscovered factors, or at least new metrics.

Armed with this superior information and superior processing speed, they transact rapidly often on large volumes of securities for short investment horizons, capitalizing on small inefficiencies that others typically can't access quickly enough. This is often referred to as a black box, an opaque system of rules that takes money and information in on one side and spits out a portfolio on the other, and investors don't exactly know why. However, these funds typically employ teams of PhDs in physics, statistics, mathematics, and computer science to design the code on which the black box runs, and they certainly know exactly how it works, if not always why it works.

Comparing the returns from these so-called quant funds versus returns from the broader Eurekahedge Hedge Fund Index of 2,500 funds,[15] we can see significant outperformance from the quants. Figure 3.7 presents the results in graphic form. Since January 2010, computers have trounced their human counterparts, annualizing at 12.9% per annum versus a mere 5.1% for the broader index. Despite having slightly higher volatility, this outperformance still represents a healthy alpha of nearly 9.5% compared with that of the overall hedge fund index.

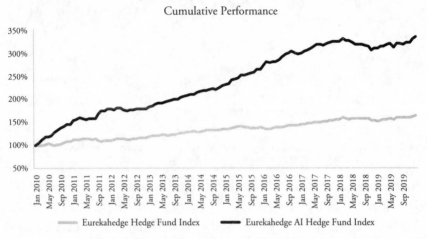

FIGURE 3.7   Computers winning at alpha

Quant appears to be the final holdout of alpha in hedge funds, as investors finally come to realize that the traditional strategies are no longer competitive with other sources of return. Classical long-short equity, fixed-income arbitrage, merger arbitrage, and convertible arbitrage strategies will all continue to shrink in prominence as investors plumb less overallocated sources of uncorrelated returns, like quantitative strategies. The search for an equation that solves the market is likely to prove fruitless to many alpha hunters. True alpha can only come from constantly researching and identifying new signals, a robust statistical process to measure and combine them, and a disciplined approach to killing the ones that are no longer working. Great quants aren't so much a fixed formula as they are an iterative research process. And since alpha is a zero-sum game, in liquid markets this quant alpha will accrue to a few winners with massive computational advantages that latecomers simply won't be able to compete with.

The objectives for hedge funds will also likely evolve once again as well, beyond equitylike returns, fixed-income replacement, or the new favorite—absolute return. Absolute return as a mandate is a fantasy, the financial equivalent of a perpetual motion machine. No investment strategy exists where you put money in one side, turn a crank, and more money will always come out the other side, at least more than the risk-free rate. You have to accept more risk to earn an excess return above that. By calling something an absolute return, you are basically tacitly endorsing an idea that doesn't remotely hold up to scrutiny. (And please, don't call portable alpha "alpha" either. It's just leverage.)

As investors continue to search for alpha, they are increasingly realizing it's simply not to be found in highly efficient markets, outside of a select few quants. The game of scouring public stocks, bonds, currencies, and commodities, even going long and short, is now a commoditized game. These strategies are almost universally known, and the returns have compressed below what investors should require relative to the risk they are taking.

Using beta to judge hedge fund returns has been counterproductive. Unable to reduce their correlation, managers of most hedge fund strategies had only one lever to keep the beta down, and that was by reducing volatility. Unfortunately, the lowered returns that resulted from this double whammy of less alpha available and reduced exposures resulted in a staggeringly inefficient portfolio allocation for most limited partners. Instead of continuing to pump money into the same old strategies, investors seeking uncorrelated strategies would be better served by finding differentiated exposures. Those wanting higher returns should give up the benchmark-linked alpha-beta fool's errand.

The search for uncorrelated returns is leading us to areas of less efficiency, with fewer competitors, less capital, and more information asymmetry. Often, semi-illiquid strategies like direct lending, litigation finance, insurance-linked securities or reinsurance, life settlements, drug or music royalties, and structured settlements are replacing hedge funds because they do what hedge funds used to do, namely provide strong, consistent returns that are fairly uncorrelated with stock markets.

These different strategies do share some commonalities, namely being less understood or widely adopted and all involving highly structured transactions and contractual cash flows. Unlike traditional hedge funds, returns of

8 to 12% are still common, but the trade-off is illiquidity instead of liquidity, and credit risk or counterparty risk in place of volatility. For the majority of these uncorrelated sectors, the duration of the underlying assets is marked in months or years, unlike public stocks and bonds, and the funds are often offered through hybrid or closed-end structures like private equity.

It's precisely this opacity and the unfamiliarity of the rules of the game to all but the most informed that creates the excess return potential. These newer sources of uncorrelated returns can replace traditional hedge funds in the asset allocation, but will require the willingness, and ability, to participate in less competitive, less widely distributed segments of the market. Of course, once they too become overcapitalized and widely known, it will be time to move on to other things.

Finding uncorrelated strategies, allocating to smaller funds, and hiring aligned managers committed to being true partners[16] remains the best way for investors to harvest some excess returns in hedge funds—basically turning them into private markets.

Notes
1. Loomis (1966).
2. Compiled from *Barron's*, *Forbes*, Wikipedia entries, hedge fund databases, and industry contacts. While certainly not exact, I would contend most seasoned market participants familiar with these managers would agree these estimates are quite reasonable.
3. The HFRI family of indexes is managed by Hedge Fund Research Inc. The indexes are among the most comprehensive performance trackers of hedge funds available. HFR has over 6,400 individual funds in its database and roughly 1,900 separate funds that report performance on a monthly basis.
4. Those early hedge fund index returns may have well overstated the performance that the average hedge funds generated. Since reporting performance to HFRI is completely voluntary, there is a self-selection bias built in to which hedge funds are included in the index returns. Aiken et al. (2013) used a data set of hedge fund returns from SEC filings to show that when so-called dead funds stop reporting to the database, the resulting superior returns of the remaining funds create a survivorship bias, upwardly inflating returns. And when relatively new funds decide to report, often after returns have been good, they fill in historical returns since inception, which creates a backfill bias. The combined effects of these biases are estimated by most research to account for 2 to 5% per annum of overstated returns (for instance, Fung and Hsieh, 2009). Still, even with nominal returns 4% lower, early hedge fund performance was at least comparable to, and probably slightly better than, equity returns.
5. Loeys and Fransolet (2004).

6. Bhardwaj et al. (2012).
7. Preqin (2015).
8. Teo (2009).
9. PerTrac (2011) found that small hedge funds (those under $100 million in assets) generated average returns of 13.6% per annum compared with large funds (or those over $500), which averaged 10.0% over the sample period. Ding et al. (2009) and Joenväärä et al. (2012) confirmed that smaller funds outperform in nominal returns, but the authors also provided evidence that they do the same in risk-adjusted returns as well.
10. Fung et al. (2008).
11. Aggarwal and Jorion (2010),
12. Schneeweis and Spurgin (2000) introduced the concept.
13. See Fitzpatrick (2015) and Steyer (2016).
14. See Kozlowski (2020).
15. The Eurekahedge Hedge Fund Index has a 0.98 correlation with the HFRI Fund Weighted Composite.
16. There is strong empirical evidence that managers that act like true partners do outperform. Liang (1999) documented that hedge funds with high-water marks outperform those without them. Agarwal et al. (2009) showed that funds with greater alignment of interests, proxied for by higher levels of managerial ownership and management investment in the fund, delivered superior performance. Joenväärä et al. (2012) confirmed these findings.

4

Private Equity— Taming the Barbarians at the Gate

Any fool can buy a company. Just pay enough.
—HENRY KRAVIS

A Brief Account of Private Equity

Much like hedge funds, the history of institutional private equity dates back to the 1940s, with the founding of American Research and Development Corporation (ARDC) and JH Whitney and Company. These first two dedicated private equity firms, venture capital funds each, were launched in 1946. Prior to this, making minority investments in and acquiring control equity positions in unregistered companies remained almost exclusively the purview of wealthy families and merchant banks.

There is some evidence that the Phoenicians, who were the major naval and trading power in the Mediterranean Sea around 1200 to 800 BC, built their merchant city-state empire on the basis of a private equity carry model, whereby kings would provide upfront resources—ships and supplies—to sea captains to conduct trade in dyes, wood, textiles, and spices across the region in exchange for 20 to 25% of their profits.[1] However, it is also equally plausible that this story is apocryphal.

Similar to what occurred in hedge funds, the notable successes of early private equity practitioners-spawned a generation of eager imitators. ARDC, for instance, landed a huge winner with its investment in Digital Equipment Corporation. Founded in the 1950s, DEC, as it became known, was one of the first, and biggest, manufacturers of personal computers. Unlike many competitors that largely built mainframes, Digital Equipment Corporation focused on much smaller minicomputers. Eventually, DEC was acquired by Compaq in 1998, but ARDC had already exited its investment after the company had gone public. This IPO reputedly bagged the venture investors 500 times their initial investment and an IRR (internal rate of return) of over 1,000%! Not too shabby.

In validating the market for personal computers, DEC and ARDC simultaneously legitimized the venture capital model as well. And subsequently, the 1960s and 1970s saw the birth of such industry stalwarts as Draper and Johnson, Kleiner Perkins, Sequoia, Greylock, and TA Associates, which in turn led to the national emergence of Silicon Valley as a global investing mecca.

At roughly the same time, several financiers led by Jerome Kohlberg, Jr., working at Bear Stearns, began investing in family-owned enterprises that were facing succession issues with no viable exit or that were strapped for cash and otherwise unable to access capital markets. The 1964 acquisition of Orkin Exterminators was one of the first examples of a true leveraged buyout transaction, or LBO.

Orkin Exterminators was founded in the early 1900s by Otto Orkin, the son of Latvian immigrants. As a young child in a large family, Otto was responsible for keeping rats and other pests away from the food supplies and animals on the family's Pennsylvania farm. After experimenting with a mix of arsenic and phosphorous paste mixed with food scraps, young Otto developed a cheap, effective poison that the rats mistook for food and fatally consumed.

Otto began peddling his concoction to neighbors and friends of the family who, impressed with both the youngster's ingenuity and the success of his creation, quickly became loyal customers. Otto the Rat Man was formed shortly thereafter.

By 1926, the firm had outgrown its early headquarters and cutesy moniker. That year, the newly renamed Orkin Exterminating Company relocated its corporate offices to Atlanta and expanded nationally. For the next 30 years, the business grew steadily as Otto began to transition management to his two sons and two sons-in-law. However, in a plot that has now been played out countless times in the private equity industry, the firm struggled with this generational transition, as Otto's sons disagreed bitterly with their in-laws over numerous issues, and Otto himself wound up getting pushed out of the business entirely. Despite record profits in 1963, Orkin was officially up for sale.

Enter the team of Kohlberg and his younger protégés, the hard-charging Henry Kravis and Kravis's more introspective cousin George Roberts.

Wayne Rollins, the CEO of conglomerate Rollins Inc. and a client of Bear Stearns, saw the impressive profitability of Orkin as well as a series of management and organizational changes that would create enormous potential value at the firm. With the help of the three bankers, Rollins put together a bid of $62.4 million (approximately $500 million in today's money) to purchase Orkin, using a healthy dose of leverage of course. In April 1964, Orkin was fully acquired by Rollins Inc., and has been a very successful wholly-owned subsidiary ever since, becoming practically synonymous with pest control.

Many similar early LBOs were executed on behalf of clients of Bear Stearns, where the bank would receive fees on advisory, transaction, and lending services for the deal. Others were financed through a series of off-balance-sheet vehicles, and some investments used the bank's capital directly. But what the bankers really wanted to do, especially the younger Kravis and Roberts, was raise a dedicated pool of capital from which to invest. The CEO of Bear Stearns at the time, Cy Lewis, had other ideas, preferring that his bankers got back to banking and generating safe fee income, just like MacCrone and Lovelace.

By 1976, frustrated by repeated rejections from their boss to create a dedicated business internally, the trio of Kohlberg, Kravis, and Roberts finally left Bear Stearns to form their eponymous company, shortened to KKR. The firm astutely utilized the recent passage of the Employee Retirement Income Security Act of 1974 to raise capital from pensions and other institutional investors that could now legally invest in the asset class, and KKR grew rapidly, raising the industry's first institutional fund in 1978 and later the first billion-dollar private equity fund ever in 1984. Today, KKR is a publicly traded firm with revenues of $1.9 billion and income of $795 million through 2017. The firm is one of the largest alternative asset managers in the world, with approximately 1,250 employees worldwide and roughly $150 billion in assets under management.

Although KKR was among the most widely known firms in this first institutional wave of private equity, other large players such as Thomas H. Lee, Warburg, Clayton Dubilier & Rice, and Welsh Carson raised their first funds during this same boom period.

The First Private Equity Wave . . . and Crash

The 1980s witnessed the first true LBO boom, financed largely by Michael Milken's junk bond department at the brokerage firm Drexel Burnham Lambert. Although high-yield bonds existed before Milken brought the asset class to prominence, most of the unrated or below-credit-grade bonds that were outstanding prior to this period were those that had experienced a material decline in financial performance and suffered a ratings downgrade as a result, so-called fallen angels.

Milken's contribution to this market was a massive increase in both the interest in and credibility of junk bonds, which led to a boom in new issuance. Not only did this investment activity provide relatively cheap leverage for private equity shops to finance their acquisitions as an estimated 2,000 LBO transactions occurred throughout this era, but the growth in the high-yield market was at least partly responsible for a surge in overall economic growth as well. Milken's high-yield desk took capital that had been otherwise locked into less productive, often inefficient old-line businesses and released it back into the capital markets to be redeployed elsewhere. Moguls such as Steve Wynn and Ted Turner went on to build highly successful firms boosted by early financing from Milken's high-yield desk at Drexel.

However, two events heralded the end of this first big wave of private equity: the famous RJR Nabisco buyout and the collapse of Drexel Burnham. If Milken gets credit for the expansion, the double-edged sword of leverage that he unleashed was also a big part of the downfall.

As chronicled in one of the most compelling business narratives ever written, *Barbarians at the Gate,* the acquisition of RJR Nabisco by KKR in 1989 at roughly $31 billion (financed nearly 90% with debt!) would be the largest LBO transaction for nearly two decades (and in inflation-adjusted terms, remains so to this day).[2] The deal, while a landmark transaction for KKR and the private equity industry at large, ultimately resulted in significant losses for investors, as the company struggled mightily with excess leverage.

And at the same time, Drexel found itself embroiled in insider trading and stock manipulation charges stemming from the actions of merger arbitrage and corporate raider clients of the bank, most notably Ivan Boesky, who bought stocks ahead of merger announcements based upon tips from Drexel bankers. Another bestselling work of nonfiction, *Den of Thieves,* recounts how Boesky cooperated with federal investigators, and his testimony regarding many illegal activities incriminated multiple executives at Drexel, including banker Dennis Levine but also Milken himself.[3] Although to this day people disagree to what extent Milken was involved, several of these executives, including both Levine and Milken, pleaded guilty to various felony charges and were sentenced to prison. The disgraceful downfall of high-profile bankers, coupled with an increase in defaults and bankruptcies from the unfolding S&L crisis and a general slowdown in the economy, left Drexel Burnham with no choice but to file for Chapter 11 bankruptcy in early 1990.

The first wave of private equity came crashing to an end.

The Internet Bubble . . . and Dot-com Bust

The 1990s saw a slow and steady reemergence of private equity, but without a return to the heady leverage ratios and headlines of the 1980s. Blue chip names such as Bain, Blackstone, TPG, Carlyle, and Apollo either launched their first funds or rose to real prominence during this period. However, still smarting from the aftermath of the 1980s, the buyout sector remained somewhat in the shadows as venture returned to the foreground. Venture-backed companies like Apple, Microsoft, Cisco, Amazon.com, and America Online soared, lifting valuations of technology stocks and taking the tech-heavy Nasdaq from below 1,000 at the beginning of the decade to roughly 5,000 by the turn of the century, spawning a generation of day traders that could do no wrong. It was easy; all you had to do was buy the latest tech IPO, or better yet call options on the latest tech IPO!

As the Nasdaq exploded exponentially upward (see Figure 4.1), the number of IPOs surged as well, with venture investors using the frothy valuations to exit cash-burning businesses. Profitability took a back seat to new economy metrics, and valuations such as dollars per click or market capitalization per "eyeballs" became all the rage.

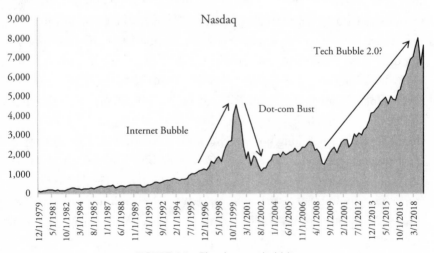

FIGURE 4.1   The dot-com bubble

Unfortunately, cash still matters, and these unprofitable businesses still needed to fund their operations. Soon investments in both venture funds and the IPO market stalled as investors came to their senses, and the dotcom bubble deflated rather precipitously. The most notorious example of this was Pets.com, which declared bankruptcy a mere nine months after its ill-fated IPO!

In just three years the Nasdaq shed approximately 4,000 points. The collapsing public equity valuations led to both IPO and M&A activity drying up even more dramatically, and venture funds were forced to write off large chunks of their portfolios. Many funds posted negative returns, and by 2003 the VC industry was a mere fraction of its prior size.

The Nasdaq would not retrace the 2000 highs until a full 15 years later, well after the recovery of the next wave. However, once it did, technology stocks would continue to soar, roaring to new all-time highs and raising concerns of another technology bubble today.

The LBO Boom . . . and Credit Crisis

Buyout activity was not completely unfazed. Although only a handful of buyout deals occurred during this time, the ones that did transact eventually performed quite well, as they were executed with modest leverage and at low valuations since equity markets remained depressed. Improving credit conditions throughout the early 2000s, combined with declining interest rates, a weak stock market, and corporate scandals at public companies, created the perfect conditions for another booming period of take-private LBO activity.

During this period, credit creation for levered businesses expanded once again. Not only was the junk bond market back open for business, but a new type of loan known as a leveraged loan, or bank debt, was also booming. These are loans extended to businesses with already considerable amounts of outstanding debt. Unlike a bond, however, these loans are not truly publicly traded. They are arranged, structured, and underwritten by a bank, and then they get syndicated out to other market participants, such as smaller banks or pension funds, that can trade them over the counter.

Often, the buyers of these leveraged loans were new structures called collateralized loan obligations, or CLOs. The issuers of the CLOs bought pools of these notes, and took what were generally below-investment-grade credits and "tranched them up" into investment-grade bonds, which sold like hotcakes. The CLOs issuers themselves took a spread on the transaction, so they scooped up these underlying loans to resell as many CLOs as they could. With such willing buyers, leveraged loans became a prime financing source for the big wave of LBOs that occurred in the mid-2000s. When added to high-yield issuance, the total supply of new debt spiked to over half a trillion in 2007—double the next highest annual amount in any period prior to 2006. You can see the spike in Figure 4.2.

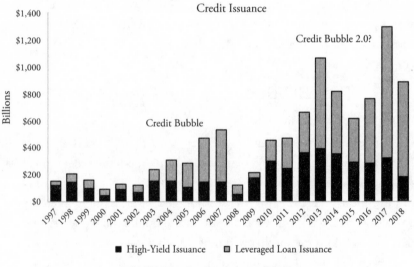

FIGURE 4.2   Credit expansion (*S&P*)

Low valuations and easy credit are the perfect conditions for private equity investment activity to take off, and fund-raising and deal activity once again surged. Buyout deal activity hit new highs through 2005, 2006, and 2007. By late 2007, equity valuations had soared, and eye-popping megadeals were once again all the rage—deals like Apollo and TPG's $27.4 billion acquisition of Caesars; the KKR and TPG–led take-private of First Data for $29 billion; the $32 billion Bain and KKR acquisition of HCA; Blackstone's

$38.9 billion purchase of Equity Office Properties; and the $44 billion TXU deal, the biggest deal of all time in nominal dollars. Unfortunately, two of those five ended in bankruptcy, two were mixed to partial exits, and only one—HCA—has been a solid winner.

And again, a massive contraction in credit activity led to a collapse in private equity transactions, and to another recession, as shown in Figure 4.3. But this recession, since dubbed the Global Financial Crisis (GFC), was slightly different from prior recessions in that it was precipitated by massive Wall Street banks unwinding excessive leverage.

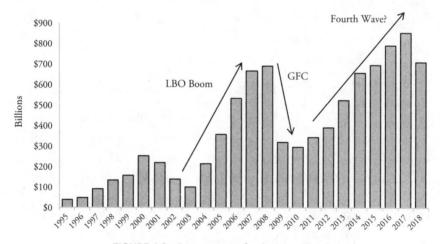

FIGURE 4.3   Private equity fund-raising (Bain[4])

Throughout the 2000s, structured products, such as CMOs, CDOs, and CLOs, had all become big business, and the investment banks were minting money selling those products to investors. However, banks had begun to retain a certain amount of the issuance from many of these securities, like a drug dealer dipping into his own stash, and as a result, their balance sheets became stuffed with them. Once some cracks began to appear in the creditworthiness of some of these securities, new issuances began to freeze. And worse, these banks came to realize that they would have to sell many of the securities that they already owned simply for de-risking and de-leveraging purposes.

I recall in the fall of 2008 that the end-of-day bond bid lists circulating around trading desks from various banks had gone from a few pages of fixed-income securities that the banks were willing to make markets in, which was typical, to phone book–sized compendiums littered with securitized products that the banks were looking to dump.

After the bankruptcy of Lehman, the cracks opened like floodgates, and structured product holders and credit investors in general sold their holdings as fast as they could unload them. The selling pressure pushed prices down even further, causing more selling in a vicious cycle that seized up credit markets and the financial ecosystem globally. This story is told with both more insight and wit than my abilities permit in a few bestselling books, such as *Too Big to Fail*[5] and *Fool's Gold*,[6] to name but a few. Suffice it to say, the death throes of the third wave of private equity threatened to bring the global economy to its knees.

The Fourth Wave of Private Equity

After the Global Financial Crisis, central banks initiated various types of monetary stimulus to keep the economic wheels from grinding to a complete stop. By pumping money into circulation through both conventional and innovative means, central bankers were able to forestall a complete economic collapse, and a gradual recovery—turned into one of the longest economic expansions, and equity bull markets, in history, that is until the recession brought about by the COVID-19 pandemic in 2020.

Since the GFC, private equity fund-raising and deal activity have recovered, surpassing the peaks of the prior cycles. Indeed, the increase in credit issuance has been far greater than precrisis levels, as the loan market has matured and high-yield issuance has exploded.

And with yet another $25 billion tech IPO, the total market capitalization of the Nasdaq index sits at roughly $11 trillion. The index is trading at 9,900—over six times the lows from 2009! More concerning are the estimated 227 venture-funded private businesses with a valuation of $1 billion or more. These businesses were called unicorns because such big winners used to be a rare occurrence. Not so anymore.

Some of these firms, such as Uber or Lyft prior to going public, command valuations in the tens of billions, while the smallest by definition is one billion. Collectively, these businesses could be worth $500 billion to $600 billion on paper, and of course, they would need to be sold at some point so their venture capitalist owners could cash out. It looks a bit like for the first time in history, we may have a substantial bubble in both venture and buy-out at the same time. (I would take odds that Lyft trades down substantially from where it trades today by the time this book hits the market!)[7]

So when will the next bust occur? That's obviously impossible to predict, but it's a virtual certainty that one will occur. I suspect we are closer to the proverbial ninth inning than the sixth. However, I think that this one is going into overtime, and it could well be a 15- or 16-inning marathon. In the meantime, investors will continue to maintain or increase their allocations to the asset class based upon expectations of outperformance versus public markets.

Now let's look at those expectations. First, it's important to understand that private equity is actually fairly cyclical and tied to broader economic conditions, despite the protestations of many in the industry. In some ways, it is no different from public equity. Private equity represents owning stock in corporations; the only difference between private equity and public equity is that private equity isn't publicly traded on a securities exchange. But the fundamental factors that generate returns are no different and often are directly linked to economic activity, just like public equity markets.

Private Equity Returns

So how has the asset class performed historically? Well, amid claims of sub-stantial alpha compared with public equity returns, private equity appears to have done a pretty good job on the whole. Despite the clear cyclicality, nominal returns have been quite strong.[8]

Figure 4.4 displays on the x axis the combined IRRs generated by the private equity funds raised during the years, as calculated by investment con-sultant Cambridge Associates. The weaker returns coincide with the funds that were raised during the tops of the cycles that we discussed previously, and funds from these years subsequently went on to underperform the long-term average return of private equity. But on the whole, we can see that the average IRRs of private equity look pretty stable and relatively strong, somewhere in the neighborhood of 13%.

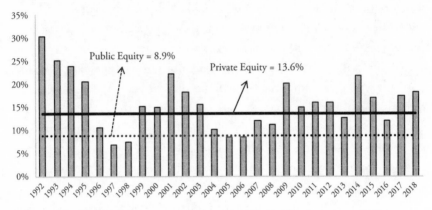

FIGURE 4.4 Private equity performance (*Cambridge Associates, S&P*)

The IRRs certainly tell a good story versus those of public equities, which have been significantly more volatile over this same period and with a slightly lower average return, closer to 9%. However, IRRs are somewhat of a misleading return number, and they can't be perfectly compared with public equity returns. The reasons are complicated.[9] But suffice it to say, they don't allow a true apples-to-apples comparison with the returns of public stocks. To do that, you need an equation called the public market equivalent, or PME, which takes the returns of public equities and makes them directly comparable to IRRs.

When you calculate this PME number for public markets—we'll use the S&P 500 for a broad set of large-capitalization stocks and the Russell 2000 for small caps—you can see that perhaps the alpha argument for private equity is not quite as powerful.

Figure 4.5 compares the Cambridge private equity IRRs over 1-, 5-, 10-, and 20-year periods versus the PMEs of the S&P 500 and Russell 2000. Over long periods, private equity does outperform public markets, generating excess returns of 2.5 to 4.0% in the 20-year comparison.

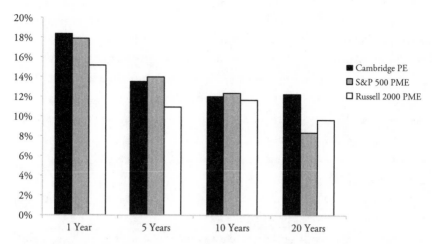

FIGURE 4.5   Private equity returns comparisons (*Cambridge Associates, S&P*)

In a 2018 report, Cliffwater, another alternative investment consultant, decided to look at private equity returns from the investor side.[10] Digging through the annual reports of dozens of US public pensions from 2000 to 2017, Cliffwater showed that the median return of the private equity asset class for these pensions over this time was 9.3%, whereas the median return for the public stock portfolio was just 6.8%. This report concluded that private equity generates the highest return for investors of all asset classes, besting public equity by 2.5% on average. And this is the alpha argument that institutional investors use to include private equity in their portfolio.

However, there are a few counterarguments that can be made from Figure 4.5 as well. First, over shorter time periods, the outperformance from private equity is nowhere near as strong as in the 20-year segment. Across 1-, 5-, and 10-year periods, the average excess return to the public equity benchmark drops to roughly 1%. And clearly, the S&P has held its own with PE over this sample.

Which brings us to the other detail that becomes apparent. In more recent times, there is virtually no outperformance for the average private equity fund relative to large-cap stocks (i.e., the S&P). The returns are statistically identical. Interestingly, private equity has beaten small-capitalization stocks by a larger margin in those periods than over two decades, an inversion in the long-term relationship.

I think there are two reasons for this. First, recall that the return to the small-cap factor has declined in recent periods. That effect is evident here. Small-cap returns have been lower relative to the returns from "average" equity ownership. The other reason is due to a bit of a change in the private equity sector itself. Like hedge funds, the private equity industry has evolved over the last two decades, and the institutionalization of the sector has brought with it substantial changes, not the least of which is just the growth from the massive amount of money that has been raised. Using estimates from Bain's 2019 annual private equity report,[11] the private equity industry has grown from under $1 trillion to nearly $4.5 trillion today, an annual growth rate of approximately 11%.

Again, similar to other alternative investment sectors, such as hedge funds, asset growth has exploded as institutions have become large-scale investors. Cambridge estimates that public pensions, with nearly $6 trillion in investable assets themselves, have today on average close to 10% allocated to PE, the highest in alternatives, and much of this occurred over the last 10 years.

Figure 4.6 shows the growth of assets under management in the private equity industry. The dark black series titled "Unrealized NAV" highlights the collective value of all the actual companies that are currently owned by private equity funds. The gray series of bars called "Uninvested Dry Powder" represents commitments investors have made to the asset class but have not yet been invested. Given how private equity works, such commitments are

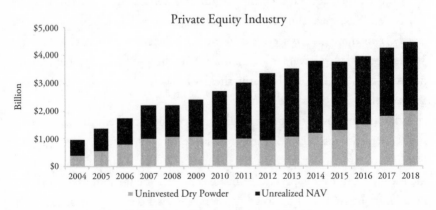

FIGURE 4.6   Private equity assets (*Bain*)

essentially legally binding and will eventually become the NAV. This second series has grown slightly faster than the first.

Figure 4.7 demonstrates clearly how fund-raising activity in recent years, largely from big institutions, has driven the growth in the industry's size. Annual fund-raising totals today are 7.5 times what they were in the nineties, and this influx undoubtedly has meaningfully changed the industry. As we've seen repeatedly, bigger pools of money chasing a strategy results in decreasing return opportunities.

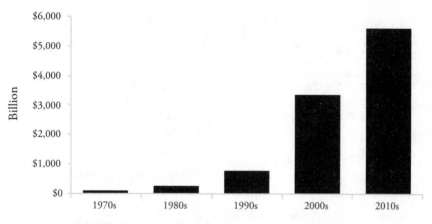

FIGURE 4.7 Private equity fund-raising decade totals (*Bain*)

The Decline of Alpha, Again

To assess exactly how alpha declined (again!), let's turn to some longitudinal analysis. Using information available from databases and consultants, I created vintage-year groupings from 1976 until 2010 for 25 of the largest private equity fund families. Specific managers were chosen to provide the longest, largest unbroken sample set, although not all had investable track records pre-1980. By bracketing funds from these blue chip firms into two- to three-year clusters, return data is anonymized. Since private equity funds can take ten years to return capital, by ending the analysis at 2010, the data contains information only for funds that have very nearly completed their full life cycle, but the data still includes some more recent information given the substantial growth witnessed recently.

Statistics were then pooled across these synthetic fund vintages and classified into decades roughly corresponding to the historical cycles discussed previously. The intent was to track the development and performance of the oldest and largest firms in the industry as they grew, rather than re-create an industry "average" or benchmark. Table 4.1 presents a periodic comparison.

TABLE 4.1   Periodic Comparison

	1976–1986	1987–1997	1998–2010
Average fund size	$217	$1,405	$7,758
Average net MOIC	4.7	2.7	1.8
Average net IRR	33.1%	26.5%	14.8%

First, it should be apparent that as the sizes of these particular funds have increased, returns have come down in lockstep. The average IRRs have fallen from an impressive 33% in the first wave down to less than half that, just under 15% in the most recent period. Of course, these returns still remain strong enough to meet most investors' bogeys.

More troubling is the decline in the multiple of invested capital (MOIC). While IRR represents a more complex time-weighted rate of return, MOIC is a much simpler calculation. Say, for example, you invested $100 and got back $300. Well, your MOIC would be 3.0x, or you returned three times your initial investment, a simple way to measure your cash-on-cash return.

This number has plunged from an average of 4.7 times your capital in the first era of private equity investing to just under 2.0x today. You may ask, how can the MOIC decline by nearly two-thirds when the time-weighted rate of return only drops by half? IRR can be manipulated. Private equity funds have had to get creative to keep returns compelling for investors as the funds have grown massively. Using fund leverage, pulling cash out quicker, and holding the companies for shorter periods has helped keep IRRs up.

Now admittedly, this is a small sample, so I now turn to broader, industry-wide data for a more representative analysis to understand what is occurring. Using fund return information from data provider Burgiss,[12] I created two separate return series: one for buyout funds below $500 million and a second data set for those above $2.5 billion. Using time series data going back to 1989, we can compare the actual compound returns of the two series. At 14.5% per year, smaller funds have outperformed their larger peers, which have compounded capital at 12.2%.

Clearly, size matters, similar to what we observed historically in hedge funds. But precisely why this effect occurs may not be exactly clear. Is it because large funds erode the very "alpha" opportunities they are pursuing, or because smaller funds buy smaller companies? Or some combination of both?

At this point, it's worth pausing to address the unspoken $64,000 question: What are the fundamental factors that drive private equity returns? Private equity is merely the ownership of stock in a corporation, so it stands to reason that these fundamental drivers of return should be highly similar if not identical to those of public stocks. After all, you make money in private equity by selling the stock for a higher price than you bought it for or by collecting earnings along the way, just like you would for public equity. There's no other way to make money. And as it turns out, these underlying factors are essentially identical.

Private equity managers argue that there are actual levers they pull to drive value creation in private companies that aren't available to the owners in public corporations. As active, hands-on owners alongside management, PE fund managers determine management's compensation structure, set strategy for the business, and closely monitor performance toward those objectives, often in near real time. As active and highly engaged board members, if things aren't going to plan, these fund managers can do something about it and change course more quickly, such as by firing the CEO or cutting costs. And they regularly do.

Private equity managers often have deep-sector experience and networks of corporate executives that they can leverage to help create operating efficiencies, reduce cost structures, and refocus growth efforts for the business. For instance, they can implement new sales plans using digital strategies or improved marketing to increase revenue growth. Or they can hire highly experienced plant managers to fix operating problems on the plant floor. Or they can manage the company's balance sheet more actively, perhaps using cheaper, and yes sometimes more, debt.

Now contrast this to public markets, where literally millions of individuals own a stock, and individual equity holders, even large institutions, rarely hold more than a 10% stake in any one company. These corporations have indifferent—I mean independent—board trustees that are much more aligned with management than with ownership. Compensation structures for management typically incentivize shorter-term behaviors that are often inconsistent with longer-term value creation plans. And equity shareholders are basically along for the ride.

So how do those ownership levers show up as drivers of return? Well, let's return to the small-fund versus large-fund debate from above. In the long run, smaller funds outperform the larger ones, as we've seen. However, they don't outperform perfectly in all periods. In fact, in certain periods, larger funds outperform the smaller ones.

In Figure 4.8, I used rolling two-year return data from Burgiss for funds below $500 million and for those above $2.5 billion. During periods of rapid economic expansion, such as the run-up to the dot-com bubble and the mid-2000s LBO boom, large funds actually outperform for brief periods. However, they drop more sharply during periods of economic contractions.

FIGURE 4.8   Rolling returns—big funds versus small funds (*Burgiss*)

If they underperform over long periods because size erodes the potential for excess returns, they shouldn't be able to outperform in bull markets. If anything, logically they might be expected to do even worse in those periods.

So why could this be? Well, larger funds do buy larger companies than small funds do, so there is a capitalization difference. But to do so, they also pay much higher prices. And they use more leverage, too. Remember how KKR used 90% debt, or $28 billion, to consummate the RJR Nabisco buyout for $31 billion in total? This means KKR put in just $3 billion of total equity or so. Leverage amplifies returns when stocks are rising, but when they aren't, like for RJR, it also increases losses.

Figure 4.9 plots the average amount of leverage used by large funds versus small funds during the acquisition of their companies over time. Similar to RJR above, it shows leverage as a percentage of the total purchase price paid by the private equity fund. This information was compiled by private equity consultant StepStone from tens of thousands of actual private company transactions across thousands of funds.

FIGURE 4.9   Leverage used—big funds versus small funds (*StepStone*)

And as my quant professor used to say, according to the theory of looking, we can observe that on average large funds slap much more debt on their companies than do smaller funds. Of course, this helps in periods where equities, and equity valuations, are rising unabatedly, but it causes problems when things move in the opposite direction. It is no coincidence that the only two periods in Figure 4.9 where large deals have less debt than smaller ones come immediately after private equity busts.

The higher leverage used by private equity funds to purchase larger companies relative to small ones results in much greater overall cyclicality and higher risk of insolvency or loss of capital. This may not hurt in boom periods, but in the long run, it's less clear if it's a net positive.

One of the problems, aside from the higher risk of bankruptcy from having to make larger and larger annual debt service payments, is the fact that higher leverage generally also equates to higher valuations. Just as the shopper who uses his credit card to splurge inevitably winds up spending more than the frugal customer who pays with cash, private equity funds that use higher leverage pay higher overall valuations for their companies.

Using the same data from StepStone, Figure 4.10 plots the entry-point valuations for the average private equity deal in the large market versus the small market from 2000 to 2018. Similar to the commonly cited price-to-

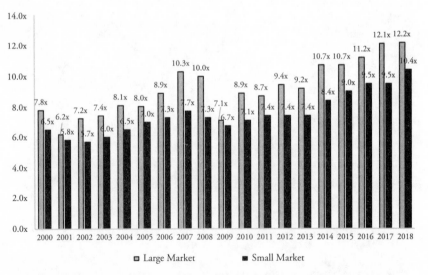

FIGURE 4.10 Purchase price multiples—big funds versus small funds (*StepStone*)

earnings, or P/E, ratio in public equities, this number is expressed as an earnings multiple (technically, an earnings before interest, taxes, depreciation, and amortization, or EBITDA, multiple), where the total enterprise value of the company is divided by the prior year's earnings. While calculated slightly differently than P/E is for public markets, it still works the same way in principle. All else being equal, paying higher valuations results in lower subsequent returns for equity investors.

Not only do we see that small companies always trade at a discount to larger ones, but the figure also graphically displays the increase in competitiveness and higher prices resulting from the increase in capital pursuing the sector. The average multiple paid in large funds has risen from 7.8 times earnings in 2000 to 12.2x as of the end of 2018, an increase of over 50%. And if these ratios were calculated the same way as public P/Es are, we would also see that large private companies no longer trade at a discount to public markets at all.

While Figure 4.10 does provide some evidence for the continued outperformance of smaller companies relative to bigger ones going forward, it also suggests that the overall average return expectations across private equity should be coming down, both big and small. It's also worth noting that although small-company valuations have surged as well, if you grow a small company to a larger company, you still could sell it a higher valuation.

Drivers of Return in Private Equity

And that brings us to another driver of returns in private equity: growth. To do that, unfortunately, we have to work through a little more math.

Let's assume we just bought a company called Super Amazing Private Company, Inc. Now, Super Amazing has a super-amazing product called a gidget that's a mix of a widget and a gadget, and it could make both of those outdated products obsolete. And it's been selling like hotcakes! Sales have doubled over the last four years. The market potential going forward is still substantial.

Currently, Super Amazing has $100 million in revenue and $25 million in EBITDA for a healthy 25% profit margin. (To keep it simple, we'll ignore many complicating factors like the effects of taxes, capital expenditure needs, and actual free cash flow.)

The prior owner of Super Amazing was looking to retire and had no one in her family to pass the company to. Thankfully, we had been studying the prospects for the gidget market and firmly believed through a combination of enhanced sales strategies and cost reductions, we could pretty easily double earnings over the next four years.

The company didn't come cheaply, however. We paid $200 million to purchase it, or eight times earnings, and we used 50% equity and 50% debt. We had to put in $100 million of our own money, and we borrowed $100 million to buy the company from its previous owner, who promptly handed us the keys and retired to a Caribbean island. Table 4.2 summarizes these financial metrics, and as you can see, things are pretty straightforward so far.

TABLE 4.2 Super Amazing Financial Metrics at Purchase

Financial Metric	At Purchase
Equity value	$100
Debt	$100
Total enterprise value (TEV)	$200
Debt-to-TEV ratio	50.0%
Revenue	$100
TEV revenue multiple	2.0x
EBITDA	$25
EBITDA margin	25.0%
TEV EBITDA multiple	8.0x

Now, let's assume that four years later, the enormous international conglomerate SuperHyperGloboChem reaches out to us about our business. It turns out SuperHyperGloboChem has been hemorrhaging sales in both its widget and gadget divisions. The company wants to talk about acquiring us to backfill some of its revenue losses, and we know that the company has cash to burn from all its other profitable business units.

In the last four years, we've more than doubled earnings. And we know SuperHyperGloboChem will pay a higher multiple than we did because it needs to hit its earnings targets, so we ask the company to make us an offer. SuperHyperGloboChem offers us 9.5 times last year's EBITDA, which we had grown to $54.8 million.

This offer represents an enterprise value of $520 million. Since we did put some more debt on the firm to help build new plants to double our production, the bondholders will get paid $270 million from the purchase. As equity holders, we will receive the remaining $250 million. This gives us a solid gross MOIC of 2.5x our original $100 million investment. Not bad.

Now, given the financial metrics at the time of sale, we can see where this 2.5x comes from. First, we grew revenue substantially, but not quite doubling it. We were able to more than double our earnings, however, by expanding our profit margin from 25 to 32.4%. Each gidget we sold was more profitable because not only did our new plant expand our production capacity, but it used new automated technology that made it cheaper to manufacture each gidget. Without raising prices, we were able to boost profitability.

However, that plant and equipment didn't come cheaply, either. As stated, we had to take out more debt to finance them, and the increase in leverage over the tenure of our ownership meant that less of the total enterprise value accrued to the shareholders. But that's still OK. Our buyer paid us a higher multiple than we paid, so that too increased our return.

Table 4.3 shows the metrics for Super Amazing Financial at the time of the sale.

TABLE 4.3   Super Amazing Financial Metrics at Sale

Financial Metric	At Sale
Equity value	$250
Debt	$270
Total enterprise value (TEV)	$520
Debt-to-TEV ratio	*51.9%*
Revenue	$170
TEV revenue multiple	*3.1x*
EBITDA	$54.8
EBITDA margin	*32.4%*
TEV EBITDA multiple	*9.5x*

Overall, a 2.5x deal is a strong outcome for a buyout transaction. But let's decompose this return into the various drivers. Figure 4.11 breaks down this return into its component parts using a method called a return bridge.[13] This method takes these metrics and breaks them down into additive pieces of MOIC, which allows us to explicitly attribute the total return to these underlying factors.

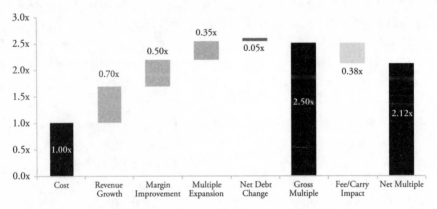

FIGURE 4.11   Private equity Return Bridge A

We can see in the figure that the multiple expansion was helpful, but it only added 0.35x of the total gains. Revenue growth and profit margin increases combined to yield a total return of 1.2x. And increasing the debt created a slight drag. (And of course, a private equity fund will have management fees, expenses, and profit sharing that would decrease the final net return. In this example, we wind up with a net MOIC of 2.12x after these were deducted from the gross return.) All in all, this return bridge looks less like it is due to leverage or valuation arbitrage and more like it is the result of actual fundamental improvement in the business. However, I don't see alpha in there anywhere.

On that point, let's compare Return Bridge A with another deal that has exactly the same gross and net MOICs of 2.50x and 2.12x, respectively. If these returns are the same—and if the holding periods were the same length, the IRRs and PMEs would be identical as well—then traditional approaches to performance analysis would argue that the two return streams would axiomatically have to be the same mix of beta and alpha, if any, because they are the same. But I don't think it's quite that simple.

Figure 4.12 sums up the return bridge for a private equity deal where the operational and financial metrics looked quite different. In this deal, there was very little revenue or profit growth, and virtually all the returns came both from paying down debt—so the equity holders got a larger share of the total enterprise value upon the sale, like amortizing down your home mortgage—and from a subsequent buyer being willing to pay a massive valuation premium.

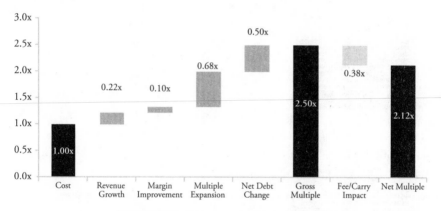

FIGURE 4.12   Private equity Return Bridge B

While the end returns may be identical, how you got there isn't. I believe one return bridge suggests greater skill on the part of the investor and provides a higher degree of predictability versus the other, which suggests more luck and provides less information about future returns. Certainly neither is a guarantee about future performance, and neither is definitively alpha or beta, but it also seems obvious that they are simply not truly the same, either.

In their 2018 annual survey, Ernst and Young asked 110 private equity firms across North America to provide information on a host of questions, and one covered the drivers of return.[14] Aggregating this information across the respondents over time allows for some interesting observations, as shown in Figure 4.13.

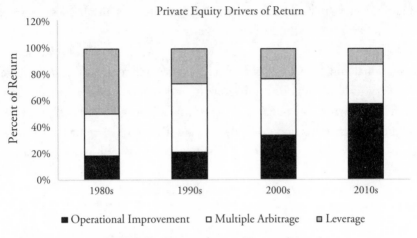

FIGURE 4.13 Drivers of return (*Ernst and Young*)

In the 1980s, by far the predominant driver of returns was simply the use of leverage. Private equity managers realized that they could buy private companies cheaply, lever them up, and flip them for a big gain. But the RJR Nabisco deal changed the industry, and moving into the 1990s, leverage came down. During this period, valuation arbitrage was the main factor resulting in strong returns for the sector. PE funds were buying cheaply, but because of the equity bull market of this decade, multiples expanded sharply in both public and private markets. Merely buying and holding was almost a can't-miss strategy.

During the early 2000s, public equity markets became much more volatile, and private equity became more competitive as fund-raising accelerated for the first time (recall Figure 4.7?). For the first time, private equity shops had to actually make meaningful operational improvements in their businesses, growing revenue and improving profit margins, to continue to generate the type of returns that investors expected. While the drivers of return were more balanced during this time, utilizing leverage and selling at a higher multiple still were certainly critical components of value creation.

Finally, during the decade of the 2010s, as many private equity shops began to implement McKinsey & Co. or Bain Consulting management strategies for executing on sales plans, optimizing production, and generally focusing on running the businesses more efficiently, operational improvements began to account for the majority of returns.

In an ecosystem where more capital is being raised and deployed against private markets, valuations have increased to a point where private equity is no longer cheaper than public equities, and leverage actually exceeds that found in public markets, I suspect improving the revenue and earnings of the underlying businesses will only become more and more critical. In that type of hypercompetitive, highly priced environment, it stands to reason that private equity shops with deep operational experience and industry expertise will stand a better chance at generating outsized returns.

Indeed, one of my healthcare-focused specialist funds described the environment thusly: "We have got to be completely focused on getting better at our job faster than the market gets more competitive."

And as PE's job gets harder, we can expect our job as the end investor to get harder, too. Average returns across the industry will probably fall, as will the excess return compared with the return for public stocks. In fact, over the last four or five years, the average excess return generated by private equity relative to the public markets has been negative, as we saw earlier. It's hard to justify locking your capital up for 10 years or more in private equity funds when the funds are not even beating public markets.

Turning back to the Cambridge private equity index data, I decided to bucket private equity excess returns into two discrete periods: returns prior to 2006 and those since. (The periods are admittedly somewhat arbitrary, but they are largely based upon both the significant increase in fund-raising that the industry has been forced to digest more recently and the clear visual evidence that excess returns have changed since 2006. This date also loosely corresponds to the Global Financial Crisis.) As depicted in Table 4.4, the differences are stark.

TABLE 4.4 Excess Return Periodic Comparison

	IRR Excess	MOIC Excess
Pre-2006	7.74%	0.5x
Post-2006	1.35%	0.0x

If that's what has happened over the last decade, it's hard to see how this will change for the better going forward with even bigger funds, more capital being raised, and ever higher valuations.

To generate returns (which will probably be lower than the past and also less compelling versus public counterparts), average managers will have to work harder to drive actual operating results at their businesses, which in turn will drive performance. And selecting which of the nearly 5,000 private equity managers out there are actually capable of doing that could be difficult.

Return Dispersion and Persistence

But this point brings up a problem with averages. The average return of private equity masks a lot going on underneath those averages. Unlike public equity-managers, private equity managers exhibit far greater dispersion of returns. In fact, the gap between top- and bottom-performing managers in private equity is nearly 10 times as wide as it is in public equity markets!

Using data from Burgiss for private equity and eVestment for public equity, I analyzed 20-year return data and grouped managers into quartiles. Figure 4.14 shows the results. Comparing the top 25% with the bottom

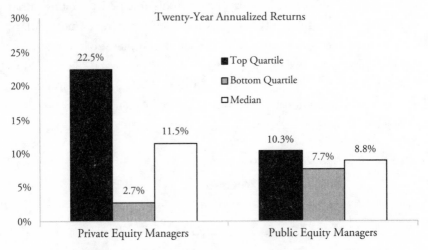

FIGURE 4.14 Manager dispersion (*Burgiss and eVestment*)

25% allows us to see the gap. In public stocks, the top managers generate annualized returns of 10.3%, solidly beating the average managers as well as the bottom performers who made just 7.7% per year, a spread of 2.6%. However, the top quartile of private equity managers made 22.5% per annum, blowing away the meager 2.7% put up by the bottom-quartile firms. The spread between these top- and bottom-performing funds is nearly 20% annually! And these top managers also significantly outperformed the average of 11.5%, roughly doubling it.

In public equities, the potential excess return available from picking better managers, or picking better stocks for that matter, is minimal. And it's very hard to do. On the other hand, in PE the potential return available when selecting superior managers is quite high, as is the risk of doing it poorly. Although it may not be easy to pick those managers, it's certainly not as hard to do as it is in public markets. In fact, private equity managers that generate top-quartile performance in one fund are far more likely to continue to be top managers in subsequent funds. This so-called persistence of performance is stronger in private equity than in just about any other asset class, and it's strong evidence of the presence of skill.

In a seminal research paper on the subject in the *Journal of Finance* in 2005, professors Steven Kaplan and Antoinette Schoar studied the returns of roughly 1,800 private equity and venture capital funds using data from 1980 to 2001.[15] Specifically, they measured IRR, PMEs, and MOICs across funds, and then they bucketed all the funds for which they were able to match subsequent funds into terciles, which is just academic speak for thirds. The findings are illustrated in Figure 4.15.

What their research demonstrated was that for those funds that performed in the top third based on IRR within a given vintage, their next fund was 48% likely to also be top tercile. Conversely, funds that came in the bottom third for IRRs were 49% likely to have a bottom-third performer in their subsequent vintage. And take a look in the table at those funds that were top quartile in one fund and bottom in the next, or vice versa. Such first-to-worst, or worst-to-first, scenarios occurred only 20 to 21% of the time, far less than the 33.3% that would be expected by pure chance.

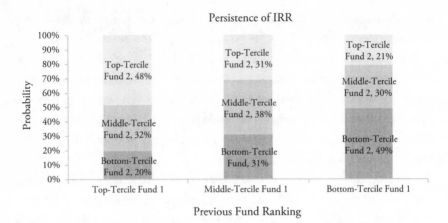

FIGURE 4.15   Persistence of performance in private equity (*Kaplan and Schoar, 2005*)

These results showed that there was a high degree of persistence in returns from one fund to the next, which also suggests the presence of skill. The persistence in bottom performers particularly is quite strong evidence for this. You can't lose a game of chance intentionally, so the fact that bottom dwellers continued to lag suggests that skill, or the lack thereof, is a dominant driver of future returns in private equity.

Selecting private equity managers that have done well in the past, unlike other asset classes, increases the odds of superior returns in the future. This research on persistence was updated in 2014 with a similar set of funds, but using performance data since 2000; the analysis suggested that persistence of returns has disappeared for buyout funds, except for bottom performers, indicating that skill still matters.[16] Interestingly, persistence of performance was also found to be strong for venture funds. Differentiated skill appears to still be present there.

However, the researchers concluded that this absence of mathematical persistence in buyouts suggests that this market has become more efficient, and PE funds cannot sustain skill or outperformance from one fund to the next because of increasing competitiveness. I disagree with this conclusion for two simple reasons. First, the researchers are using the brand name of the private equity firm as a proxy for the same team. They assume that because Private Equity Fund ABC II is the same firm that ran Private Equity Fund

ABC, it also means it is the same team investing the fund, and this assumption simply no longer holds.

From 1980 to 2000, investment teams largely stayed together, and persistence was in fact accurately measured using the firm. If you were on the partnership track at KKR or Apollo, you stayed at KKR or Apollo. However, by the late 1990s and early 2000s, many of these senior investment professionals realized that Henry Kravis and Leon Black weren't going anywhere anytime soon (indeed, 20 years later both men remain active at their respective firms!), and in order to really make the type of money they wanted to, they would have to launch their own funds, a process referred to as a "spinout." It's no coincidence that Ares, today one of the largest private equity managers in the world, was one of the first big spinouts, leaving Apollo in 1997.

According to some estimates, prior to 2000, less than 10% of private equity funds raising capital in any given year were first-time funds. And these were true first-time funds. However, more recently nearly 25% of funds in the market were "fund I," and the vast majority of these emerging managers were spinouts from existing firms. Since 2000, the number of private equity firms has more than doubled, with thousands of these startups being launched by professionals with extensive experience investing at prior firms.

In one particularly stark example, a large brand-name private equity firm is currently in the process of raising money for a fund III. However, after a successful fund I, the managing team spun out to launch its own firm and raise a competing fund. And after the brand-name shop hired a new team to manage fund II, upon witnessing the financial success of its predecessors, that new team spun out to launch its own firm, too!

Of course, during its most recent fund-raising, the brand-name parent claims that none of the departures were a meaningful loss, and fund III will be just as good a product as fund I because of the strength of the institution. I'm hesitant to believe such claims, and I note that during the course of my due diligence on the first spinout team (Figure 4.16), the performance of that team's first fund (not surprisingly!) nearly perfectly matches the performance of the parent company's fund I, which of course the team actually invested!

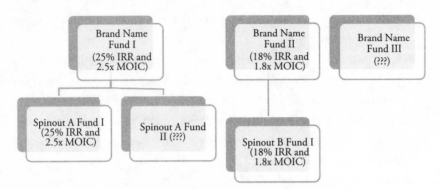

FIGURE 4.16   Spinout misattribution of persistence

This family tree appears to be clear evidence in support of strong per-sistence of returns. (Anyone care to place odds on the performance of Spinout A Fund II? We can follow up in six or seven years . . .) Unfortunately, such effects would show up in the new research as lack of persistence at the parent company, and unpredictable strong returns would be credited to the new startup manager. Regardless of being raised under a different flag, persistence follows the team, not the brand!

As one GP told me after spinning out from his prior firm, "Institutions don't do deals; people do deals." No longer can one assume that the name brand has any relationship to the team. And prior attribution for performance must include a detailed analysis and understanding of the actual investment professionals who did the deals. When corrected for this inaccuracy, I believe persistence remains nearly as strong as it was in the earlier research.[17]

The second reason for this apparent disappearance of persistent returns is that the research does not control for fund size. Interestingly, venture funds did not increase much in size from 2000 to 2010, and it's no coincidence that persistence there remains strong. Buyout funds, as we have seen in Table 4.1, have not maintained such fund-size discipline. With these funds often more than doubling from one fund to the next, we've also seen that such increases in fund size absolutely erode returns.

In fact, private equity consultant StepStone has conducted research on fund-size increase that measures this impact specifically. Looking at a sample of over 2,600 funds for which StepStone had mature performance information for both an initial and a subsequent fund from the same manager, the firm was able to explicitly quantify the effects of fund-size increases. StepStone's research showed that managers who raised substantially larger funds experienced lower IRRs in the subsequent bigger investment vehicles. As you can see in Figure 4.17, the worst performance results were observed in those funds that were more than double the prior vintage; such managers posted returns 5.8% lower on average.

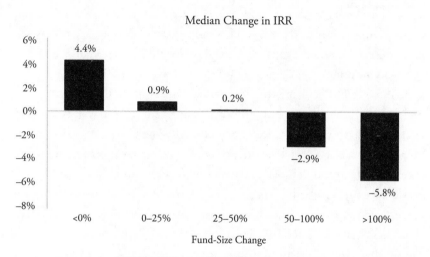

FIGURE 4.17 Fund-size effect (*StepStone*)

On the other hand, those managers who raised funds no more than 25% larger than their earlier partnerships were actually able to increase returns modestly, and funds that shrunk saw returns jump meaningfully, up by 4.4%. Interestingly, private equity funds that were 25 to 50% bigger than the previous fund produced returns that were virtually unchanged since the last go-around. Persistence can only be logically expected to endure if you have the same investment professionals executing on the same strategy, and going from $700 million to $2 billion to $5 billion is difficult to argue that it's the same strategy. If a fund is now doing expensive large cap instead of cheap small cap, of course returns will be different, even more so when it's a totally different team!

The Future of Private Equity

As valuations push inevitably higher, the returns that the average manager generates will not be as strong as they have been in the past and may not compare as well with the returns of public markets, either. With more and more capital pursuing the strategy, the spreads between the best and worst performers will tighten even further. And as more new participants enter the space, competitive edges will become harder and harder to sustain.

For a few years, it appeared this had already come to pass, leading pundits to proclaim that excess returns in PE were a thing of the past,[18] perhaps a bit prematurely. These assertions were based upon another period of strong public equity returns—from January 2009 until December 2017, the S&P 500 annualized at 15.8%—and they were also compared with the performance of highly immature private equity funds. More recent research has shown that as these later vintages have started to come through the J curve, they have posted better relative results, and almost all vintages have generated positive excess returns to public markets across multiple metrics, such as KS-PME and Direct Alpha.[19] Comparing the ILPA Private Markets Benchmark horizon pooled return over to the Cambridge Associates Modified Public Market Equivalent for the S&P 500 over different time horizons in Figure 4.18, we can see that excess returns in private equity do appear to have revived a bit.

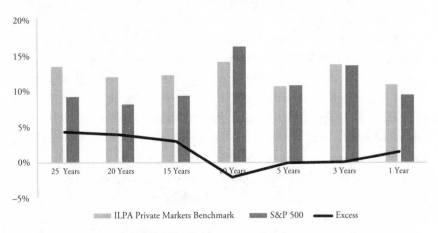

FIGURE 4.18   Public versus private returns

Private equity is becoming more and more competitive. However, it is still possible to identify managers with durable skill who can consistently outperform the average return. It requires investors to forgo capital allocation as an objective of the asset class and not spray money out on a top-down basis. The big funds are paying higher multiples and are using more leverage, and they are less motivated to continue to generate returns going forward.

On the other hand, smaller managers have likely taken the alpha that used to be found in the lower market capitalization range of public stocks and transferred it to investors in private equity. These funds are buying cheaper companies, with lower leverage, and growing them faster than larger firms are. Further, if you can find managers that have generated returns more from operating value creation than leverage or multiple expansion, and it's the same team implementing the same strategy at the same fund size that has performed well recently, I think your odds of generating consistent strong returns are probably still pretty good.

While I suspect big funds—and perhaps even average ones—will disappoint investors in the future, unlike what many of the most ardent detractors of the industry would argue, I believe it is still possible to generate substantial rates of return in private equity, and top-quartile managers will outperform public markets. It remains far easier to generate acceptable outcomes in private equity than it does in hedge funds. But doing so will require accessing the fundamental drivers of return that appear attractive on a prospective basis, as opposed to just doing what worked in the past.

And these underlying factors can still be found, albeit perhaps in different amounts and areas than in the past. Now none of this means that it is alpha or, in truth, ever was. (But neither was tilting toward value in public markets!) In Part II, I'll present a better framework for thinking about alpha, one not dependent upon benchmarks as much as market dynamics. Alpha as an investment skill is only as good as one's ability to consistently produce it. Framing alpha as a hierarchy of investment skill may provide greater insight into its durability, which will also help us understand the disappearance of traditional alpha across markets.

Notes

1. Between 1200 BC and 800 BC, during a period of decline for both the Egyptian and Hittite Empires, a series of independent city-states sprang up around the Mediterranean Sea led by loosely allied kings that history has called the Phoenicians. Archaeological evidence, including stores of silver that came from all across Europe, suggests that these port cities controlled trade along the most important shipping routes with their oared warships, and thus dominated merchant activity. In 539 BC, the Persian king Cyrus the Great conquered the Phoenician Empire and divided up the kingdom among his generals. However, Cyrus allowed the sea kings to continue managing commerce, so long as they supplied warships for his Persian commanders. Then in 332 BC, after the Persians were defeated by Alexander the Great, the Macedonian brutally over-threw the Phoenician leaders, slaughtering thousands and installing his own commanders. Thereafter, the Phoenician culture went into terminal decline.
2. Burrough and Helyar (1990).
3. Stewart (1992).
4. MacArthur et al. (2019).
5. Sorkin (2009).
6. Tett (2009).
7. Lyft is currently trading at $35.83, nearly half the IPO price of $72. Indeed, the tech IPO market is clearly showing signs of broad stress, with multiple issues trading down, not to mention the whole WeWork debacle.
8. There has been a great deal of academic research on the topic of private equity performance. Covering it all isn't the objective of this chapter or this book. However, for those more curious readers, I'll summarize a few of the more seminal works. Kaplan and Schoar (2005) showed that venture returns beat the market both before and after fees, whereas buyout funds only beat it before deducting fees. However, they showed that top managers do outperform consistently. Phalippou (2009) also provided evidence that the average buyout manager does not generate excess returns to public markets. On the other hand, Ljungqvist and Richardson (2003) used a different data set and showed substantial outperformance for private equity. I think problems with incomplete data sets, challenges scrubbing the data, and the difficulty of comparing public to private equity returns make it hard to draw a conclusion. I also believe the "average" private equity fund did beat public markets at some point in the past, but probably no longer. Suffice it to say, the data is mixed, but if there is a clear conclusion to draw, it should be that one should not invest in private equity with the objective of generating the industry average return. The goal should be to exceed public equity returns substantially and to beat the average PE fund as well. I believe PE is the one asset class in which this is actually achievable.
9. The internal rate of return represents the discount rate at which the net present value of the sum of a series of cash flows is equal to zero. It is often referred to as the asset-weighted rate of return. There is no closed-form solution to IRR, as the answer is found iteratively. The formula for calculating the discounted net present value, however, is simply the sum of all the discounted cash flows:

$$\text{NPV} = \sum_{n=0}^{N} \frac{C_n}{(1 + r)^n} = 0$$

So IRR is the r that yields a zero NPV. As the formula suggests, the timing and size of cash flows can result in dramatically different IRRs. Traditional public equity returns, on the other hand, are typically reported as geometric rates of return. These are sometimes also called time-weighted rates of return. The simplest formula used is

$$Geometric \; Return = \sqrt[n]{(1 + r_1) \times (1 + r_2) \times \dots (1 + r_n)} - 1$$

Time-weighted calculations allow you to link together returns from different periods to create a true compound return as the way of addressing cash flows. The big difference between the two is the impact of cash flows over the investment period. In the presence of many substantial cash flows, which occur early in the life of a private equity fund, the two calculations can differ dramatically. However, when cash flows relative to the size of the portfolio are quite small and infrequent, the numbers will converge over time. In fact, for a return where cash flows are negative $100 at year 1 and positive $250 at year 4, the IRR of 25.7% is identical to the continuously compounded rate of return of 25.7%. While IRRs certainly can be misleading, the media hype around them as being completely meaningless is simply uninformed hysteria. Most limited partners that calculate both can show you that for a mature portfolio, the differences between IRR and geometric return are negligible.

10. Nesbitt (2018).
11. MacArthur et al. (2019).
12. Today, Burgiss's database contains over 8,900 private capital funds dating back to 1978. The data has been aggregated from limited partners, or investors in private equity funds, which reduces some of the self-reporting and survivorship biases in other databases. With over $6.3 trillion of cumulative capital represented, it is also probably the largest private equity database in the market.
13. There is some "dirty" math involved, and one can find several different methods of constructing a return bridge. Some are even more complex, and separate idiosyncratic results from those caused by market factors. At TMRS, we certainly don't have the best model, but it's better to be kind of right than dead wrong.
14. Engert et al. (2018).
15. Kaplan and Schoar (2005).
16. Harris et al. (2014).
17. During the course of writing this book, some excellent academic research has come out showing strong evidence for this theory. Braun et al. (2019) took a look at 3,977 individual buyout managers and 5,030 unique transactions, matching deals with actual individual investors, and what the authors found was staggering. It turns out that the individual responsible for the deal is up

to four times as powerful statistically for persistence of performance than the PE organization is! This replicated prior research in venture capital (Ewens and Rhodes-Kropf, 2013) that demonstrated that the individual venture capitalist was two to five times as important in explaining performance as the VC firm was. People have skill, not institutions!

18. Applebaum and Batt (2016).
19. Brown and Kaplan (2019).

PART II
Deciphering Alpha

5

The Hierarchy
of Alpha

*Skeptical scrutiny is the means, in both science and religion,
by which deep thoughts can be winnowed from deep nonsense.*
—CARL SAGAN

OK, we've walked through public markets, hedge funds, and private equity and observed how all these have evolved over time. One common thread through all their histories is that alpha opportunities come and go. Some asset classes still present an opportunity for investors today to continue to access these excess returns, whereas in other markets, the outlook is not quite as good. We've also seen how increasingly competitive these asset classes have become as they have grown, with large institutional allocators plowing hundreds of billions, even trillions, of dollars into them. Such capital growth can only erode future return expectations.

Problematically, moving such huge pools of capital is a bit like captaining an aircraft carrier. It takes a long time to get up to speed in one direction, and once started it cannot stop or turn on a dime. Switching metaphors, this dynamic unfortunately means that large asset owners are usually the last to arrive at the party, and all too often once they've gotten there, the music has already stopped.

Given these challenges, a number of institutional investors have begun to rethink their allocations to such strategies, in some cases divesting from hedge funds or private equity entirely.[1] For some of the largest investors, with hundreds of billions to deploy, a small relative allocation to alternatives cannot possibly have enough portfolio impact to justify the mindshare spent on managing the allocation, let alone the ensuing headaches. Others have made the rational decision to exit an asset class where they have found results to be unacceptable. Unfortunately, in a few cases, political forces are driving the investment or divestment decisions, which typically results in suboptimal outcomes for the ultimate beneficiaries.

One way to combat the consequences of falling expectations for future returns is to use scale to negotiate lower fees for the end investor. This has been a very effective means of keeping net returns, or returns to the investors after all fees and expenses, steady in efficient asset classes when gross returns decline. However, I'm not certain such a beta strategy is effective in alpha-seeking allocations.

In theory, a service provider in any competitive industry must contend on either quality or price. Investment management is certainly a highly competitive industry, and searching for the lowest-cost provider may be perfectly rational in the commoditized world of beta returns. For instance, when picking an index provider, selecting the manager with the lowest overall cost structure is guaranteed to yield the best net results because all the competitors will have the same gross returns—that of the index. The dispersion of returns, or the difference between best and worst performers, is quite small in such markets, which makes trying to pick managers based on superior skill pointless.

However, this same decision is counterintuitive at best, or outright counterproductive at worst, when searching for alpha generators. Unlike beta managers, managers in less efficient market segments have a far wider dispersion of returns between the best and worst managers. As we've also seen, top-quartile private equity managers outperform bottom-quartile managers by almost 10 times the relative differential of public equity managers.

Dispersion and Persistence

Figure 5.1 plots this same dispersion data for public equity and private equity and also adds similar points for venture capital specifically, as well as data from consultant Cambridge Associates for hedge funds. As is readily apparent, these asset classes present entirely different pictures of competition. Going from public equities on the right, which is highly efficient and demonstrates very little performance differentiation between top and bottom managers, all the way to venture capital on the left, where the difference between the best and worst managers, 42.8% from top to bottom quartile, overwhelms the average return of 13.3%. In such a market, managers are competing on investment performance or on return quality.

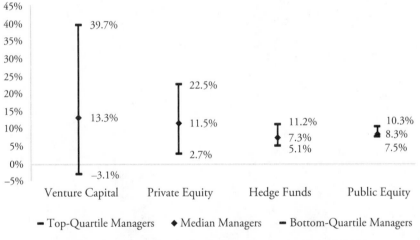

FIGURE 5.1   Dispersion of annualized manager returns, 1994–2014
(Burgiss, Cambridge, and eVestment)

We have also seen evidence that the tendency for top performers in one period to remain outperformers in subsequent periods follows this same pattern. In public equities, there is virtually no persistence found.[2] Research on hedge funds suggests modest persistence over a few months to a few years,[3] while private equity is the one asset class where persistence has been shown to last five years or longer.[4] Clearly, competition varies across these markets, as does evidence of skill.

But if alpha does exist, one could hardly expect a manager that truly possesses such an edge to give it away cheaply. It is a high-quality, high-value service and should be priced appropriately. Indeed, one should question any firm purportedly selling true alpha at a significant discount to the competition. It's perfectly irrational to expect the highest-quality provider (true alpha generator) to also be a discounter (beta provider/asset gatherer).

Interestingly, recent research by Preqin, an alternative assets data provider, shows that quality managers aren't competing on price.[5] Preqin investigated hedge funds in its database by performance fee and bucketed the funds into three separate groups: those charging carry less than 20%, those with the standard 20% split, and those charging an even higher profit share.

Examining performance over three- and five-year periods, Preqin found that the managers who generated the strongest returns net of fees were the ones who charged the highest incentive fee. As shown in Figure 5.2, the relationship was a step function, with net returns higher in all periods for progressively higher fee buckets.

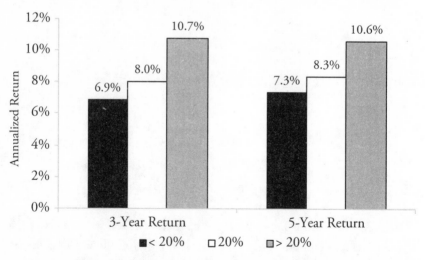

FIGURE 5.2   Hedge fund performance by fee load (*Preqin, 2013*)

And ensuring that this was not simply evidence of higher risk, Preqin then sorted these returns by Sharpe ratio, as well. The higher the Sharpe ratio, the greater the level of returns per unit of risk taken. Those hedge fund managers in higher-incentive brackets achieved progressively higher levels of risk-adjusted returns. Hedge fund managers who charged more than 20% of profits generated Sharpe ratios of 2.5, by far the highest risk-adjusted returns in the sample. Conversely, the lowest-incentive basket, hedge funds charging less than 10% profit share, had the lowest Sharpe ratio at 1.22, about half that of the premium funds. Figure 5.3 displays these results.

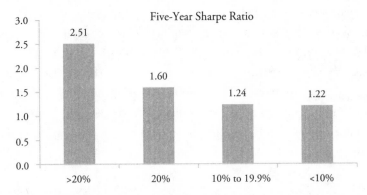

FIGURE 5.3 Hedge fund risk-adjusted returns by fee load (*Preqin, 2013*)

Incentive fees, unlike fixed management fees, incentivize profits, and the evidence suggests you get what you pay for when trying to select from managers competing on quality as opposed to price. In fact, institutional investors, such as the Texas Teachers Retirement System,[6] have even devised a new model—called 1 or 30—to increase the carry and, it is hoped, drive higher returns. This fee structure pays a flat 1% management fee unless returns exceed a certain threshold, at which point the fixed fee is rebated in favor of 30% of the profits for the manager. Time will tell how effective this new fee structure is.

However, for institutional investors wishing to continue to deploy assets into alternatives, success as always is likely to revolve around selecting top-quartile managers, not merely negotiating improved economic terms. The challenging search for alpha has become harder as the costs associated with being average have gone up along with the resources needed to scour an increasingly large universe of managers amid a similar rise in the amount of capital pursuing the same strategies. In effect, the needle has gotten smaller while the haystack has gotten bigger. Investors continuing the search for true alpha should proceed with an abundance of caution and skepticism.

Opportunities for excess return still exist, but not all alpha is created equal. As I hope I've shown in earlier chapters, alpha in and of itself is an overly simple construct. The concept of a clean, binary separation between alpha and beta is far too simple a paradigm for the complex realities of active investing. Alpha to beta would be better conceived of as a spectrum, and often what once was the former eventually becomes the latter.

This skeptical scrutiny about true alpha calls for a better framework for the classification of investment skill. This classification mechanism should not only describe the nature and source of the return stream, identifying the manager's ability to access this return and the probability of it continuing in the future. But even more importantly, the framework should present investment skill as a true spectrum. I propose such a framework, as shown in Figure 5.4.

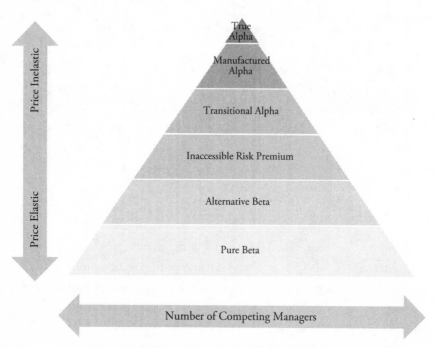

FIGURE 5.4   Hierarchy of investment skill

The rarest investment skill would be creating a return stream that has no observable correlations to other known returns. For instance, picking a portfolio of public equities that has a correlation of zero with all other stock market indexes would fall at the top of this hierarchy. This holy grail of investing would be pure alpha, and it would very valuable if it existed. Indeed, such a product could command the highest management and profit-sharing fee structures in the market. Now, finding such an uncommon return stream is improbable to say the least. And managers capable of doing so would be few and far between. The Renaissance Medallion fund is probably the best (only?) example of such a manager.

In 1982, a mathematics professor, Jim Simons, at Stony Brook University in New York, launched a hedge fund called Renaissance Technologies.[7] At the time, Simons was known for his work on string theory and pattern recognition, and he also worked for the National Security Agency as a codebreaker. However, he was utterly unknown in investing circles.

The most successful fund managed by this company is a fund called the Medallion fund. The fund employs quantitative strategies built over decades by teams of mathematicians and computer scientists combining proprietary mathematical, pattern recognition, and natural language processing algorithms allowing it to beat the market. While highly complex, the strategy searches through petabytes of data to uncover little trading signals that provide statistical probabilities about the direction of securities prices across a range of markets. And then it profits based on those movements.

For nearly 30 years, Medallion has yielded net returns around 39%, without hardly a down year. In fact, it is believed that the fund has only had two or three down months since its inception. These net returns have come after fees that reportedly went as high as 5% management fee and 40% of profits, which means Medallion has generated gross returns of nearly 70% for three decades!

Today Renaissance manages close to $65 billion across numerous hedge fund products. However, the Medallion fund is no longer offered to external clients. All the money in the fund today, perhaps $5 billion or so, belongs to employees of Renaissance, and in fact preferential access is a retention tool for the most valuable employees. If you actually find true alpha, it is so valuable you probably don't want to sell it, even for the highest fees in the industry!

On the other hand, the most common return stream would be one that is highly price competitive, with thousands of managers providing nearly identical products. Managing a portfolio of stocks to perfectly track the S&P 500 index is certainly still an investment skill, and it requires professional experience and competence to execute the strategy. Pulling someone at random off the street to run a fund to do this would probably yield worse results than hiring any of the numerous professionals who currently offer products in this space. But clearly, this latter investment skill is far less valuable than the return stream that the Medallion fund provides.

Conceptually, the hierarchy displayed in Figure 5.4 has two separate continua. The first is the number of competitors, indicated from left to right, and the second is price elasticity, indicated from top to bottom.[8] On the top of the pyramid, the hierarchy goes from very few competing products that are highly price inelastic, such as Medallion, to products with hundreds and even thousands of competing offerings at the bottom that are nearly identical and hence highly price elastic.

And not surprisingly, a quick Yahoo! Finance search for "S&P 500" yields hundreds of competing mutual fund and ETFs. Many of these funds can be bought for extremely low fees—for example 0.1% instead of 5% and 40%. At the extreme end of this spectrum, mutual fund giant Fidelity has begun to offer several mutual fund products, including a passive large-cap equity fund, with no fees at all.

However, the argument for hedge funds or private equity does not rest on the head of a pin. Instead, most asset managers across the industry have structured return streams that fall somewhere in between. Understanding the skill required to generate these returns is critical to manager selection and pricing for such complex strategies, as it is for all investment managers. So let's start at the top and walk through the hierarchy.

True Alpha

True alpha is generally what most market participants mean when they refer to "alpha." This is superior skill generating outperformance solely from the active selection of securities that differ from the market. This kind of alpha is truly beating the market, or outsmarting the competition, without embed-ded style tilts. For instance, stock pickers who do not take value, dividend, growth, capitalization, or sector bets but still generate excess returns are actually creating true alpha. However, as we've seen historically, virtually all managers that have appeared to do so were merely accessing one of these tilts before the advantages of the factor had become widely known by other market participants.

This form of alpha, from pure security selection with no discernible fac-tor bias, is also the rarest. Managers that generate sustainable, repeatable true alpha are few and far between, the Medallion fund being perhaps the lone example. True alpha is harder to underwrite with confidence, precisely because it so rare. A much larger sample set is required to ensure that what appears to be alpha is not merely a misidentified beta or, worse, mere luck. At best, if the return is durable, that is probably evidence of a durable factor exposure that the market has not yet discovered more broadly.

Again, does that mean it was actually alpha at all? Perhaps, if only tem-porarily. But underwriting a manager based on the expectation of this con-tinuing should be done only after a great deal of skeptical scrutiny, if at all.

Manufactured Alpha

The next type of skill, manufactured alpha, is easier to underwrite with a higher degree of confidence. Manufactured alpha can also be thought of as value creation. Picking which specific securities to purchase, while certainly not unimportant, is not the main driver of excess return in this category of skill. Unlike the purely passive buy-and-hold approach of security selection, manufactured alpha requires an investor to make an investment with a view to impart structural changes or operational improvements that will unlock or actually create value and then ultimately execute on that vision. This usually involves repositioning the asset for resale to another buyer with a different cost of capital (similar to transitional alpha, as we'll see below), but only after some actual value enhancement from the asset owner.

Remember the return bridge from the previous chapter, where private equity managers create value from growing revenue or expanding profit margins? That is manufactured alpha. In this skill category, the investment manager has to actually do something to change the investment. Other examples could include value-added real estate strategies. In these funds, the manager will often buy an underutilized property in need of some significant improvements with a concrete plan to do so. For example, a slightly rundown apartment building with out-of-date furnishings running with very low occupancy rates but in a good location could be a very attractive investment (at the right price, of course) to a real estate manager capable of upgrading the rooms and refurbishing the facade and lobby to look more modern and upscale. After the renovations are completed, the objective would be to get occupancy rates up and have a significantly better-performing asset.

Other related strategies that could fall into this class would include shareholder activism, where a meaningful equity holder of a public company will advocate that management sell off underperforming assets or improve the composition of the board, among other things, or even more esoteric investment strategies such as servicing receivables and reperforming loans. In these strategies, the investment manager will typically purchase a large portfolio of underlying loans, like home mortgages or auto loans, from a bank where the borrowers have begun to fall behind on payments or miss them altogether. Oftentimes, banks aren't equipped to deal with these borrowers one by one and figure out a workout plan, whereas the investment manager will dedicate resources directly to servicing these loans. These types of funds often have teams that will call the individual borrowers one at a time and come up with payment solutions to get the borrower back on track, sometimes lowering the interest rate or even taking principal reductions. Once the borrower establishes several periods of making payments on time, these loans are considered cured and worth substantially more money to a broad pool of potential new investors.

Which takes us directly to the next type of skill, transitional alpha. Given the operationally intensive, process-oriented nature of manufactured alpha strategies, managers who have executed successfully on them in the past tend to demonstrate stronger persistence of performance in the future, resulting in more predictable outcomes. They literally have a blueprint for value creation. However, while improving the asset should drive the majority of this type of alpha, repositioning and selling the asset to new buyers also often increases the returns.

In the example described above, once the real estate manager has fixed the run-down apartment complex and turned it into a fully occupied Class A property, a totally different universe of potential buyers would emerge. These new buyers generally have a lower cost of capital and are willing to accept lower returns. And with the property now fully leased, the risk is substantially lower, and the buyers are willing to pay more. When this increase in value from a higher eventual earnings multiple being paid by the next owner is highly predictable, it is transitional alpha.

Transitional Alpha

Transitional alpha is the excess return that can be generated from short-term market changes or specific temporal inefficiencies where the typical, long-term owners of a specific asset are prevented from owning it, and the pricing trades down significantly as a result of their departure from the pool of potential buyers. Nimble investors, able to step in and provide liquidity by purchasing the asset and holding it until the natural buyers are able to return, can earn this abnormal return.

Often, these inefficiencies result from massive regulatory changes that sweep across markets, for example, Basel III and the Volcker rule,[9] or other sociopolitical events that alter previous market dynamics. For instance, after the Global Financial Crisis, banks were prevented from engaging in many of the riskier, highly leveraged activities that had precipitated the correction by these newly enacted policies almost overnight. This meant the banks had to sell some assets that were on their balance sheet, sometimes at losses, just to get their leverage ratios in line. And they couldn't issue new loans in certain financing areas. Investors able to buy the discounted assets off the bank's balance sheet were able to earn an excess return simply by being this transitional owner.

Other times, economic changes or even technological shifts can change the cost of capital or utility functions of market participants, which impacts their ability to transact in a given marketplace. And sometimes, such transi-

tional alpha can simply occur from shifting levels of risk aversion or changing investment fads.

Several other examples of these transitional opportunities include stock
spin-offs and post-reorg equities. In these situations, the stocks of a specific
company wind up in the hands of unintentional owners as a result of mergers
or legal proceedings, often resulting in these shareholders simply selling their
positions without much thought. Spin-offs occur when a publicly traded
company decides to divest a wholly-owned subsidiary into a completely separate stand-alone business, issuing shares for the equity ownership in the new
company to shareholders of their own stock. This may be done because the
two businesses make more sense apart than they do together, and the new
spin-off company can usually focus on maximizing growth or profitability,
whereas it may have been lost in the shuffle in the larger parent. However,
these smaller stocks are usually not a fit for owners of the parent corporation,
who likely wanted a large-cap stock in one sector and now find themselves
holding a small-cap stock in another sector entirely. As a result, they sell,
depressing prices in the new firm.

Research shows that buying equity spin-offs after the initial shareholders
liquidate can result in excess returns. In one report, researchers examined
every spin-off that occurred in US equity markets from 2001 until 2013,
and they showed that buying all of them as soon as possible after they were
traded outperformed public equity benchmarks significantly.[10] The article
suggested that by using this strategy it was possible to achieve excess returns
of 0.5 to 1.0% per month for almost two years after the spin-off. After that
point, the stocks revert to the mean and begin to pace the index, once market
participants more fully vet and fairly value the new business.

This would happen in our example above once small-cap research analysts
and mutual funds had time to analyze the separate financial statements in
the newly independent business, an effort the prior large-cap owners did not
undertake. Upon doing so, their collective purchasing power, informed by
more fulsome valuations, would push the price of the spin-off up, earning
the excess return for the transitional owner and depressing the returns for
future investors back down to the mean. (And if the argument is that these
spin-offs are simply not fully researched and understood initially, I'd sug-

gest that bears a striking similarity to what we've observed in private equity spinouts. Those teams are often unloved by their original parent company investors and are underappreciated by the market, which gives investors the opportunity to generate excess returns.)

Similarly, post-reorg equities are typically private shares that are issued to certain bondholders of a company after it has successfully emerged from the grueling process of a bankruptcy. Most bondholders do not want to own stocks, and so these entities often quickly sell out of these positions as well, creating another opportunity for transitional alpha.

And even to a certain extent, downgraded high-yield bonds can fall into this category of transitional alpha. Many institutional investors and mutual funds have well-defined limits on the credit ratings of bonds they are allowed to own. In some instances, pensions were legally prevented from owning bonds that were not rated or were rated below investment grade by credit ratings agencies such as Moody's or Fitch. When a bond suffers a credit downgrade, like an investment-grade bond going from BBB to junk status at BB, such entities are often forced by policy or statute to divest the bond. I worked at a mutual fund company where the high-yield fund had a policy to automatically sell a bond that had been downgraded from B to CCC, which is extremely speculative.

However, as we witnessed during the Global Financial Crisis, credit ratings are not always accurate representations of credit risk. And in cases where the downgrade has occurred without any real impairment in the credit quality of the borrower, an opportunity to buy bonds that are trading below fair value creates the potential for alpha, because the previous owners can no longer hold the asset regardless of price. In such situations, somewhat shorter-term, ephemeral circumstances cause forced selling from current holders while simultaneously removing other natural buyers from the supply-demand equation.

In short, transitional alpha can be generated from holding certain assets until such time as natural buyers can come back into the equation and prices normalize. One may consider this a form of alpha, as the temporary nature of the inefficiency requires active, sometimes rapid, analysis and execution to capture the opportunity. Often, it is difficult for an institutional investor to assess the opportunity set before it is gone, making it key that an investment manager have the ability to identify and shift from one transitional investment to another. However, the transitory nature of these opportunities often makes returns more unpredictable and episodic.

Inaccessible Risk Premium

An inaccessible risk premium may not be true alpha, but this category logically sits between transitional alpha and alternative beta. Similar to transitional alpha, an inaccessible risk premium exists where structural forces prevent many market participants from investing in specific investment segments. However, unlike the shorter-term, temporary nature of transitional alpha, an inaccessible risk premium is quasi-permanent in nature.

In prior chapters we discussed hedge funds and private equity funds, vehicles that for decades were only available to accredited investors. These were wealthy individuals, presumed to understand the risks of these private markets, who were required to have a net worth of at least $1 million, or to have an income of at least $200,000 per year for the last two years or if married a family income of $300,000 annually for the last two years. Individuals who did not meet this litmus test were simply prohibited from investing.

Sometimes investors are unable to allocate to illiquid investments due to short-term cash flow needs or investment minimums. Retail investors simply cannot invest $5,000 directly in a privately negotiated commercial mortgage even if they wanted to. To make such direct loan investments, an investor would need the scale to write multimillion-dollar individual investments. In other circumstances, certain investors are prohibited from using derivatives or have significantly higher costs of leverage than other market participants due to suitability requirements or exchange rules. Some investors, such as some state pensions, are precluded by law from using leverage at all.

Any such legal or structural barriers to entry obviously reduce the potential buyers for an asset and create an uneven playing field. Some investors can participate, and some cannot. Unlike transitional alpha, these types of structural constraints tend to be long term in nature and widely known. Not much analysis or timely response is needed to interpret their effects. In the loan market for example, privately originated corporate loans often have yields around 6 to 8%, while similar broadly syndicated loans—which are far more actively traded and are often even held in mutual funds—might have yields of 4 to 6%. The risks of these two loan markets are nearly identical, and it doesn't take complicated quantitative analysis to understand which is a better deal.

Thus, these inaccessible risk premiums have barriers to entry that require some active management in order to access, making them, if perhaps not actual alpha, something other than simple beta. These investments tend to be easier to underwrite with confidence, as the market dynamics don't really change overnight. However, as we saw with hedge funds and commodities, as these barriers can and do slowly erode over time, inaccessible risk premia can become more correlated with other risk premia, at which point they begin to look more like beta.

Alternative Beta

An alternative beta is by definition not alpha, nor is it beta in the purest sense. Alternative betas are investment opportunities that at one point in the not too distant past were one of the above categories of alpha, but since have become more accessible and more broadly understood over time. Today, these opportunities have liquid, registered products including mutual funds, closed-end funds, and ETFs that allow access to a much wider array of potential investors, retail individuals included. Such products create relatively low-fee, low-minimum, investable, and benchmarkable return streams similar to pure betas.

These products attempt to replicate investment strategies that were previously solely the purview of hedge funds and private equity funds. As more market participants learned what hedge funds were doing, they realized they could offer similar strategies at far lower cost and could do so in a way that was accessible to a deeper pool of possible investors. Examples of alternative betas could be catastrophe bonds, merger arbitrage mutual funds, long-only commodities, and systematic trend-following products. There are even a few ETFs that build portfolios of public equity spin-offs.

Collectively, such funds have come to be known as liquid alternatives, and interest in them has skyrocketed, as Figure 5.5 clearly shows. (A quick Google search for "liquid alternatives" yields 119 million pages in 0.6 second.) According to data from consultant RVK and financial research firm Morningstar, assets in these vehicles have also risen sharply, growing from just under $14 billion in 2003 to nearly $300 billion as of the start of 2019, a growth rate of 21% per year.

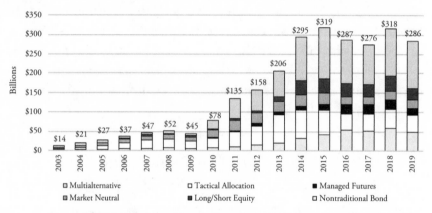

FIGURE 5.5   Rise of liquid alternatives (*RVK, Morningstar*)

These strategies are typically far cheaper than hedge funds or private equity funds. While 1 to 2% management fees (with no profit sharing) are common, some liquid alternatives can be found for 0.5%, cheaper than many active equity mutual funds. Unlike pure betas, alternative betas are less widely researched, less widely championed, and subsequently less widely adopted in investor portfolios. These return streams simply have shorter track records and fewer adherents than do the completely ubiquitous pure betas. And while there is more performance differentiation among managers in alternative betas than pure betas, the rapid increase in investor appetite, accessibility, and changing market structure makes future returns less predictable than when they were inaccessible return streams.

Pure Beta

Finally, pure betas are quite simply basic asset class exposures that have been around for a long time. Pure betas have decades of price history and extensive research that is widely available. These betas are broadly accepted as the basic investment strategies appropriate for nearly all portfolios. Pure betas are usually offered via thousands of competing low-fee products and are available to investors of any experience level or asset size. In short, pure betas are entirely commoditized return streams that anybody can buy. Think of a standard S&P 500 index fund or a broad market investment-grade core bond portfolio.

Factors

Where do factors fit in this investment hierarchy? Factors are themselves the fundamental underlying building blocks of the investment return streams that go into all investment products. Market beta is itself a lazy and naïve concept since betas by themselves have no "average" expected return. In essence, betas are merely rules for accessing factors, as indeed are all forms of investment skill. As such, factors themselves don't represent skills; they are the atomic material that asset managers use to create return streams. What we purchase when we hire investment managers are packages of these factors. We are buying the manager's rules for accessing these factors, and betas are the simplest, most widely known rules.

This hierarchy of skill also works similar to a waterfall in terms of tracking the migration, or evolution, of investment skill from alpha to beta. In theory, the process goes like this: Initially, a select few individuals adept at pattern recognition are able to identify and implement a highly successful investment strategy (recall Warren Buffett, Bill Gross, Alfred Winslow Jones, Henry Kravis). The process becomes systematized and institutionalized as others at the firm are taught how to implement it, and the business grows.

Competitors take note, as they try to chase the returns put up by the sector's top performer. Others gradually learn the strategy and begin to replicate it. Perhaps a few lieutenants spin out on their own, taking their inside knowledge of the approach with them, and begin to compete with their former mentors. More and more market participants begin to imitate it, academics begin to write about it, and the skill becomes more broadly understood. Eventually it becomes widely implemented and ultimately turns to beta, whereby relative performance and costs are dominant considerations when hiring a manager.

As we observed in Chapter 2, such a scenario is more than mere theory. Competition drives changes in market efficiency over time. As Professor Andrew Lo argued so brilliantly in his book *Adaptive Markets,* it is in fact how financial markets evolve.[11]

Market participants learn and adapt, and the efficiency of a market changes accordingly. Not all asset classes are equally, or statically, efficient. This reality has to be incorporated into our assessment of strategies and the managers who implement them.

Recall the Morningstar style boxes from Chapter 2? Well, what was intended to be a descriptive approach to investment strategies has become proscriptive, and it dominates how many allocators think about the investment landscape. No institutional investor is indifferent to public equity or private equity, or stocks versus bonds. We make asset allocation decisions, and hire managers to invest in a given asset class, in a very well-defined, "stay in your box" approach, for right or wrong. Managers are discouraged, if not outright prevented, from switching to large-cap growth if they are small-cap value, let alone from public to private equity. Hence, if asset classes are stratified and style-boxed inputs, then it stands to reason that market efficiency itself must be a stratified, style-boxed output.

Large-cap value stocks and US Treasury bonds, for instance, are highly efficient markets, no matter how you measure it. These markets have very low commissions, are highly liquid, and exhibit tight spreads between top and bottom managers. Investors should be highly skeptical of managers claiming that they can generate true alpha in these asset classes.

Even for strategies that are far less efficient, it's critical for end investors to understand the competitive dynamic in that particular market and the source, scope, and nature of that alpha. At the end of the day, you probably don't want excess return to be true alpha. True alpha, if it even exists, is statistically indistinguishable from luck. It is idiosyncratic, fleeting, and unpredictable. If you really want durable, predictable sources of excess returns, you want it to be an as-of-yet unidentified beta by everyone else—yourself included!

But perhaps this is all a foolish effort. The more investors search for the next new source of alpha, the faster and faster it will disappear, making the exercise a wild goose chase. The paradox of alpha is that the harder we search for it, the more efficient the markets become and the less there is to be found. I think this framework of alpha—that of beating a benchmark—is probably no longer worth the effort. Does this then mean the inevitable demise of alpha?

In the next chapter I'll discuss the end of alpha, at least the way we've been discussing it so far, before turning to a new way to reset our investing mindset and focus on what really matters in investing.

Notes

1. For instance, in 2014 the California Public Employees' Retirement System publicly announced it would be redeeming its $4 billion hedge fund portfolio, exiting the asset class entirely (Fitzpatrick, 2014). A few years later, the New York City Employees' Retirement System (NYCERS) came to the same decision, stating that "hedge funds can be removed from the NYCERS asset mix to achieve targeted levels of return and maintain consistent levels of volatility" (Steyer, 2016). More recently, legislators in Pennsylvania have proposed legislation that would require their state pensions, both the Pennsylvania Public School Employees' Retirement System and the Pennsylvania State Employees' Retirement System, to invest far less in illiquid investments, like private equity (Cumming, 2018).
2. See Carhart (1997) and Detzel and Weingard (1998).
3. See Boyson (2008), Ammann et al. (2013), Jagannathan et al. (2010), and Kumar (2015).
4. See Kaplan and Schoar (2005).
5. See Preqin (2013).
6. See Rose-Smith (2017), or https://www.institutionalinvestor.com/article/b1505qmcspbw8p/new-fee-structure-offers-hope-to-besieged-hedge-funds.
7. This story is told in greater detail in a fantastic book, Gregory Zuckerman's *The Man Who Solved the Market: How Jim Simons Launched the Quant Revolution.*
8. Price elasticity of demand is another technical economic term that measures how sensitive consumers' demand for a given product or service is relative to changes in price. If the demand for something does not change when the price rises, that item is said to have inelastic demand. Think of products like life-saving medicine in this category. Sellers of such items have pricing power. On the other end of the spectrum are things where an increase in price results in a

substantial drop in demand for the good. Newspapers are an example of such products. There are many competing venues (some of which are free) where we can receive news today, and a rise in newspaper prices (indeed, even keeping prices flat!) has resulted in demand dropping significantly. Like most things in life, the majority of products and services fall somewhere in the middle, such as gasoline and pork, where customers can accept some price increase, but they can also easily change consumption patterns if prices rise too much.

9.   Basel III was a set of international banking rules designed in 2010 by the Bank of International Settlements to restabilize the financial system after the Global Financial Crisis. These rules basically meant banks had to use less leverage and raise more equity. The Volcker rule was a section of the Dodd-Frank Act of 2010 that limited how banks could invest depositor capital, and prevented them from doing certain investments that looked more like proprietary risk taking or merchant banking. The combined effect of these regulations was that the banks had to reduce the amount of leverage they used, reduce the risk they took, and reduce the amount of loans they held.

10. McConnell et al. (2015).

11. Lo (2017).

6
Alpha and Omega

In stock market affairs, the popularity of a trading theory
has itself an influence in the markets behavior,
which detracts in the long run
from its profit-making possibilities.
—BENJAMIN GRAHAM

Alpha is disappearing everywhere it has been found, turning into beta faster than ever before. Figure 6.1 traces the decline. Active mutual funds are losing market share to factor-based or smart index strategies, while masters of the universe like Bill Gross, Warren Buffett, and the luminaries of the hedge fund and private equity industries are no longer able to replicate the eye-popping returns of the past.

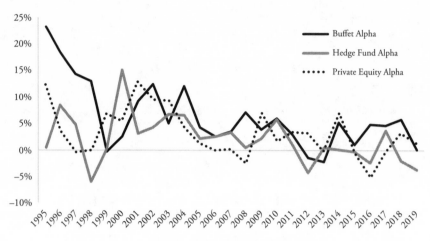

FIGURE 6.1 Decline of alpha

We are witnessing the disappearance of traditional alpha, and it is happening more quickly today. The rapid acceleration in the decay function of alpha is shortening the half-life of alpha, turning it to beta faster and faster over the last decade. This coincides with the rise of factors observed in Figure 2.4. Since alpha is a residual—the part of Equation 1.2 from Chapter 1 that can't be identified—the more factors that are identified, the less there is left over for alpha.

And the rates of the discovery of factors and the disappearance of alpha have clearly accelerated since the mid-2000s. The rules around what makes up alpha don't remain secret for long anymore. So that's where we are today. But let's pause and take a little trip into our past to see how we got here.

In 1965, a young researcher at Fairfield Semiconductor named Gordon Moore authored an article in *Electronics* titled "Cramming More Components onto Integrated Circuits." Moore's critical insight was the realization that the falling cost and shrinking size of transistors due to gains from increasing manufacturing efficiency suggested chips could contain more and more components over time and, hence, would have far greater processing power.

Moore predicted that while the average chip had around 50 components in 1965, he believed by 1970 the chips could contain 1,000 transistors and perhaps as many as 65,000 by 1975, as manufacturing methods would continue to advance. History has shown this prediction, subsequently titled

Moore's law, to be fairly accurate, and because of this insightful observation, Moore went on to a highly successful career in semiconductors, ultimately becoming CEO of Intel.

Indeed, as Moore's law predicted, the number of transistors on an integrated circuit doubled roughly every 12 to 18 months for about a decade. Since then, the rate of growth has slowed to a doubling approximately every 2 years, and today it's closer to 2½ years for the transistor count to double. Still, this growth has resulted in an exponential increase in computing power. Today the most advanced chips on the market have roughly 20 billion transistors on them. Using information on transistor growth from Wikipedia,[1] we can plot this exponential growth in chip component density, graphically showing Moore's law in the scatterplot shown in Figure 6.2.

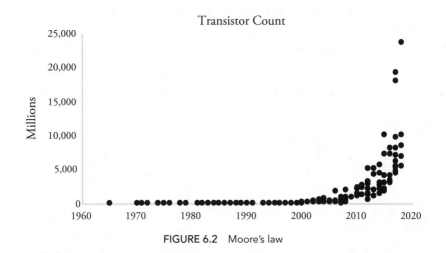

FIGURE 6.2   Moore's law

And in a fairly poignant example of supply creating its own demand—largely because of this increase in computing power—the amount of data to feed these machines has exploded in nearly perfect lockstep with it. Today, as a society, we create roughly 2.5 exabytes of new data each day.[2] For perspective, an exabyte is 1 quintillion bytes, which is a 1 with 18 zeroes after it! Or put another way, 1 exabyte is 1 billion gigabytes, a number more familiar to most of us. My current iPhone has a storage capacity of roughly 125 gigabytes, which would mean I would need 8 million iPhone 7s just to store

1 exabyte of data, and 20 million iPhone 7s just to warehouse the new data created every day. Data is now ubiquitous.

To put this incredible data creation in context, let's turn to what during my formative years represented basically the collective storage of humanity's knowledge, the Library of Congress—the United States' answer to antiquity's great Library of Alexandria.

Established in 1800 at the suggestion of Founding Father James Madison, the Library of Congress is our nation's oldest federal cultural institution. Initially housed in the US Capitol, it grew slowly at first. During the War of 1812, much of its original material was destroyed by vengeful British soldiers who set fire to the collection. Thankfully, another Founding Father, Thomas Jefferson, sold his entire personal collection of books, an amazing total of nearly 6,500 works, to the library, helping to lift its profile from a specialty government library to a true scholastic institution.

Unfortunately, another fire in 1851 destroyed much of Jefferson's original collection. And for some time, the library languished under restricted leadership and weak funding, but by the late nineteenth century, under the leadership of Ainsworth Rand Spofford, a legend in library science, it had grown from 60,000 books to 850,000.

Spofford's masterstroke was the Copyright Act of 1870. In petitioning Congress for this law, Spofford argued that any applicant for copyright protection from the federal government should be required to submit two manuscripts—one to the copyright office and one to the Library of Congress, for posterity. By the time of his death in 1908, nearly half of the 1 million books the library then housed had come via this copyright registration deposit.

Today the Library of Congress contains more than 32 million cataloged books and other print material, across 470 languages, and more than 61 million rare manuscripts in addition to millions of periodicals and magazines. According to various estimates, if all the printed material contained within the Library of Congress today were converted to digital data, it would be about 10 terabytes.[3] Each day then, the world creates new data equivalent to roughly 250 Libraries of Congress. It took us 200 years to store one Library of Congress's worth of human knowledge, and now we create 250 of them daily.

Now, admittedly, not all data is created equal. I hardly think history will assign the same value to Henry David Thoreau's opus *Walden* that it will to your television viewing history. However, not all this data has come from content platforms tracking your internet viewing habits or from social media monitoring your shopping preferences. Some of this increase in data has also resulted from more productive venues.

For instance, a decade ago the cost of sequencing a genome was approximately $100 million. Today this same sequencing costs just $1,000. This massive decrease in cost has created an explosion of genetic data available for scientists and researchers, opening up opportunities for the advancement of new and innovative therapeutic technologies that would not have otherwise been available.

Figure 6.3 shows the rise of global data in zettabytes.[4] Given the rapid speed of new data creation, the total amount of global data is expected to hit 100 zettabytes over the next three to five years.[5] This blistering pace means that more than 99 percent of all data in existence over the course of human history has been created since 2007, which corresponds to nearly the same date that this alpha erosion pattern has been observed across markets, a fact that is not a coincidence. During this same time, the amount of information available on liquid financial markets has proliferated identically. For instance, there are now about 3.7 million different indexes available on pub-

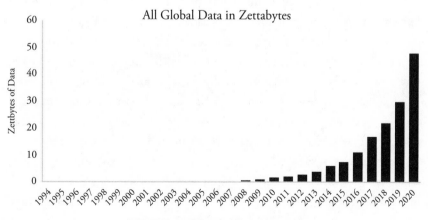

FIGURE 6.3   Rise of global data (*IDC*)

licly traded assets globally, and over 400,000 created in 2018 alone.[6] Again, axiomatically, it becomes harder and harder to find alpha the finer and finer you can slice beta. And this rise in computing power clearly parallels the rise in factor discovery and beta production.

But more problematically, we simply cannot keep up going forward. We can't aggregate, synthesize, and analyze this information fast enough, parsing through it all to find new sources of outperformance before the competition. Computers on the other hand can, or more accurately, have, and not just in financial markets.

We saw the incredible outperformance that Renaissance Medallion's computing power has generated. However, computers are now consistently winning in other intellectual domains as well. Indeed, in 2016, Google's fittingly named AlphaGo program beat world champion Go player Lee Sedol in four games out of five. With more potential game configurations than estimated atoms in the known universe,[7] Go is a very complicated game—10 raised to the power 100 times more complex than chess—but it's still a board game with fixed rules. AlphaGo's decisive victory coming after IBM Deep Blue beating Gary Kasparov in 1997 and IBM's Watson defeating Ken Jennings on *Jeopardy!* in 2011 means computers now reign supreme in all existing board or puzzle games.

Similarly, finding value by analyzing loads of financial and operating metrics for public companies—searching for assets trading at 95 cents on the dollar—is something that humans simply do not have an edge in anymore. Sifting through this structured financial data is something that computers are great at, and that doesn't require anywhere near the horsepower of AlphaGo. But even if the specific metric used for implementation of value (say, a price-to-book or price-to-earnings ratio) changes due to either market conditions, competitive dynamics, or the financial reporting tendencies of corporate executives, computers are far better positioned to identify the shift than we are, with their machine learning enhanced pattern recognition.

Computers are also winning in arbitrage-style hedge fund strategies, where an asset worth 95 cents is bought in one market and a quasi-identical one is sold in another market for $1.00. Most of those traditional hedge fund strategies are rules-based, and if anything, data ubiquity means computers have a huge advantage parsing through ever-increasing amounts of data to step in front of slower investors for a smaller spread if necessary, essentially beating them to the punch.

It would be prudent for investors to be skeptical of an investment firm's ability to harvest replicable excess returns in the future from simplistic, highly transparent rules-based strategies amid data ubiquity, where computers now have the clear advantage. As the saying goes, if you can't spot the sucker at the table in the first 10 minutes of the game, then it's you. And if that game involves the ordinal ranking of numbers and all the other players are computers, you're in big trouble. Alpha of any type comes from only two sources: (1) an informational advantage or (2) a processing edge; and in public markets and traditional hedge fund strategies, neither is possible anymore.

In public markets, accessing beta exposure cheaply is a better use of investment resources than the search for alpha. If you are still determined to find excess returns, the only place left to look for alpha is in less liquid, esoteric markets where data asymmetry still exists. But whether this means first-time funds, small market buyout, litigation finance, or even more esoteric private strategies, you have to be willing to go where others aren't and to move on once the jig is up. I have a friend who in the past worked for a massive alternatives shop on Wall Street and now is the head of alternatives for a small wealth management firm in Atlanta. He puts it bluntly: "In New York, there were a thousand people like me who could cut $100 million checks. In Atlanta, there are only five people like me with the same level of sophistication who can cut $5 million checks."

Alpha in private markets doesn't scale. The firms that have become asset managers in private equity and hedge funds are providing (expensive) exposure management today. I don't think it's worth the cost. If you want alpha, you have to go where others aren't and where capital *and information* are in short supply.

Even better than just finding pockets of inefficiency where asymmetric information exists in undercapitalized segments of the private markets is finding the opportunity to manufacture alpha in those sectors. Manufactured alpha is where changes made to an asset result in future returns, a far more durable and predictable driver of future returns than the mere identification of attractive factors and passive ownership of an asset. Think of manufactured alpha as an assembly line, where several components are added together to create the final return stream. Or think of it perhaps as a recipe. As long as the ingredients are still the same quality and combined in the same amounts, you have a good probability that the final product will also be the same.

Chapter 4 provided an example of manufactured alpha in private equity in our return bridge analysis, where a company generated strong equity returns from several components, such as revenue growth + margin enhancement + multiple expansion + leverage = gross multiple of capital. Things like revenue growth are somewhat predictable if the strategy is to consistently purchase businesses that don't have a dedicated sales staff and then the private equity owner subsequently builds out that resource. Revenue growth should follow.

However, underwriting to explicit building blocks of return is possible in other private market strategies as well. For instance, some real estate assets combine both income and some light refurbishing for capital gains, sort of in between core plus and true value added. In these strategies, there is often the potential to generate income immediately but also the ability to enhance both occupancy rates and rent prices through some modest enhancements before reselling the property. Perhaps it is by upgrading the lobby of a hotel or some light kitchen remodeling in an apartment complex, but such improvements typically lead to higher rent rolls through both higher occupancy and pricier rents. In such a scenario, the total return stream would look like the following:

$$\text{Rental income} + \text{improvement in occupancy} +$$
$$\text{increase in rent} - \text{capital expenditures} +$$
$$\text{cap-rate compression} = \text{total gross return on capital} \qquad (6.1)$$

A similar approach is possible in private debt strategies but can be applied to the rate of return as opposed to the multiple of capital. For instance, let's imagine a mezzanine lending strategy with the following portfolio characteristics. Let's say for the portfolio as a whole, the average tenor of the loans is three years, they are issued at 97% of par, and the average coupon is floating rate at LIBOR (with a 1% floor) + 7.5% spread. Let's assume some equity upside participation that has historically created a few points of return, less average credit losses (either historical or projected[8]) and fees. This would provide the annualized return bridge shown in Figure 6.4.

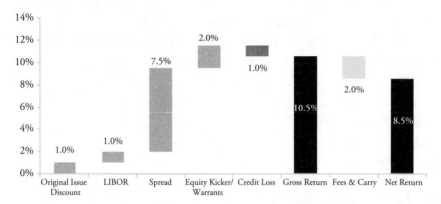

FIGURE 6.4 Private debt annualized return bridge

This manufactured alpha process allows the investor to investigate the individual components of the return stream today, see how they compare with the past, and assess how likely the manager will be at constructing desired returns in the future. This provides for more predictable and durable future returns. It's worth noting that these return drivers look a lot like factors (income, value, growth). If you are just constructing portfolios of them, even in higher doses than "average," it's still basically a type of beta.

So that's it. Now, for a book about alpha, perhaps this is not a rosy outlook for the hero of our story. It has been absolutely eviscerated in public markets, is recently deceased in hedge funds except in select quantitative strategies, and is probably on life support in private markets, at least in the more developed segments. And if our framework of alpha inexorably evolving—or perhaps devolving—into beta is correct, then it is probably doomed everywhere it is to be found, as it is precisely the act of discovery that leads to imitators and the degradation of future returns.

However, it is possible that this story still has a happy ending, but to do so will require that our antagonist goes through some difficult self-discovery before redefining itself in the end.

You see, very finely tuned computing engines, like Google's AlphaGo, are great in one specific domain with structured data and rules, and although these computing engines can improve their performance at that one task, they have yet to truly show anything remotely resembling the humanlike intelligence required for creative, unstructured thinking. AlphaGo, for example, cannot tell a cat from a table, nor can it beat me at checkers. Although the brain is prone to certain errors, it is still more powerful at combining information from otherwise unrelated domains to make creative and intuitive leaps of discovery than any computer to date. And these errors are often predictable, and frankly it's because of these errors that scientific discovery and creative leaps occur.

If alpha versus a benchmark is a fool's errand today, we must search for it from a processing perspective instead. In Part III, I'll provide some tools we can use to overcome or at least harness these predicable cognitive processes, and in so doing improve portfolio outcomes. In the story of alpha, I believe this is the new way we should be thinking about excess returns instead of the fruitless quest to beat a benchmark.

If a simple 60/40 indexed portfolio gives us a 50% chance of meeting our goals, can we do things differently to increase those odds? I believe we can, and over the remaining chapters, I'll try to redefine alpha as *making investment decisions that yield a higher probability of meeting or exceeding our required return objectives.* This is eminently doable, unlike beating a computer in a race versus a benchmark.

Alpha is dead! Long live alpha!

Notes

1. https://en.wikipedia.org/wiki/Transistor_count.
2. According to data from DOMO's Data Never Sleeps 5.0 Report, https://www .domo.com/solution/data-never-sleeps-6.
3. Estimates for the size of the data needed were the Library of Congress to be fully digitized vary tremendously—from some outdated numbers of 20 years ago, as low as 10 terabytes, to 20 petabytes for more recent assumptions. Librarian Leslie Johnston, posting on the Library of Congress blog page, states the LOC has over 50 petabytes of storage, of which only 5 petabytes is used. Further, not everything is currently digitized. Using some assumptions about the size of an average digitized book, and how many books are not yet stored digitally, 10 petabytes is as good a ballpark guess as any.
4. Reinsel et al. (2018).
5. See note 2.

6. According to an article published in *Bloomberg Markets* on November 14, 2018 (Evans, 2018).
7. Renowned physicist Michio Kaku provided this estimate in his book *The Future of Humanity*, p. 113 (Kakio, 2019).
8. The assumed credit loss rate allows an investor to model more realistic assumptions if default rates have been low for an extended period of time, providing more conservative underwriting. For instance, if a specific credit manager has never had a credit loss, one could still model 10% default rate with an 85% recovery rate as [10% default rate × (1 – 85% recovery rate)] = 1.5% net credit loss assumption, to better capture the environment of a credit contraction.

7
Behavioral Biases— Negative Alpha

[Market] participants act not on the basis
of their best interests but on their perception
of their best interests, and the two are not identical.
—GEORGE SOROS

If alpha is dead, then why do so many investors still spend so much time picking stocks or managers in a futile attempt to beat the market in highly efficient asset classes? What is the point of all the frenetic activity of the millions of individuals involved in investment activity, especially when it often results in worse outcomes than doing less? To try to answer that question—which is necessary before we return to how to find alpha again—we'll turn to a discussion of behavioral finance.

Introduction to Behavioral Finance

For many years, classical economists struggled with a glaring flaw in one of their basic underlying premises. When they tried to model decision-making behavior, the mathematically sound methods describing the optimal behavior of rational market participants they had created failed consistently to predict actual market participant behavior.

Utility theory was the conventional model that classical economics used to predict market behavior, and it was first described by Daniel Bernoulli in 1738. Bernoulli was a brilliant Swiss mathematician and physicist, and much of his work lives on today in ways most people may not appreciate. He described in detail how the law of conservation of energy applies to fluid dynamics, and many of his calculations are still used in mechanical applications as well as statistics and probability theory.

This utility model was a formula that was supposed to be a proxy for how people make decisions about risky outcomes, weighing the expected utility received from a good or service versus the price and/or risk. Unlike the simple value of something, utility can have elements of personal preference that vary from individual to individual and can incorporate different amounts of risk aversion. This model had its limits. It was expected that some of the underlying assumptions would not work in all circumstances, but it was good enough and held for hundreds of years, largely unchanged.

Then in 1979, psychologist Daniel Kahneman and his long-time collaborator and friend Amos Tversky published "Prospect Theory: An Analysis of Decision Under Risk" in *Econometrica*,[1] and behavioral economics was born. Kahneman and Tversky had long studied judgment and decision-making and realized how complex people were. The coauthors didn't think existing models on rational decision-making were accurate, because real decisions often seemed wildly inconsistent with optimal outcomes. Moreover, they had recognized some of this suboptimal behavior in themselves as well. In one anecdote in Kahneman's *Thinking, Fast and Slow*,[2] he describes how as a young officer in the Israeli army, he was given the task of assessing the aptitude of incoming recruits to predict who would be better suited for officer training school. Despite having no real objective knowledge of the matter,

Kahneman's education in psychology got him picked for the gig, thankfully for the Israeli Defense Forces, as it turned out.

At first, Kahneman used a standard questionnaire developed from the accumulated tribal knowledge of past officers. This subjective approach relied heavily upon the judgment of the evaluators, basically allowing them to interpret responses through their gut instinct of whether they thought the candidate would be a good officer. Realizing the folly of this intuition-based approach for assigning military roles after trying it unsuccessfully himself, Kahneman decided to implement a new, data-driven method, which nearly caused a mutiny among his team of evaluators.

This second approach was limited to a series of factual questions that systematically generated a score on six personality traits. After just a few months, the superiority of this approach became obvious to all. This method was so effective the army used it nearly unchanged for decades. Later, when Kahneman wrote "Prospect Theory," he used elements of cognitive psychology to explain the failings of classical economics regarding rational decision-making as he had observed firsthand and documented empirically.

One of the key tenets that differentiated prospect theory from utility theory was that the personal preference individuals displayed in making decisions under certainty were themselves inconsistent across choices, but largely dependent upon how the choices were presented. These irrational or imperfect elements of decision-making were also not random, but were highly predictable.

Fundamentally, he and coauthor Tversky showed that actual market participants were not perfectly rational, robotic logicians. Rather, they were subject to a litany of biases and cognitive shortcuts that resulted in suboptimal decisions. Ultimately, prospect theory won Kahneman a Nobel Prize in Economics, even though he never took an economics course in his life!

In *Thinking, Fast and Slow*, Kahneman describes two systems of thinking. His System 1 is a quick, intuitive processor that favors the efficiency and speed characteristic of snap judgments. This system, although fast and decisive, is prone to errors in many complex situations. Kahneman's book is packed with examples of where our intuitive, gut response leads us astray.

On the other hand, System 2 is a more deliberate and logical process, but it is also much more effortful. System 2 is the cognitive engine we engage when reading a textbook, taking an exam, or writing an essay. In short, it is intentional, measured thinking, and because it is far more energy intensive than System 1, our natural proclivity is to bypass it, much to our detriment.

While Kahneman showed that people were not even close to the perfectly rational economic agents previously assumed, unknowingly the mathematician Bernoulli had already given us another principle about finance. Bernoulli's flawed model proved that unlike physical sciences where mathematical models can describe what must happen with certainty, finance and economics are social sciences and deal in human behavior. There is a big difference between what is likely to happen and what must happen.

In physics, net force equals mass times acceleration. In equation form, $F_{net} = m(a)$, always. In chemistry, hydrochloric acid plus sodium yields sodium chloride (salt) and hydrogen gas, with certainty. On the other hand, in finance, math can provide relationships that are only tendencies, not certainties. For example, geometric Brownian motion, a model used to simulate price movements in assets, doesn't hold perfectly because stocks exhibit discontinuities, or price gaps. Value in the earnings of a company is not mathematically guaranteed to be reflected in stock price appreciation. Finance is probabilistic, not deterministic.

This also means it is often impossible to separate the dependent variable from the independent variable in social sciences or to determine the cause from the effect. In fact, this circular "reflexivity" where an effect strengthens itself through a feedback loop has long been noted by no less an investment luminary than George Soros. Soros believes that markets are driven by participant behavior, and the market activity itself stimulates certain participant behavior, which in turn drives market activity, and so on.

This is precisely the sort of feedback loop that creates price momentum, or trends, in markets. Traders observe a stock continue to rise in price, and they become more confident in that investment as an attractive opportunity. When they actually decide to invest, their purchasing power bids up the price even further, which increases their confidence in the investment thesis, creating a virtuous cycle, a positive self-fulfilling prophecy.

Sociologist Robert Merton coined the term "self-fulfilling prophecy" in a 1948 article based on this theory of reflexivity developed by earlier scholars in his field.[3] Behavioral confirmation is a type of self-fulfilling prophecy whereby people's social expectations lead them to behave in ways that cause others to confirm their expectations. A financial example of a self-fulfilling prophecy that Merton used to describe his concept was a bank run.

In a bank run, depositors become concerned that a bank may be running into solvency problems and decide that to protect themselves, they should withdraw their assets immediately. Other counterparties of the bank hear of this activity and also become alarmed. Given how fractional banking works, where banks only have a portion of their obligations on hand in cash at any time, if enough depositors demand to withdraw their assets, an otherwise liquid bank could become an insolvent one and be forced to declare bankruptcy, a scenario memorably depicted in the film classic *It's a Wonderful Life*.

The objective of this chapter is not a comprehensive review of all the work that has been done in recent decades. Investors wishing for more information on the subject can peruse any number of research papers or books by Terrance Odean, Richard Thaler, or Daniel Kahneman. *Thinking, Fast and Slow* by Kahneman and *Nudge* by Thaler are virtually canon in my mind. Another good overview is *The Behavioral Investor* by Daniel Crosby.

Nevertheless, the point here is to show that in spite of all the evidence regarding the absence of alpha or the extreme difficulty in finding and accessing it, many if not most investors (myself included!) still try to do so. We will review some of the reasons why this is the case, and why in many ways System 1 processing is our own worst enemy. We are creatures of instinct and habit, and this instinctual processing often leads us astray.

Inherence Heuristic

While conducting research at the University of Illinois at Urbana-Champaign, psychologists Andrei Cimpian and Erika Salomon introduced the concept of the inherence heuristic in a paper published in the journal *Behavioral and Brain Sciences*.[4] Building on Kahneman's two types of thinking—fast and intuitive versus slow and deliberate—the authors explored the fast, intuitive cognitive process of identifying causal relationships. They set out to discover how our System 1 intuitively answers "Why?"

According to the authors' concept of the inherence heuristic, people process easily accessible information relating to a pattern they've identified and intuitively arrange it into a compelling narrative to explain causality. It's a mental "shotgun" approach to reasoning, as opposed to the more systematic, rigorous approach that goes into deliberate thinking.

Our quick mental processes prefer the path of least resistance, with the easiest answer derived from superficial characteristics that are labeled inherent features. Here's how it works in practice: A primitive human drops rocks and logs into a river. The rocks always sink, and the logs always float. Hence, he concludes rocks are inherently heavier simply because, well, they're rocks.

Despite the shallow reasoning, the patterns are deemed stable and inevitable precisely because the identified characteristics are believed to be immutable and inherent. In other examples, people tend to view blue as masculine and pink as feminine. If you feel such relationships are natural and inevitable, that's the inherence heuristic ascribing gender as intrinsic to the colors.

In an investment context, I've observed something very similar regarding the so-called equity risk premium and illiquidity premium. The equity risk premium is the excess return that stocks produce compared with the risk-free rate of return provided by US government bonds. Similarly, the illiquidity premium refers to the surplus return that illiquid investments generate relative to comparable publicly traded assets, like private equity versus public equity. These assets have outperformed historically, but the belief that such premia are immutable, inherent features of the asset classes is simplistic thinking, the result of lazy System 1 processing.

The scientific method—a very deliberate, System 2 process of thinking—has given modern humans a deeper understanding of causality. Unlike primitive humans, we've discovered that rocks and logs are composed of similar elements such as carbon, oxygen, iron, and potassium. It's the density of atoms in solid objects, or the amount of matter per unit of volume, that determines what floats or sinks, not any inherent feature of rock.

Correspondingly, as we established when we discussed factors, there are only two ways an investment can generate returns: by generating income while you own the investment or by appreciating in value so it is worth more than you paid for it. That's it. We know over the long run that stock market returns come from underlying factors such as dividend yield, corporate earnings growth, and the expansion of price-to-earnings multiples. Private equity is no different. While I suspect stocks will continue to outperform bonds over the long run, and private equity should still beat public equity, that will certainly only be the case as long as the levels of these fundamental factors allow. There is no inherent reason to expect such premiums to look anything like they have in the past simply because, well, they're equities. System 1 processes such as the inherence heuristic are cognitive mechanisms for jumping to easy and often erroneous conclusions.

Confirmation Bias

Another shortcut for jumping to conclusions is known as the confirmation bias, the tendency for humans to selectively overweight information that agrees with their views and de-emphasize any information that conflicts with them.

When Austrian philosopher Karl Popper wrote *The Logic of Scientific Discovery*, he argued that the only way of truly testing a hypothesis was to form a view and then search for evidence that could empirically falsify the hypothesis, as opposed to searching for evidence to support it. You can never prove something right, but you certainly can prove it wrong. Science can advance on the assumption that the current working hypothesis is correct, and if you continue to accumulate evidence consistent with it and none contrary, it may well be. However, true scientific discovery comes by embracing the reality that a piece of conclusive evidence can come along someday and utterly debunk prevailing views.

Even some of the greatest scientists of all time—such as Nicolaus Copernicus and Isaac Newton—were eventually proved wrong when elements of their theories were disproved. Copernicus correctly put the sun at the center of the solar system instead of the earth, arguing against the previously held geocentric view. His resulting calculations of planetary movement were more accurate than earlier models, thereby disproving them. However, his calculations weren't perfect.

Isaac Newton's application of calculus to the problem showed that these elliptical, not circular, paths required some sort of centripetal force to slightly alter the orbits, and hence his introduction of the law of universal gravitation. Ultimately, even the great polymath Newton's views were replaced by Einstein's general theory of relativity, which corrected inaccuracies in the Newtonian model. That's how science works. Unfortunately, searching for contrary evidence is not the way our minds work. Instead, we form our views and spend the rest of the day finding all the information that agrees with them.

An interesting study of this bias occurred during the 2004 US presidential election. According to an article published in the *Journal of Cognitive Neuroscience*,[5] researchers selected participants for the study who reported having strong feelings about the candidates—Republican candidate George W. Bush and Democratic candidate John Kerry. These subjects were presented with a series of apparently contradictory statements, from either candidate or from a politically neutral public figure. They were also given further statements that made the apparent contradiction seem reasonable. They were then asked to decide whether they believed the candidate's positions were inconsistent. Subjects were much more likely to justify the exact same apparent contradiction for a candidate they supported, while interpreting the statements from the candidate they opposed as contradictory.

Of course, this behavior appears in many forms in investing; from the hedge fund manager who is convinced her returns come from "100% Pure Alpha," to the technology-sector specialist that always argues it's a great time to invest in tech, and even to the bearish economist who can point to the decline of at least a few economic indicators as proof that the next recession is imminent. Humans really enjoy listening to their own internal yes-man!

While there are no foolproof ways to completely circumvent such biases, implementing a scientific method–based approach to investing—coming up with a thesis and looking for evidence to disconfirm that thesis—can help to reduce the effect of this particular one.

Illusory Pattern Perception

Illusory pattern perception is another interesting foible of the human mind. It has to do with seeing what we want to see, not unlike the confirmation bias. Have you ever looked at a cloud and seen a fluffy dog running across the sky? Or swore that you heard hidden voices buried in otherwise unintelligible static? It's a nearly universal experience to look at an oddly shaped tree trunk or a random patch of shadows on a window and feel that you can see a face staring back at you. That's illusory pattern perception. The technical name most often used is pareidolia, the tendency for our minds to see a meaningful pattern emerge in otherwise random data or images.

Some evolutionary psychologists have argued that it's an adaptive behavior. Those among our early ancestors who presumed that the slight scent wafting on the breeze coupled with the soft rustling in the bushes nearby was a meaningful pattern—a predator about to strike—were less likely to get eaten than their peers and thus more likely to pass on their genes. Certainly, the risk of being wrong in that scenario and doing nothing far outweighed any risk from the pattern being merely illusory.

This theory has some support in the animal kingdom, where many animals have evolved defensive adaptations to take advantage of this phenomenon. For example, many species of moths and butterflies have spots on their wings that look startlingly like eyes. These eye spots have been shown to scare off birds that otherwise would eat the butterfly by appearing to be the face of an owl, a natural predator of the smaller bird. Pareidolia put to good effect.

However, in financial markets the effect is not so benign. With nearly instantaneous bid and offer quotes and volumes into the millions on thousands of individual securities trading daily around the world, financial markets generate an overwhelming amount of discrete data points daily. Much of this data is random noise. But many people are convinced that they have found patterns in that data.

Several researchers have found an interesting link between our perceptions of patterns that aren't there and a need for a sense of control. When we feel as though we do not have control over our environment, our tendency to perceive nonexistent patterns increases, which in turn provides us with a false sense of control.

In an article published in *Science* in 2008, psychologists Jennifer Whitson and Adam Galinsky constructed a clever experiment to measure this effect.[6] They divided their subjects into two groups based on this idea of a need for control. Those in the in-control group were given a menial test with accurate feedback on their performance, allowing them to understand and attribute their performance on the test.

On the other hand, the lack-of-control group experienced random feedback from the same project, with the feedback being disconnected from the actual performance. In short, the subjects in this group had no idea why they scored as they did. Subsequently, the lack-of-control crowd scored much higher on a test designed to measure both groups' need to structure the world. This important distinction led to interesting results.

When presented with the actual experiment, this lack-of-control group demonstrated far greater illusory pattern perception relative to the in-control group, reporting to see more images that didn't exist in digital pictures and consistently selecting certain stocks based on what was actually random, uncorrelated data. Time and again, the group that felt less control claimed to see images where there were none and found stock patterns that didn't really exist.

In capital markets, humans are confronted with decision-making about an unknowable future given an imperfect set of mostly random data and compensated based on the outcome—a perfect condition for increased illusory pattern perception based on a need for control. Unfortunately, just as one's response to a Rorschach inkblot test provides more insight into the mind of the respondent than the actual image, alpha too is in the eye of the beholder. Take some illusory pattern perception, throw in a dash of data mining, a hint of statistical overfitting, and heaps of overconfidence, and voilà—alpha appears!

Familiarity Bias

Among the many cognitive biases we all have is the familiarity heuristic, the tendency to favor the familiar over the unfamiliar. On an instinctual level, we conflate familiarity with safety, and vice versa. In short, we tend to pick the devil we know instead of the devil we don't. When deciding which berries to eat in the wild, this bias may serve us well. But in a modern, information economy, it often works against us, particularly when we are under stress.

In an article in the *Journal of Psychological Science*, Stanford University psychologist Ab Litt and his colleagues described an elegant experimental paradigm they conducted that demonstrated how this mental shortcut works.[7] Researchers solicited a pool of online volunteers to participate in what they were told was just a challenging word puzzle. To create a sense of urgency, they offered a cash prize to those who did well. Some of the volunteers were told that they could take as long as they needed to complete the puzzle, while others were told they had only four minutes to finish, putting those participants under greater pressure.

Next the candidates were given the option to select between two puzzles: a short one created by a stranger or a longer one generated by a person familiar to the candidates. To any rational, external observer, the choice should be simple—for those candidates under the time constraint, the shorter puzzle should be the logical preference. However, just the opposite was true.

The volunteers under time pressure were more likely to select the lengthier puzzle from the known author, even though it should be expected to take longer. Those with more time picked the shorter challenge. When asked why they perversely selected the more difficult choice, participants offered justifications such as the choice felt like the "safer" option, it was "less risky," and, perhaps most telling, the decision simply felt right, down in their "gut." Clearly, these gut instincts are unreliable.

Not only is familiarity a maladaptive heuristic for decision-making; it leads to choices that actually exacerbate stress, thereby increasing the likelihood of poor judgments, creating a vicious cycle of counterproductive actions. So how does this bias affect investors? There is a decent amount of financial research that has documented a local or home country bias in portfolio construction, a perfect financial corollary to the familiarity heuristic. For example, American investors have on average about 82% of their total equity exposure in domestic stocks even though the United States makes up just 44% of global equity market capitalization. Investors in smaller countries are even worse offenders.

Further, an article published in the *Journal of Finance* in December 1999 by researchers Coval and Moskowitz showed that not only do US institutional investors overweight domestic stocks in general, but they also tend to invest more in companies headquartered close to their offices.[8] Another paper by Ning Zhu at Yale studied the same effect for retail investors, revealing that the tendency to invest in local companies was even stronger for individuals than for institutions.[9] Unfortunately, most of these studies clearly demonstrate that the results of this biased decision-making tend to be lower returns for investors. Sticking with the devil we know generates negative alpha, perhaps on the order of negative 1 to 3% per year.

Saliency Bias

A closely related concept to the familiarity effect is what's known as the saliency bias, our tendency to use readily available features and characteristics to make snap judgments, as the inherence heuristic suggests. While that particular mental shortcut applies to determining cause and effect, the saliency bias deals with our predisposition to pay attention to certain factors to begin with. Like the magpie drawn to shiny buttons or sparkling jewelry, as human animals we quickly focus our attention on headline-grabbing news and other prominent material that stands out. Since we have limited processing power, we naturally prioritize these conspicuous features of our environment as being the most important things to focus on.

Salience has been shown to significantly influence people's perception of the causes and frequencies of events. For instance, media coverage that sensationalizes relatively uncommon events can cause people to massively overestimate the frequency of relatively unusual dangers (such as airplane crashes) and underestimate much more common threats (for instance, colon cancer) that do not get as much press. Once again, in the modern knowledge-based economy, this unconscious bias is even more damaging as we struggle to prioritize the most important facts and figures out of the endless stream of information and data overload that we face.

The impact of the saliency bias on investors has also been well documented. Researchers Brad Barber and Terrance Odean demonstrated that investors tend to buy stocks that have been recently featured in the news, although more informed institutional investors tended to have more disciplined screening processes than individual traders.[10] Retail investors showed abnormally high purchases of stocks featured in the news. The more actively these individual investors scooped up these headline-making stocks, the worse they performed.

Further research from Werner Antweiler and Murray Frank revealed a similar phenomenon looking at internet message board activity.[11] Sorting through nearly 35 million messages posted to Yahoo! Finance from 1999 to 2001, the authors found that the stocks with the highest levels of posting activity exhibited higher trading volumes, unusual volatility, and poor subsequent returns, even when controlling for a host of other characteristics. Once again, those investors who were wowed by headlines and frenetic message activity did worse than average, generating negative alpha by falling victim to their biases.

Numerous other studies have confirmed the same effect. By allowing what Carl Sagan called our reptilian brain to determine where we should focus our decision-making, we are probably paying attention to the wrong things.

Endowment Effect

The endowment effect, sometimes known as the endowment bias or ownership effect, refers to the predisposition to attach a higher value to things we already own versus similar items we do not own. Clearly, there is a close relation between the endowment effect and confirmation bias, as they both relate to favorable feelings we have toward preexisting views or items we own.

The endowment effect has been shown in many fascinating studies. In one example, students who participated in an experiment were separated into two groups: one group who received a coffee mug and another group who received a chocolate bar. When the experimenters later offered to trade one for the other, the subjects in both groups refused. The students who owned a coffee mug were unwilling to part with the mug in exchange for the candy, and those who already had the chocolate bar weren't willing to swap it for the mug. Both groups claimed to value the items they had more than the ones they did not.

In another example, Ziv Carmon and Dan Ariely, then both professors at Duke, published an article in the *Journal of Consumer Research* in 2000 detailing a study that took advantage of the Duke student body's rabid support for the university's basketball team, the Blue Devils.[12] Duke runs a lottery to allocate tickets to students, as there are not enough seats for everyone to attend. In 2000, Carmon and Ariely reached out to those who had signed up for the lottery for NCAA Final Four tournament seats, which were in high demand.

The researchers asked subjects two questions. The first question was, assuming you didn't have a ticket, how much would you pay for one? Second, they were asked, how much would it take for you to sell the ticket if you had one. The results were telling. On average, students said they would be willing to pay $166 for the tickets, but if they had them, they wouldn't let them go for less than $2,411—a differential of more than 14 times!

Later research has shown that the spread between these two prices can be much lower when there are other substitute goods available or when the item doesn't have as much demand. Clearly, this has implications for thinking about bid-ask spreads in financial markets. It's especially important to consider in light of the significant differences between highly efficient markets, such as public equity where, for instance, Amazon has 491.2 million shares outstanding and the bid-ask spread is inside of a penny (or about 0.0005%) as I type these words, and less liquid ones, such as your house where it would probably take an offer at least 20 or 30 percent higher than what you paid in order for you to even consider selling it.

The endowment effect can also be observed in manager selection, where it manifests as a sort of decisional inertia. At times, investors do churn through managers too quickly, but at other times, they also can stick with underperforming managers for far too long. The reasons given to not let go often echo what many of the subjects in the studies above say. They just like them more because they already have them.

Loss Aversion

Loss aversion refers to our tendency to dislike losses far more than we like gains. It's sort of the flip side of the endowment effect. We feel that losing

$500 is far more painful than winning the same $500 would be, in part because we attach incremental value to the mere ownership of the $500. Daniel Kahneman's prospect theory, in comparison with utility theory, was able to more accurately account for the unequal way people price gains and losses. In yet more research recounted in *Thinking, Fast and Slow*, Kahneman presented the scenario below to people and recorded their responses.

Scenario: Imagine you are offered a gamble on the toss of a coin.
If the coin shows tails, you lose $100.
If the coin shows heads, you win $150.
Is this gamble attractive? Would you take it?[13]

Despite the fact that this gamble has a positive probability-adjusted value of $50, most people said they would need a 50 percent chance of a $200 gain in order to willingly accept the deal. This research yielded the famous chart seen in Figure 7.1, showing people experience losses roughly twice as much as equal potential gains.

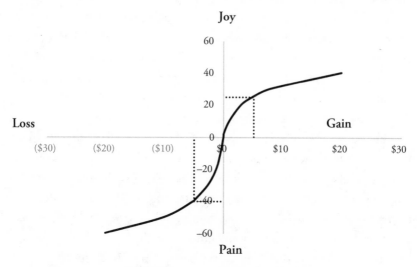

FIGURE 7.1   Loss aversion function

In Figure 7.1, the psychological value is the vertical axis, and the dollar gain/loss is plotted on the horizontal axis. The line thus describes a function where the pain of losing $5 is roughly twice the joy we feel from gaining the same $5.

Like the marginal utility curves that prospect theory replaced, not every individual has the same loss aversion function. The relative steepness of the curves on the two sides of the equation is modestly to significantly different for all of us and probably can also be affected by life experience. Some studies clearly show that loss aversion can increase in competitive situations. It is a complex equation. Our attachment to the ownership of something via the endowment effect isn't the only reason we feel losses more sharply.

Some research using brain imaging to investigate the neural activity involved in processing gains and losses indicates that different regions of the brain are activated for each. Gains or rewards, or even the anticipation of them, are associated with the neurotransmitter dopamine stimulating a portion of the brain called the ventral striatum. This "pleasure center" is what is responsible for the sensations we receive from eating chocolate, for example, and is the same mechanism that creates addiction when it malfunctions.

On the other hand, losses, as well as the mere anticipation of negative outcomes, are felt more acutely in a section of the brain called the amygdala. The amygdala is where emotional responses such as anxiety, fear, and aggression emanate. It controls what is known colloquially as our "fight-or-flight" response, a very different neural pathway from how we process rewards.

In *Thinking, Fast and Slow,* Kahneman argues that loss aversion evolved as an adaptive cognitive characteristic of humans. Those individuals who were more attuned to avoiding immediate threats in their environment, perhaps forgoing optimizing prospective gains, likely had a higher survival rate and thus passed on the genes more than those whose priorities were reversed.

Imagine a group of Australopithecus foraging on vegetables and tubers in a clearing. As they feed, the group benefits from the shared watchfulness of its members. Each member can eat comfortably, content in the knowledge that should a predator appear, many other individuals will alert the group to the predator's presence and likely provide ample time to escape.

On the other hand, the benefit to straying outside of the group to find a modestly better grazing ground is extremely limited. More importantly, it comes with a much higher risk of being the one animal to get caught. As the theory goes, over time, the prospect of losses has become a more powerful motivator of your behavior than the promise of any potential gains.

One financial behavior related to our predisposition to avoid losses is sometimes referred to as the sunken-cost fallacy. In traders' parlance, it's called getting married to your position. This happens when an investment position, such as an individual stock or fund manager, suffers significant underperformance. Instead of rationally assessing what potential recovery value remains or returns going forward could realistically be, people tend to hold on too long, hoping the trade will come back. The thought of crystallizing the loss by selling below our cost basis is too painful. To avoid this, it is helpful to establish relative and absolute parameters around expected returns and drawdowns over various time frames on an ex ante basis in order to remove the subjectivity and emotion around selling losers. As Peter Lynch advised, "Selling your winners and holding your losers is like cutting the flowers and watering the weeds."

Hindsight Bias

We've all heard the quote "Hindsight is 20/20," or had the feeling after something went wrong that you really should have known ahead of time. This effect is known as the hindsight bias. Human beings tend to perceive events as being more predictable than they actually are. After the event, this effect results in distortions to the memories of how much we knew beforehand.

A recent example of hindsight bias played out in the national media after the shocking election of Donald Trump in 2016. Nearly every political commentator on both sides of the political spectrum believed Hillary Clinton, the Democratic nominee, would cruise to an easy victory over Republican candidate Trump. Few pundits even gave him a chance. Statistician Nate Silver, founder of the election forecast website FiveThirtyEight, put the odds of a Trump victory at precisely 28.6% on November 8, 2016, and his odds were higher than most, some of which gave Trump as little as a 1 percent chance of victory.

Immediately after this result, hundreds of articles were published trying to explain away this outcome. Soon, the consensus emerged that Trump had a groundswell of support from disillusioned voters not captured in traditional polling metrics. It was obvious; we all should have seen it coming.

In a related study, when college students were asked to predict the outcome of a certain election, 58 percent of the participants correctly predicted the winner. When asked later about what they had predicted, somehow 78 percent claimed they had known who would win. This is why it's also sometimes called the "knew it all along" effect.

In another interesting study, Gilad Feldman,[14] professor of psychology at the University of Hong Kong, gave his undergrad students two different versions of the following handout:

Version A—Researchers have found that people with *low* self-confidence are more susceptible to flattery than those with *high* self-confidence. In a sentence or two, why do you think this is true?

Version B—Researchers have found that people with *high* self-confidence are more susceptible to flattery than those with *low* self-confidence. In a sentence or two, why do you think this is true?

After coming up with a causal narrative for why the result was true, students were then asked to rate the extent to which they found the result surprising or predictable. No matter which of these mutually exclusive pamphlets they had received, 75 to 80% of Feldman's students recounted that the results were predictable.

The hindsight bias is very evident after major financial crises, when policy makers tend to implement new regulations and tools, with the intention to prevent whatever triggered the crisis from happening again. Despite their assertions that next time they will see it coming, such macroprudential policies rarely work. More often they help cause the next crisis . . .

Another way this bias appears in the financial ecosystem is in the back-testing or paper trading of an untested strategy, where an investor creates a hypothetical or pro forma return stream. Often, slight tweaks or assumptions made in creating the theoretical returns are justified by hindsight bias. Investors convince themselves they would have really known to avoid that one underperforming stock or to reduce leverage at that one convenient point in time. However, once live trading of the strategy is initiated, suddenly such decisions are not quite so easy. For this reason, I ascribe no weight whatsoever to backtesting when researching potential investment strategies. If it's not live trading, it's probably riddled with hindsight bias effects.

Fundamental Attribution Error

Social psychologist Lee Ross coined the phrase "fundamental attribution error" in 1977 based on earlier work of other researchers that looked at how individuals attribute the behaviors and attitudes of themselves and others.[15] What all this research collectively showed was that humans have a propensity to credit intrinsic reasons for positive things but extrinsic reasons for negative ones in ourselves while doing the exact inverse for others.

Let's look at a classic example of this tendency to describe how this bias works in layperson's terms. We'll assume a situation where one driver, Sally, experiences being cut off by another driver, Joe, in heavy traffic. Sally attributes Joe's actions to intrinsic characteristics, similar to how the inherence heuristic works. Joe cut her off because he is selfish or inconsiderate or is just a terrible driver. However, when Sally had to do the same thing, it was only because of the situation. She had to change lanes because she was running late for a meeting, or she would be late in picking up her son from school. It wasn't because she was a bad person. It was situational.

On the other hand, when Sally does something good, like aces a particularly difficult test, she does attribute that to an intrinsic reason. She is smart and hardworking; she earned that A. Joe, however, just got lucky with his A—it was the exact same essay question on the test that Joe had written his paper on! Or when Sally holds the elevator door for her colleague running down the hallway, it's because she is thoughtful and kind. When Joe does it, it's only because the boss is watching, and he wants to look good.

To put it prosaically, when I succeed, it's because I'm good, but when I fail, it's bad luck. When you succeed, it's good luck, but when you fail, it's because you're really not that great.

The investment analogue is clear. When Sally significantly outperforms the market, it's a clear sign that she is a brilliant investor and finally has the evidence to prove it. However, if she trails the benchmark, it is only because of idiosyncratic events that she can't be responsible for. She just happened to be concentrated in a stock that missed earnings, or she had an overweight to a sector that was temporarily out of favor. Or her analyst had just quit, and she hadn't time to update her models on her own. It's only temporary, and situational. She'll bounce back.

On the other hand, when Joe outperforms his peers, Sally knows it's only because he got lucky. He just had a value tilt in his portfolio, and value stocks were all surging. Or he was too concentrated, and his biggest position rallied sharply. That's just taking more risk. At some point, his true mediocrity will shine through, and he'll start trailing the market again.

It shouldn't be difficult to see how this particular bit of mental gymnastics results in the consistent misattribution of beta as alpha across the industry, and why so many managers think they can beat the market, despite the overwhelming evidence we presented in Chapter 2 that approximately 90% of them don't!

Overconfidence Effect

Despite all these various biases and cognitive errors we make—or more accurately precisely because of them—we humans are notoriously overconfident in our own abilities. We all think we're great! This well-established bias is appropriately named the overconfidence effect. Research convincingly shows that people tend to overestimate their own performance in absolute terms and overstate their relative performance compared with that of others. One often-cited statistic in this field is that 90% of drivers score themselves above average. The effects of overconfidence on investing behavior have also long been documented, for professionals and amateurs alike.

In 2006, the former stand-alone investment bank Dresdner Kleinwort Wasserstein sent out to clients of its macro research team a survey that included several behavioral questions. Over 300 investment fund managers responded. The resulting strategy piece, written by behavioral finance researcher, author, and now head of asset allocation at GMO James Montier, is itself a fascinating read on the effects of various behavioral biases and cognitive heuristics.[16] On overconfidence specifically, one of the questions asked these managers "Are you above average?" To which, 74% of the respondents answered yes, an unequivocal and mathematically impossible response!

Terrance Odean, one of the leading experts on behavioral finance, argued in a 2002 white paper that mildly overconfident executives may actually outperform, whereas shareholder returns may be eroded by the decisions of excessively overconfident management.

His later research also looked at the effect of confidence on investment returns. Using brokerage data that covered over 65,000 households, Odean and Barber first divided these retail investors into five buckets based on how frequently they traded, and then the researchers measured the performance of each group.[17] The 20 percent of investors who traded stocks the most actively earned 5.5% less than those investors in the least active quintile—substantial negative alpha.

Further, if men tend to be more overconfident than women—and research suggests they are—and if overconfidence is a cause of excessive trading as the study presumed, then one could reasonably expect men to trade more than women. And boy do they! This research found that on average men trade 45% more than women, and single men trade 67% more than single women.

Excessive trading reduced returns for all the investors in the study, but men did even more poorly on average. Men's overconfidence eroded their returns by about 1% per year. That may not seem like a lot, but think how much you could save if you shaved 1% off your mortgage rate. Unhappily, the group of single men did even worse, giving up 1.4% for their testosterone-fueled hubris. And the effect is not constrained to individuals.

In an article published in the *Journal of Finance,* finance professors Amit Goyal and Sunil Wahal investigated the selection and termination of investment managers by institutional investors.[18] Looking at the behavior of a group of 3,400 pension plans and other allocators over a 10-year period, the authors demonstrated some familiar counterproductive behavior.

They were able to show that plan sponsors tend to hire managers after they outperform and fire the ones that underperform. But as we have seen, these decisions are driven largely by emotions instead of logic. And not surprisingly, it was precisely the wrong thing to do, as the managers that were terminated went on to outperform the managers that were hired. And those institutions that churned managers the most aggressively, overconfident in their own fund-picking abilities, did even worse. They would have been better off just sticking with the same funds the entire period.

Later research published in the *Journal of Finance* showed some remarkable, and clearly related, results regarding the fund-picking abilities of investment consultants.[19] Looking at 13 years' worth of recommendations on active US equity fund managers, the authors of this research calculated the performance of the funds that the consultants had recommended to their clients versus those they had not.

Not surprisingly (but certainly alarmingly, given that 80% of institutional assets globally are advised by investment consultants!), the fund managers that the consultants recommended underperformed those they did not support, lagging by 1% per year, negative alpha rearing its ugly head yet again!

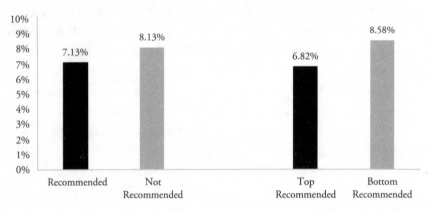

FIGURE 7.2   Investment consultant recommendations

Worse, as Figure 7.2 illustrates, the consultants' top recommendations did even more poorly, trailing their bottom picks by 1.76% per year. However, none of this stops investment consultants from running a business model largely reliant upon their earnestly professed ability to add value for their clients through manager selection. We may scoff at the absurdity of the fact that 90% of drivers believe they are better than average, but if we are being honest with ourselves, many believe *we really are* one of the individuals above average. We still think we can pick stocks or pick managers that will beat the market. (Some of us have the ultimate hubris to write a book on investments!) We all still suffer from overconfidence. And the Dunning-Kruger effect shows exactly how overconfidence works.

Dunning-Kruger effect

In an article entitled "Unskilled and Unaware of It: How Difficulties in Recognizing One's Own Incompetence Lead to Inflated Self-Assessments," published in the *Journal of Personality and Social Psychology* in 1999, authors Justin Kruger and David Dunning revealed some interesting tendencies about peoples' perceptions of their own competence, tendencies that are very important for investors to understand.[20]

These two psychologists created a series of tests measuring participants' abilities in certain functional areas, such as humor, logical reasoning, and grammar. This experiment measured two things: first, the actual scores on the tasks participants were given, and second, participants' self-reports of how they believed they scored. Like most psychological experiments, the real design of the study was not what participants thought it was. The researchers were trying to quantify the gap between performance and our perception of our own performance, and their results were striking.

The first test measured participants' ability to recognize humor. Subjects were presented with a series of jokes and were asked to rate how funny they were. These participant scores were then compared against the scores of a panel of professional comedians whose ratings were based upon their own judgment and their personal experiences based on audience reactions. Although somewhat subjective, it is not an entirely unreasonable standard.

Then respondents were grouped into quartiles based on the accuracy of their scores versus the professional benchmark, which was then compared with the performance that subjects thought they got. The results are shown in Figure 7.3.

The second skill measured was logical reasoning. In this test, the subjects—undergraduate students at Cornell University—were given 20 logical reasoning questions drawn from the Law School Admissions Test. Grading of the results was straightforward and entirely objective in this case. And once again, participants were asked to report how they thought they did. These responses are tabulated into quartiles in Figure 7.4.

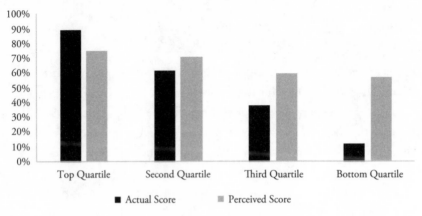

FIGURE 7.3   Humor recognition scores

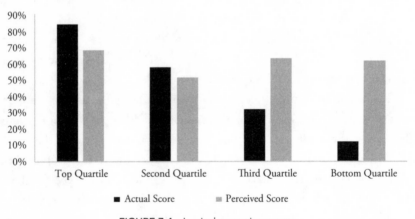

FIGURE 7.4   Logical reasoning scores

The final domain measured was grammatical ability. In this study, 84 students were asked to answer 20 grammar questions drawn from a National Teacher Examination preparation guide. The results are compiled in Figure 7.5. As you can see, the main result of the study was the discovery that competence on a specific domain was inversely correlated to the degree of misperception. That is to say, people worse at one thing thought they were much better at it than they actually were, and vice versa. And this result held across social and intellectual exercises.

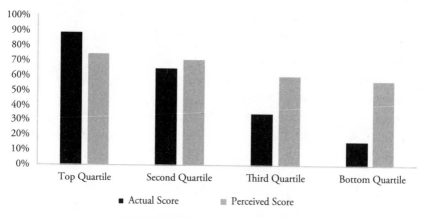

FIGURE 7.5 Grammatical ability scores

The behavioral pattern that emerged is simply undeniable. As summarized in Figure 7.6, top performers across every functional test consistently underestimated their own performance. Whether this is from modesty, false humility, or simply the rational approach of competent individuals building a margin of safety by underpromising and overdelivering is for further research, but clearly, the best performers understated their own capabilities.

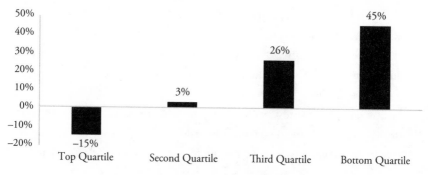

FIGURE 7.6 Average perception-reality gap

Second-quartile groups were nearly spot-on in their own self-assessment. It's once you get below median that the really interesting results begin to appear. The third-quartile performers significantly overestimated their performance. But bottom-quartile participants exhibited a self-reported competency that moves beyond merely unjustifiable confidence and squarely into utter delusion. These subjects on average scored roughly in the fifteenth percentile but assessed themselves to have scored in the sixtieth percentile—a whopping difference of forty-five percentage points!

As Charles Darwin said over a century ago, "Ignorance more frequently begets confidence than knowledge." And the Dunning-Kruger effect showed that overconfidence is indeed most prevalent among, and most detrimental to, those who are least competent. They lack both skill and the metacognitive ability to recognize their own incompetence. They are literally so bad that they don't even realize how bad they are!

Unfortunately, our cognitive abilities have not evolved to effectively make strategic decisions in a complex information economy. They evolved to efficiently make quick decisions in a relatively simple ecology. And that is an enormous difference.

Our primitive brains focus on prominent, familiar features we intuitively believe to be important. The more stress we feel from data overload, time constraints, and mental overexertion, the more we rely on these untrustworthy factors to make snap decisions. We just can't help ourselves. Despite the fact the evidence is incontrovertible, we remain obstinately overconfident in our own abilities, convinced we are above average, unlike everyone else.

I hate to break it to you, but you can't time the market, you can't pick stocks better than the market, and you can't consistently pick managers who will beat the market. In fact, as we've seen, the majority of those that try actually earn *negative* alpha, trailing simple passive buy-and-hold strategies in most asset classes.

So how can we address these shortcomings when we make investment decisions, as we still must? Thankfully, the news is not all bad. The good news is that awareness of any bias is the first step toward the defense against its effects.

Unfortunately, counteracting such effects can be quite difficult, and completely eliminating them is likely impossible. However, there are tools we can use to make sure the asset managers we hire to invest capital on our behalf are doing their job. First, we simply should expect most of them will not generate alpha, and so we should begin by assuming it's probably not alpha. Instead of searching for evidence that confirms our subjective opinions about why we like a certain manager, we should hold our research to the higher standard of having to disprove that the result is not just either beta or luck.

But more important, the best tools we have are intellectual honesty and emotional awareness. By accepting that we are emotional beings, and acknowledging our emotions when we experience them, we may be able to avoid reactive, System 1 processing during the heat of the moment. Emotions, which are chemical in nature, pass with time, and simply waiting until cooler heads prevail can mitigate some of the effects of biases. We also need to be realistic and self-aware of our own strengths and weaknesses. This means not only our individual capabilities, as Dunning-Kruger showed, but also the collective behavioral biases that affect us all. We are humans, not computers, and we are imperfect.

Context-specific knowledge helps to reduce the effects of overconfidence, so ongoing education about investment strategies and best practices for manager selection are a must. Try to stay humble and continue to learn every day. Warren Buffett has famously said he reads on average eight hours each day. That may be a high bar, but if the greatest investor of all time does that, should we strive for less? If you want to catch up to someone who has a head start, do you do it by running slower than the other person is running?

Humans are not perfectly rational, but that doesn't mean we shouldn't try to be, particularly when it comes to investing. And it's exactly in this way that disciplined investment decision-making processes can help improve our odds of investment success. In the next three chapters, I will describe three different layers of a better kind of alpha investors can harvest in their own portfolios, namely behavioral alpha, process alpha, and organizational alpha.

Notes

1. Kahneman and Tversky (1979).
2. Kahneman (2011).
3. Merton (1948).
4. Cimpian and Salomon (2014).
5. Westen et al. (2004).
6. Whitson and Galinsky (2008).

7. Litt et al. (2011).
8. Coval and Moskowitz (1999).
9. Zhu (2002).
10. Barber and Odean (2008).
11. Antweiler and Frank (2002).
12. Carmon and Ariely (2000).
13. *Thinking, Fast and Slow* (2011), pp. 286–284. Just go read the whole book, seriously.
14. https://mgto.org/in-class-experiments-5-hindsight-false-consensus-confirmation-biases/
15. Edward Jones and Victor Harris published research in 1967 in the *Journal of Experimental Psychology* that investigated how people ascribe the attitudes of others to either dispositional or situational factors. Ross (1977) later researched how people attribute causes of behaviors to these separate factors in both themselves and others, and he coined the phrase "fundamental attribution effect" to describe effects from both sets of experiments. However, some researchers continue to refer to it as the correspondence bias, and others use that term interchangeably with the fundamental attribution error. I prefer the latter, as I find it more apropos.
16. Montier et al. (2006).
17. Barber and Odean (2008).
18. Goyal and Wahal (2008).
19. Jenkinson et al. (2016).
20. Kruger and Dunning (1999).

PART III
Evolving Alpha

8
Behavioral Alpha—
Smart Thinking

The real problem of humanity is the following:
we have Paleolithic emotions; medieval institutions;
and god-like technology.
—E. O. WILSON

Since our primitive brains and emotional tendencies lead us astray when making financial decisions, we have to find ways to work within our abilities and effectively use processes to overcome or at least mitigate these weaknesses when investing. That's where behavioral alpha comes in.

What exactly is behavioral alpha? It is the excess return that investors can earn by beating their behavioral biases, as opposed to beating the market. In the last chapter, we learned about how quick, System 1 thinking often leads us astray. System 2, on the other hand, is our rational, deliberate processing mechanism and tends to result in more accurate outcomes when complex thinking is needed. So just use System 2 instead, right?

Unfortunately, it's not that easy. You cannot simply engage System 2 thinking all day long precisely because it requires much higher effort and energy. That would be like trying to sprint all day or like taking the bar exam eight hours a day every day. That's just not possible, no matter how confident you are in your own stamina and willpower.

In an article in the journal *Current Directions in Psychological Science* in 2007, psychologist Roy Baumeister described a model of willpower where self-control was viewed as a depleting resource.[1] When confronted with repeated tough decisions, the quality of decision-making declines as the self-control resource depletes, similar to the long-distance runner whose later mile splits are slower than earlier ones. Human energy, mental or physical, is finite.

Baumeister showed how this effect works in a number of laboratory settings. In one experiment, subjects were presented with the temptation to eat chocolates, a healthier option (radishes), or nothing at all. After this opportunity for self-control, participants were then given a frustrating, and ultimately unsolvable, mental challenge. The experiment measured how long the candidates continued to persist in their attempt to solve the impossible task, and those candidates who had resisted the urge to eat the chocolate, arguably using up limited mental energy, gave up twice as quickly as those candidates who were never presented with this tempting option.

Those who had made a tough decision had less left in the tank for the next mental challenge. That's called decision fatigue. It impairs our ability to engage System 2 thinking. When the mental energy required to activate System 2 thinking is depleted, we switch on System 1, reverting to our heuristic-driven decision-making.

Other research has shown similar results, but in settings more comparable to investment decision-making. One 2011 study on decision fatigue looked at Israeli parole hearings.[2] This study explored all the factors that went into determining whether an inmate would receive parole. While the authors expected that the judges would analyze the facts of the case and deliberately apply relevant laws, they found the single most important factor affecting probability of parole was the time of day. Roughly 65% of parolees who had their cases heard in the morning were granted parole, whereas those souls unfortunate enough to have their case drawn toward the end of the day had success rates dropping down to zero. Tired judges operating on System 1 chose the easiest option: saying no to everything. Interestingly, after a late-day break, approval rates abruptly jumped back up to roughly 65%. System 2 was back on.

Mental energy differs from physical exertion in some ways; it's not exactly like fuel in a tank that runs out. However, the quality of our decisions declines as we're faced with more and more choices throughout the day, without a break. Decision fatigue also causes stress, which can further decrease task engagement and productivity, creating a vicious cycle of poorer, slower, and inferior decision-making. Perhaps that marathon, six-hour investment committee isn't a testament to our stamina so much as it is to our folly.

This is a real problem for employees in today's information economy. Experts estimate that the average worker makes between 10,000 and 40,000 decisions daily, switching between tasks no less than 300 times throughout the workday. Humans are just not capable of effectively engaging System 2 processing at that rate for extended periods of time.

Nor are humans parallel processors either. We are serial processors. Despite our well-intentioned attempts to work on spreadsheets, respond to emails, and type investment memos all at once, we are not actually capable of multitasking. Instead, we are engaging in rapid task switching, shifting our attention from one job to the next. At each switching point, friction from the mental effort of stopping one thought process and returning to another, trying to pick up where we left off, causes us to complete each individual project slower and less accurately than if we simply worked on the projects one at a time. In fact, research on multitasking shows exactly that.

In an article published in the *Journal of Experimental Psychology* in 1995, researchers showed that people who were forced to switch between two tasks either every two or four trials were far slower on the tasks they did immediately after switching than they were on the repeat tasks in between switching.[3]

Later work in the same journal described a set of experiments in which young adults switched between different tasks, such as solving math problems and classifying geometric objects.[4] Once again, for all tasks, the participants lost time when they had to switch from one task to another. Moreover, as tasks got more complex, participants lost even more time because it took significantly longer to switch between the more complex tasks. The time lost was also greater when the participants switched to tasks with which they were relatively unfamiliar.

Perhaps the most applied study on the subject that I've encountered was an article published in the journal *Information Systems Research* in 2012.[5] The article, authored by a trio of IT professors, used applied econometric methods to measure the productivity of workers at a midsized executive recruiting firm. These researchers looked at nearly 1,300 projects over a span of five years and found that performance peaked at around five or six hiring projects per recruiter per year. At increasingly higher levels of multitasking, as measured several different ways, project completion rates and revenue generation both declined more and more.

You may think you are being superproductive as you toggle between working on that financial model you are building, flipping through the investment pitchbook, and checking emails as you write up the investment memo before your next call, but the truth is, you are probably doing each of those individual jobs slower and worse than if you focused on them one at a time. And that has a cost. Jonathan Spira, chief analyst at Basex, a business information research firm, estimates the opportunity cost of lost productivity due to multitasking and other distractions for US businesses is around $650 billion each year.[6]

So the question is, when making investment decisions, how do we try to mitigate the failings of System 1 thinking without simultaneously overexerting the limited resources of System 2 decision-making? Well, one of the best ways is to just not use System 2 so much. When it comes to investment decision-making, we need to prioritize the biggest, most impactful decisions and systemize as much of the rest as we can. We all have limited time, resources, and mental acuity. People who are rational would never allocate equal mindshare to a $1,000 expense and a $100 million investment, if they stop and consider it plainly. Yet investors often make analogous mistakes with resource allocation in investment decision-making.

We need to be parsimonious with System 2 resources and to prioritize active decision-making for only the biggest, most impactful items to limit the amount of discrete decisions we have to make. To do that, let's start with a framework for the investment process, since there are multiple steps and layers of decisions, each of which necessitates judgment and discretion to implement the desired investment portfolio.

The investment process has four major components:

1. **Policy and objective setting.** This includes establishing the risk tolerance, liquidity needs, investment time horizon, and return objectives for the portfolio. It is generally a one-time, organizational decision.
2. **Asset allocation.** This step involves selecting the various asset classes to invest in and at what relative weights. Generally, institutions construct a strategic asset allocation, which sets longer-term targets for each asset class, as well as a tactical asset allocation, which includes ranges that permit some allocation shift due to changing market valuations, implementation lags, or intentional temporary portfolio tilts. Long-term strategic asset allocation decisions are typically made at three- to five-year intervals, although some institutions revisit them more frequently. On the other hand, tactical decisions could be monthly or weekly, depending upon how dynamic the return assumptions are. Or they could be driven by formulaic quarterly or semiannually rebalancing back to the long-term strategic targets. Generally, research shows that long-term asset allocation decisions drive 90 to 95% of the differences in risk and return across portfolios.
3. **Manager or security selection.** This involves the selection of the specific external managers, or if asset classes are managed internally, the individual securities within each asset class to implement the desired portfolio. Although asset allocation drives 90% of the risk and return of an investment portfolio, the majority of work hours of investment professionals is spent on manager or security selection, probably three-quarters of the total personnel time and resources for most institutional investment teams.
4. **Portfolio management.** This step is not really a discrete process, but an ongoing iterative function of measuring, monitoring, and reviewing the existing portfolio to ensure that risks are consistent with objectives and that performance is meeting required returns. During this process, external investment managers may be terminated or replaced, cash lev-

els could be increased, or tactical asset allocation ranges could change, among other things.

At investment organizations, different individuals have different responsibilities for these various stages of the process, but managing our cognitive weaknesses at each step still remains critical for effective collective investment decision-making.

The first thing we can do is to make fewer, bigger decisions. The less frequently a decision gets made, the more appropriate it is to implement deliberate System 2 thinking. The more frequently a decision gets made, System 1 will invariably take over regardless of our intentions. So highly impactful and infrequent decisions such as setting policy and selecting the asset allocation clearly deserve System 2 decision-making efforts.

Policy Setting

This strategic decision to determine the investment objectives of an organization is certainly one that deserves dedicated, System 2 efforts. When making the policy decision, behavioral alpha can be achieved with some simple concepts.

First, the investor must structure the decision process in an informal setting, where every individual with relevant information is empowered to participate. The goal is to bring the best thinking to the forefront, and the stilted, formal conversations typical of most committees often stymies this. I've observed many investment organizations, including professional asset managers, where the committee discussion is merely a kabuki performance, the opposite of behavioral alpha.

There should also be three steps to a policy-setting exercise:

1. Discussing the desired outcomes, determining how success will be measured, defining risk, and establishing process and timelines
2. Setting aside dedicated time for research and deliberation engaging System 2, iterating as needed
3. Making the final decision

During the first step, the desired outcomes of the process need to be defined. For a pension, that may seem easy at first glance—selecting the actuarial required rate of return. However, this requires modeling the impact of different investment returns on the liabilities, understanding the actual cash flow needs and liquidity constraints, and identifying any likely changes in demographics, such as the increasing number of retirees to active members over a known time horizon, which could change the liquidity needs dramatically. All these factors affect how success is defined and how risk is measured.

Alternatively, an individual investor may have a liquid pool of wealth, say from an inheritance, and no clearly definable objectives. Determining if this money will be used for a down payment on a home in six months or for retirement savings that won't be touched for at least 30 years will effect very different policy return objectives and should have equally different metrics for risk. The objective of the former would be to minimize risk of a drawdown, while the latter should be focused on maximizing the probability of meeting income needs in retirement, independent of short-term volatility.

In either case, the initial project definition stage should focus on thinking about real-world uses of the capital, identifying the actual risks that will need to be faced, and trying to ensure that the best knowledge is incorporated into the process.

Once a timeline is established, the individuals responsible for making the policy decision need to set aside dedicated time—and not merely a few minutes, but hours!—to deliberate. During this time, distractions should be limited and task switching avoided. Incorporate industry and academic research into the process. Recall that Warren Buffett is known for reading an average of eight hours each day! Make an effort to find out what others addressing similar challenges have done, and acquire the knowledge for yourself. It's out there; don't just take financial providers (me included) at their word. You may even find additional considerations—ones that hadn't even crossed your mind before—that improve how you think about the objectives.

After sufficient research and deliberation, the decision makers need to reconvene and select the objectives. This part of the process should document all the research and deliberation that went into the decision and should demonstrate how objectives were selected, including discussions of the cash flow needs and liquidity profile of the organization, as well as the investment time horizon. The final deliverable should be an investment policy statement, or IPS.

An IPS is a written statement that specifies the investor's goals, priorities, and preferences. It should define risk tolerances such as liquidity needs, volatility targets, and concentration limits; set roles and responsibilities; and establish clear and specific parameters around asset allocation, and it should establish a systematic review process that enables the investor to remain focused on the long-term objectives. The IPS details what monitoring and control procedures will be followed and who is responsible for what roles in the investment process. This includes formalizing the frequency of monitoring, specifying benchmarks for evaluation of portfolio returns, and establishing procedures for making future changes to the policy statement. An IPS should evolve proactively over time as markets and objectives change, but it should not be edited reactively to near-term dislocations or other temporary factors.

While an IPS is typically used by institutional investors, individual investors would be well served by adopting the same process. By determining in advance what steps to take in what situations, investors reduce the potential for short-term market fluctuations, and our imperfect behavioral responses to them, to impair long-term decision-making.

Ultimately, determining what investment return an investor should target requires establishing a personalized understanding of your risk profile to set reasonable financial goals across realistic time horizons. To best achieve this, asset allocation inputs should also be used to inform the policy discussion. The process should not just be unidirectional, where the objective drives the asset allocation and you blindly implement what the optimizer says. You can't set realistic return objectives and risk thresholds without an understanding of what's realistic. That requires making capital markets assumptions and looking at model portfolios while thinking about what risk-return objectives should be.

Asset Allocation

Asset allocation is the process of selecting the specific investable asset classes and relative weights for the portfolio.[7] This first requires an investor to decide what constitutes an asset class, and although this may seem simple, it is no trivial matter. Traditional portfolios often include an abundance of various assets, such as domestic equities, international equities, investment-grade bonds, high-yield bonds, real estate, private equity, and sometimes curiosities such as absolute return, uncorrelated strategies, or opportunistic investments. I'm not sure this complexity has served all investors equally well, and the paradigm of Occam's razor may convey some behavioral alpha here.

Asset classes are types of investments that behave similarly in the marketplace and share similar characteristics. Arbitrary distinctions and false classifications abound in the typical portfolio. Some of these asset classes have characteristics that make them empirically difficult to distinguish from others, like domestic versus international equities for instance. Other asset classes contain very heterogenous assets lumped together under one misleading category name, such as hedge funds or opportunistic strategies. In short, I doubt most investors have quite achieved the desired benefits from the ever-increasing number of "asset classes" used as building blocks of portfolios, when many of them don't meet the basic criteria of a true asset class.

Reverting to our previous description of drivers of return, let's try to create a simpler framework for investors to rationally define their opportunity set before moving forward to next steps. Since investments can only generate returns from capital appreciation or income, these major characteristics, along with the investor's level of sophistication and capabilities, should be the driving factors underlying the selection of asset classes, with tweaks to consider specific needs of the investor as well.

For instance, some institutional investors have high liquidity needs, and may not have dedicated investment staff, yet still require an aggressive return target. For such investors, public equities may be the only realistic venue for accessing capital appreciation. I would argue, even for a plan with a sophisticated staff and little near-term cash flow requirements, private equity still does not represent a separate asset class per se. It is simply a different mechanism for accessing capital appreciation versus the same equity ownership factors present in public equities, which is why it has such a high lagged correlation with traditional equity indexes. Private equity is merely a different implementation of the same underlying financial instrument, namely equity ownership. But it's equity nonetheless.

Investors must fundamentally consider their own liquidity needs, cash flow needs, time horizons, and sophistication when deciding upon asset class definitions. I would propose the basic building blocks for most investors are actually three components: (1) capital appreciation (for a small, domestic investor, a US stock index is a good proxy), (2) income (at one time, traditional investment-grade bonds provided more of this; today more exotic credit instruments can be used), and (3) liquidity and/or principal protection (some people implement explicit hedging strategies for this, some use "absolute return" thusly, and others use simple US Treasury bonds, which have historically proved a decent hedge to equities). Basically, investors need appreciation, income, and capital preservation. Everything else is window dressing.

The absolute simplest representation of these three needs can be found in a two-asset class stock/core bond mix. Stocks are the capital appreciation, and core bonds provide both a little income and some ballast in down markets. This is defensible for less sophisticated investors. And even for more experienced investors, it still should be what the "asset allocation" looks like; strategy selection is implementation, not different asset classes. Choosing what index to proxy for the asset classes requires consideration of resources and relative skills and advantages.

For instance, picking the S&P and Barclays Aggregate as the two indexes for equities and bonds can make sense for a small individual IRA. A pension fund for a large global corporation may instead prefer a global equity index, as well as adding some private equity, but the fund is still accessing capital appreciation from stocks. It just requires a slightly more complex benchmark and implementation. We will discuss performance analysis in greater depth below, and we address manager selection in Chapter 9. Next we'll highlight some tools to improve portfolio construction after the asset classes have been defined.

When choosing the relative mix of assets to be invested in to achieve the policy objective, investors can increase their odds of obtaining behavioral alpha by doing the following things:

1. Setting realistic, data-driven risk-return assumptions
2. Thinking about upside and downside scenarios as opposed to just base cases
3. Targeting an appropriate portfolio instead of an optimal one

This process requires setting assumptions about what returns and what sorts of risk can be realistically expected from these assets, and about how they might interact with one another, in order to select the best mix. Clearly, such risk-return expectations should not be made entirely independently of the policy decision, as they are important considerations to have when determining what return objective is realistic or what level of risk is acceptable. However, it is critically important that both steps are done honestly.

For example, the intellectually dishonest way to integrate both steps would be fixating on a certain policy return objective that necessitates a higher return expectation from public equities than is reasonable to get there, and then rationalizing the subsequent, likely too high, equity return assumption. Often, this justification is done to keep contribution rates from going up. Making up an expected return to justify how much you hope to earn so you can save less is not smart thinking; it's negative policy alpha.

In a more appropriate way to integrate the two steps, feedback flows in the opposite direction. This means that returns for individual asset classes should be based on realistic expectations that include historical analysis and incorporate forward-looking ranges as opposed to merely point estimates. And if this requires a reduced policy return expectation, which may in turn require a higher savings rate or longer investment horizon, then so be it.

Capital Markets Assumptions

Using public equities as a case study, and returning to our discussion of factors, we recall that the returns to any investment can come from only two sources: income and capital appreciation. For equities, this means dividend yield plus capital gains equals total return.

We know what the dividend yield is in real time; that part is easy. Today, the dividend yield for the S&P 500 stands at 1.9%. Price appreciation unfortunately is quite a bit harder to project. However, it can only come from two sources: from financial metrics improving or from the market assigning a higher value to that specific financial metric. A company's earnings can grow or shrink, or the market can pay a higher or lower price-to-earnings ratio or some combination thereof. But mathematically it's a tautology: Price = (price/earnings) × earnings.

So this gives us a calculation for equity returns of

$$\text{Equity return} = \text{dividend yield} + \text{earnings growth} \pm$$
$$\text{multiple expansion/(contraction)} \qquad (8.1)$$

If we look at the earnings growth of the S&P 500 over the last 30 years, it is about 6.2%. Assuming no change in the market earnings multiple, total returns for the S&P 500 might be 1.9% + 6.2% + 0.0%, or 8.1%. However, this may or may not be a reasonable assumption going forward. Earnings growth comes from two sources as well: revenue growth and changes in profit margin. Perhaps expectations for slower top-line growth and reduced margin (itself a combination of factors such as tax codes and productivity) may mean that a lower assumption for earnings growth overall is more prudent, such as 5.0%.

Now let's look more closely at the earnings multiple assumption, which we held constant at first. Today the cyclically adjusted price-to-earnings (CAPE) ratio is 30.86 times. This means for every $1 of earnings, the market is willing to pay $30.86 for the equity.

Over the last 30 years, the CAPE ratio has averaged 25.5. The market is 21% overvalued compared with historical norms. If our policy investment period is 20 years, it is likely prudent to assume a reversion to the mean over that hold period, which requires roughly −1.0% capital appreciation annually attributable to multiple contraction.[8]

So a 1.9% dividend yield plus 5.0% earnings growth less 1.0% in valuation contraction provides a total expected return of 5.9%. However, perhaps a longer time frame makes more sense as a frame of reference for expectations on multiples. (Remember thinking about ranges of outcomes and downside scenarios?).

Going back to 1923 when Standard & Poor's launched its first stock index, the CAPE ratio has averaged just 17.9 times (see Figure 8.1). If you believe this is the real long-run average, multiples would then be 72% overvalued today. Over that same 20-year future investment horizon, regression to the mean would yield just over –2.7% a year from multiple contraction.[9] This gives us a total expected return for the S&P 500 of about 4.1%. There's a big difference between compounding at 4% per annum and 8% per annum. So which is correct?

FIGURE 8.1   The CAPE ratio

Behavioral alpha from setting capital markets assumptions is not about being correct. It's about using data, thinking objectively, and looking at ranges of outcomes. One way to do just that is to look at subsequent equity returns relative to the beginning CAPE ratio. Figure 8.2 plots the average 10-year return for different valuation levels, with CAPE below 10 (the most undervalued) on the right and when the S&P 500 index is trading above 25 times (the most overvalued) on the left.

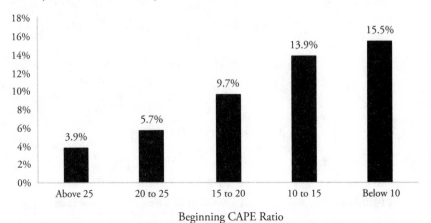

FIGURE 8.2   Ten-year returns versus CAPE ratio (*www.multpl.com, Bloomberg*)

When beginning a 10-year investment period with equities trading at a CAPE of 25 times or more, stocks go on to average just 3.9% per annum. This is similar to our second, more realistic assumption. Perhaps the average historical outcome is not the most likely average future outcome. Such a thought exercise not only introduces objective data into the decision-making process, but presents realistic ranges of outcomes. Thinking about what could go wrong is far more helpful to successful outcomes than planning based on everything going perfectly.

US public pensions are a perfect example of negative policy alpha. According to the National Association of State Retirement Administrators (NASRA), the average long-term US public pension return assumption as of the end of 2019 was 7.2%.[10] Often, individual asset class return assumptions are chosen to ensure a return target can be validated, and hence, higher contributions aren't needed. For example, in a 70/30 stock/bond portfolio, a 9% stock return and 3% bond return would get you that 7.2%. A 7% assumption for stocks would only yield a portfolio return expectation of 5.8%. That just wouldn't fly, because the implied cost would be too high.

Unfortunately, the same research from NASRA shows the average 20-year return of public pensions is just 6.2%. However, the risk of being wrong and undersaving is much greater than the risk of being wrong and oversaving. Not having enough money to retire is much worse than successfully retiring only to find you have a bit more than you needed. In part because of this negative policy alpha of 1.0%, US public pensions today find themselves only 72.7% funded, with approximately $1.8 trillion of liabilities they haven't saved enough for.

This highlights the need for a better approach both to defining risk and to constructing portfolios to better meet our objectives.

Portfolio Construction

When selecting the mix of assets based on these expectations, the typical portfolio construction approach used by institutional investors is mean variance optimization (MVO), which was introduced by Nobel Prize winner Harry Markowitz in 1952.[11] Without getting into needless detail on how this process works, MVO takes the expected returns, volatilities, and correlations from asset class assumptions, such as above, and combines them to produce the mix that generates the highest expected return for a targeted level of volatility.

This approach is reasonable and certainly objective, but in my opinion it has two flaws. First, it is heavily dependent upon the assumed rate of return. To examine this, let's build a two-asset portfolio using an 8% expected return for equities and 3% return for bonds. Utilizing common inputs for volatility and correlation, and targeting the highest level of return for an 11% volatility objective, a mean variance optimizer generates a 60% stock/40% bond portfolio with an expected return of 5.95%.[12]

Let's investigate what happens if stocks subsequently make just 4%, as is reasonable to expect. Well, instead of 5.95% as modeled, that 60%/40% portfolio will return a mere 3.6%. Of course, hindsight is 20/20, and in a two-asset portfolio, using the lower assumption of 4% initially may not have changed the allocations much anyway. However, in a real-world MVO, with many asset classes, using a lower-return assumption would have resulted in vastly different allocations to other assets. Those resulting other portfolios probably would have performed better than the so-called optimal one.

Such is the problem of optimizers in general, which is why rather than calling it "mean variance optimizers," I say "error term maximizers" instead. MVO does a great job if all the return assumptions are close to what actually happens, because the portfolio is literally optimized to that scenario. But if those assumptions are imperfect, MVO puts the biggest weights into the things you were the most optimistic about. Ultimately, that 8% expected return for stocks is not much better than a guess. Since an optimizer is highly dependent upon essentially an informed guess, it hardly seems to me a prudent strategic tool, particularly since we've seen how persistently over-optimistic we tend to be.

Which leads us to the second problem. Constructing a portfolio that is likely to achieve the policy objective is the goal. And while the future is uncertain, it probably won't exactly match your assumptions. A portfolio that generates acceptable returns across multiple likely outcomes, like what happens if equities dramatically underperform, is better than one that is optimized perfectly for one exact scenario. That means ditching the idea of an optimal portfolio altogether in favor of robust one.

Doing so necessitates not only looking at ranges of outcomes but also rethinking what risk means. The two-asset MVO we modeled required an 11% volatility target to optimize toward maximum return for that level given of risk. But why choose 11% as the volatility target instead of 11.2% or even 11.5%?

Picking a volatility target is rather arbitrary. Further, what does targeting a certain level of volatility have to do with risk? The volatility, or standard deviation, essentially measures how wide a distribution is. It's a measure of the dispersion of returns around the mean, and it certainly matters. In a normal distribution like that shown in Figure 8.3, 68% of the total distribution falls within ±1 standard deviation of the mean.[13]

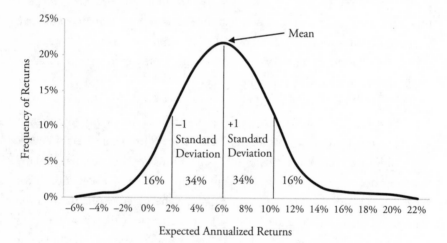

FIGURE 8.3   Expected return distribution 1

The output of a mean variance optimizer is a mean expected return—an average—based upon inputs that are no better than guesses. And for a normal distribution, this means that the expected return is the fiftieth percentile outcome; half of the distribution lies above that return, half below. If your required rate of return is 6%, the mean in the distribution shown in Figure 8.3, you have a 50% chance of falling short of that number.

No one would reasonably argue that building any strategic plan with only a coin flip chance of success is a sound policy. But for some reason, that's how strategic asset allocations are selected. To me, real risk is the total amount of the distribution that falls below the required rate of return. Risk, or the odds of failure, is equal to 1 minus (probability of success).

Hence, increasing the odds of success means reducing the probability of failure, thereby reducing risk. Why not choose a portfolio with a 75 or 80% chance of meeting or exceeding that 6% required return objective, even if it means accepting a bit more volatility to do so? Decreasing the total cumulative probability of not hitting your required rate of return is a far more practical way to think about risk than just how wide the standard deviation is.

Take, for example, the return profile graphed in Figure 8.4. With a higher volatility than the prior return distribution, it would typically be considered a riskier portfolio. However, since the mean expected return is just above 8%, over three-quarters of this distribution falls above the required 6% return level. Just 24% lies below.

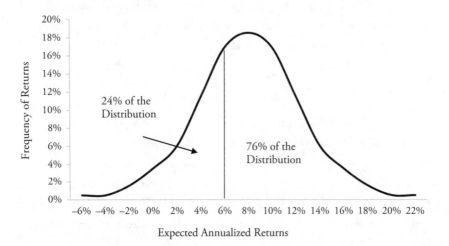

FIGURE 8.4 Expected return distribution 2

Since this return profile has a lower cumulative probability density below the required return, and a higher probability of success, it's a less risky portfolio. It's explicitly safer, a portfolio with a margin of safety built in. As we've seen, humans are predictably overly optimistic. This manifests itself in assumptions that are consistently incorrect in specific directions. We under-estimate time, risk, and costs and overestimate ease, returns, and benefits. It's why CEOs invariably predict higher future earnings than what they deliver,[14] why the average public pension investment returns have not met their actu-arial required rate of return over longer periods,[15] and also why the chores on my to-do list always take longer than I plan.

Moreover, this framework allows an investor to specifically target a mar-gin of safety, instead of arbitrarily picking some level of volatility. Do you want a 25% probability of failure and a 75% chance of oversaving, or are you comfortable with 40%/60%? I doubt that many investors would happily choose 50%/50% once they think of it this way, particularly after they realize how pernicious the overconfidence effect is.

The asset allocation smart thinking takeaway is this: If you need 6%, and you build a portfolio with an expected mean return of 8%, you may wind up being wrong but still hit 6.8%. For long-term investors, volatility is not risk. It is short-term noise, and a higher probability of long-term success is what you get for accepting more noise in the short term. Establishing realistic goals, properly contextualizing risk, and sticking with the plan are drivers of potential behavioral alpha in asset allocation.

Manager Selection

Now it's time to change course a bit. These approaches are helpful for policy and strategic thinking, but they cannot be extended to investment processes that require many more decision points. The more that active decisions are required, the more that System 1 will routinely take over. So how do we execute cognitive tasks that require more frequent decisions if we can't just brute-force them through System 2, and we still want to overcome the biases inherent in System 1?

It is fairly hard to do, but you can in fact train System 1 to get better at making intuitive responses. In the 1990s, researchers at the University of Iowa conducted a study where participants could draw from one of four decks of cards for a cash reward.[16] However, the decks were rigged. Two decks were stacked with small gains and no risk, and the other two decks had high risk but high gains. On average, after 50 cards, participants were able to respond intuitively, demonstrating that they recognized the patterns in the cards. However, it took a full 80 cards on average before they could clearly articulate what the pattern was.

Even more remarkable is that after only 10 cards, participants displayed a measurable increase in anxiety, including faster pulses and increased perspiration, when reaching for the high-risk deck of cards. A subconscious, emotional process was already aware of the pattern far before they could consciously act on it or describe it. Sounds a lot like our System 1.

And articles in medical literature that reviewed the clinical assessment procedures of experienced nurses in mental health and medical-surgical settings have come up with some interesting findings. Although the National Health Service currently places great emphasis on purely evidence-based practices when making clinical assessments, experienced nurses often incorporate other factors into their process. Several studies have shown that a holistic approach incorporating the tacit knowledge and intuition gained from experience improves diagnostic speed and accuracy.[17] These studies support the idea that intuition when used in conjunction with evidence-based practice achieves better outcomes and should play a role in clinical practices.

However, not all processes respond as favorably to this sort of intuitive training. The research on improving System 1 thinking has identified three critical characteristics of the nature of the task that makes training your intuition possible. The successful improvement of rapid, intuitive decision-making requires:

1. Lots of trials
2. Clearly definable outcomes
3. Relatively rapid feedback

When those things are in place, System 1 can be trained. For really high-frequency, immediate-feedback tasks, like identifying patterns in decks of cards, training can occur quite rapidly. In other situations, where feedback on performance may take months or even years, such as identifying traits of chronic disorders, teaching System 1 can take much longer to achieve.

The clinical diagnostic processes of nurses bear a striking similarity to selecting managers. Both processes combine quantitative, evidence-based factors with a host of other softer, qualitative considerations. Likewise, both benefit from years of experience and lots of repetition, particularly on the qualitative side, because feedback takes a lot of time.

Whereas clinical assessments involve nurses gathering information about patients to identify the most likely current and future patient needs, manager selection, also often referred to as due diligence, involves researching characteristics of asset management firms, and the individuals that manage the portfolios, to assess the most likely short-term and long-run relative investment returns. In both clinical assessments and manager due diligence, checklists are effective tools not necessarily for improving your skills but for ensuring that your skills are applied consistently and rigorously.

Broadly speaking, this process consists of a series of inquiries meant both to address the investment thesis around why you might hire a manager and to identify any potential risks of doing so. Where smart thinking comes into play in due diligence is not in making a decision about each manager, but rather in designing the process initially. It helps to start with a better checklist.

System 2 thinking must be used to separate signal from noise and identify which characteristics to look for and which to avoid. Manager researchers with significant asset class experience are likely to have developed an intuition based on pattern recognition for some of the softer characteristics. For instance, an analyst that has met thousands of alternative asset managers certainly has a more applied concept of what best practices look like for deal sourcing for small market buyout funds, or what level of in-house restructuring expertise is standard for a distressed-for-control fund, than does someone who has only met a handful of funds in either strategy.

But our ability to train System 1 is limited, and in some cases waiting years to acquire the experience firsthand is impractical. Thankfully, even where System 1 can't be trained, smart thinking is about acquiring high-quality knowledge and implementing that knowledge to develop smart habits. If you can't train System 1 to automatically process something, you have to systematize it. Using System 2 to design a process that essentially takes the thinking out of the hands of its impetuous sibling is what I call smart habits, or process alpha.

This is more than merely creating checklists or standardized procedure manuals. Smart habits involve creating learning processes that continually evolve and incorporate new knowledge and changing market dynamics. Just like policy setting profits from asset allocation inputs in an integrated fashion, taming System 1 with smart habits requires reevaluation of the process at intervals with a System 2 lens for a virtuous cycle. Smart habits drive smart thinking, and smart thinking creates smart habits. In the next chapter, we will discuss a framework for creating process around manager selection and how to generate process alpha from smart habits.

Notes

1. Baumeister et al. (2007).
2. Danziger et al. (2011).
3. Rogers and Monsell (1995).
4. Rubinstein et al. (2001).
5. Aral et al. (2012).
6. Lohr (2007).
7. For those readers interested in reading more on these topics, I would recommend Ilmanen (2011) for asset class return assumptions and the establishment of capital markets projections and Swensen (2009) for asset allocation and overall portfolio construction.
8. The formula to calculate the annual capital depreciation (ACD) from an overvalued market multiple is

$$ACD = - \left[(\text{current multiple/average multiple})^{(1/\text{time horizon in years})} - 1 \right]$$

   This formula allows an investor to mathematically link the expectation for future multiple to an annualized return number based explicitly on one's time horizon. A longer hold period allows a regression to the mean to be less punitive on the annualized return expectation.
9. Evaluating what equity multiple is appropriate is of course an impossibility, and there is no question a lower interest rate environment can support higher multiples. Prudence, however, dictates conservativeness. It seems somewhat counterintuitive to criticize investors "reaching for yield" when they purchase assets with an explicitly higher income, and yet justify higher return expectations for equities on the basis of lower yields alone. This seems very similar to the "This time it's different" argument, which does not have quite such a strong track record in investing. Behavioral alpha is about not trying to justify unrealistic return assumptions based on mental gymnastics like this. It is applying a reasonable margin of safety to establishing those expectations, which provides

a probability of outperforming them. Over very long time periods, real yields are mean-reverting. Equity multiples may remain elevated for a long time; it remains to be seen if that will be the case forever.

10. Brainard and Brown (2020).
11. Markowitz (1952a).
12. I used 8% expected return for equities with a volatility of 18%, 3% return for bonds with a volatility of 4%, and a correlation of 0.15 between the two assets. Optimizing for highest Sharpe ratio with a target volatility of 11% yielded roughly a 60%/40% portfolio with an expected return of 5.95%.
13. And this is another problem with MVO. Financial asset returns, particularly in alternatives, do not conform to a normal distribution. Using the cumulative probability distribution above a specific return threshold also captures nonnormality more directly.
14. Malmendier and Tate (2015).
15. Confirming the NASRA findings, Aubry et al. (2018) documented that over the last 15 years, public plans have made an average annualized rate of return around 5.5%, well below the average assumed rate of return of 7.6% for the same period.
16. Bechara et al. (1997).
17. For instance, see Welsh and Lyons (2001), Smith (2009), and Pearson (2013).

9

Process Alpha—
Smart Habits

We are what we repeatedly do.
Excellence therefore is not an act, but a habit.
—ARISTOTLE

Selectively using structured System 2 thinking can add behavioral alpha for the more strategic parts of the investment decision-making process, like setting policy objectives and choosing an asset allocation. Since asset allocation drives 90% of the risk-return, it's important to get that right. On the other hand, the impact of manager selection is far less, and these more frequent, higher-volume decisions require a more resource-efficient approach.

We briefly discussed how System 1 can be trained with lots of repetition and rapid feedback on performance. At a minimum, doing this type of training in a manager selection context entails meeting as many managers as possible and monitoring their performance over time, but even that is far from a panacea. Building smart habits requires acquiring high-quality knowledge and implementing process around that, but it doesn't all have to be firsthand knowledge.

In this chapter, we will lay out a framework for due diligence that includes smart habits gleaned from high-quality knowledge to select managers with a high probability of meeting investment objectives. And that should be the ultimate metric for success in picking managers—ensuring outcomes meet objectives instead of beating a benchmark. But building such a due diligence process requires prioritization around two things: which asset classes to focus on and what characteristics to look for.

As we have seen, not all asset classes offer the same opportunity for outperformance. Some asset classes are far more efficient than others, such as public equities, where the average active manager generates negative alpha. So deciding where to allocate manager selection efforts, particularly if resources are limited, is the first challenge. Frankly, given the general lack of alpha in most asset classes, does it even make sense to try to pick managers?

In select instances, I think the answer is yes, but it depends on separating luck from skill, which is not a trivial task, even if we've pinned down where on the hierarchy of alpha we believe the skill fits. Skill and luck both play a role in success, and figuring out the relative contribution of each isn't always easy.

Recently, I heard behavioral finance researcher and author extraordinaire Michael Mauboussin discuss how to untangle the effects of luck versus skill, or signal from noise.[1] During his speech, Mauboussin laid out a framework for assessing the relative impact of luck as compared with skill on the outcome of an activity.

Mauboussin starts with the concept of inside view versus outside view, borrowing from the grandfather of behavioral finance, Daniel Kahneman. Kahneman describes the inside view as how we view our own situation. When doing this, we rely on our own limited experience to make decisions, and we overestimate our own ability, ascribing any success to our unique skills and knowledge.

Conversely, the outside view is how we perceive others. We tend to be more objective, searching for patterns and situational context, which allows us to make more informed decisions based on prior probabilities—the so-called base rate—as opposed to merely our own anecdotal experience.

Now, successful outcomes at anything always combine some percentage of both luck and skill, and Mauboussin argues that it's a spectrum. For instance, look at Figure 9.1. On one end, you have certain activities, such as playing the lottery or slot machines, where success comes entirely from luck and participants' actions are irrelevant. Outcomes are determined randomly according to the odds, and the most important item to know to predict individual success rates is what the outside view of the base rate is. On the other end of the spectrum are activities where skill is a dominant factor in determining success, things like playing chess or the Chinese game go. Here the inside view of the specific attributes of the individual matters a great deal. Investing in general probably falls somewhere in between, but not all asset classes are the same.

Inside View Matters   Outside View Matters

Skill   Luck

Chess, Go   Lottery, Slots

FIGURE 9.1 The skill-to-luck continuum

In investing, market efficiency has traditionally been defined as the degree to which all publicly available information is already reflected in the clearing price of a security. In theory, the more efficient a given market is, the harder it is to outperform a passive basket of all the securities in it. But perhaps another way to think of market efficiency is where a given asset class falls on Mauboussin's spectrum of luck versus skill.

One way to evaluate where asset classes may fall on this skill-to-luck continuum is to look at the persistence of returns. We've talked about it in previous chapters, so let's bring it all together. The seminal equity factor research from Fama and French in 1996 showed that persistence of performance was almost entirely attributable to a handful of underlying factors such as capitalization and value as opposed to skill.[2] Smaller-cap and deeper-value stocks generated consistently higher returns, whereas more expensive, large stocks predictably had lower returns. Later research has shown that top-performing mutual funds may continue to outperform but only for short periods, perhaps up to a year. And even then, more and more research has shown that this is because of predictable factors, just betas or alternative betas. And at longer periods, even just two to three years, persistence in mutual fund returns disappears entirely.

Hedge fund research on performance persistence has evolved as the asset class has grown. Earlier research demonstrated strong persistence over short periods and even moderate persistence at up to three years. However, as the asset class has become more efficient, that effect is disappearing, and top managers are no longer able to consistently best their peers time after time. Nevertheless, in research from just a few years ago, less liquid hedge funds may still have this ability to outperform more reliably. This leaves us with the one asset class that still has definitive empirical evidence of persistence of returns over periods longer than three years—private equity. Although there is some evidence this is eroding, the effect is still there. Table 9.1 summarizes some of the research we've discussed in prior chapters, and the cumulative evidence suggests luck, or the randomness of the market return itself, matters much more in public markets, whereas skill is rewarded with differentiated returns in private equity.

TABLE 9.1   Persistence of Performance

Asset Class	Research	Summary
Mutual Funds	• Fama and French (1996) • Carhart (1997) • Detzel and Weingard (1998) • Fama and French (2010) • Bryan and Li (2016)	• Weak short-term persistence, up to a year, but mostly due to factors • No persistence at longer periods
Hedge Funds	• Boyson (2008) • Ammann et al. (2013) • Kumar (2015)	• Modest-to-strong short-term performance • Some persistence up to three years • Persistence disappearing, except for less liquid funds
Private Equity Funds	• Kaplan and Schoar (2005) • Gompers et al. (2010) • Harris et al. (2014) • Cavagnaro et al. (2019)	• Strong persistence of performance for top-quartile managers across vintage years • Some evidence of effect weakening

Another way to plot asset class efficiency is by examining manager dispersion, or the spread between manager returns, across different asset classes.
If we return to data provided in earlier chapters, we can clearly observe different competitive dynamics at play across various markets. Using 20-year
return data from Burgiss and eVestment, the difference between top- and
bottom-quartile managers in private equity is nearly 20% per annum,
whereas in public stocks the top managers beat the bottom group by just
2.8% annually, as displayed in Figure 9.2.

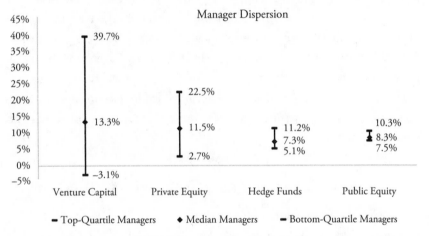

FIGURE 9.2   Dispersion of returns

Not only is the gap between the best and worst performers markedly different for these asset classes, but the percentage of return of the top managers
explainable by the average is far different as well. The average public stock
manager's return of 8.8% accounts for a full 85% of the total 10.3% return
that the top-quartile managers posted.[3] Only one-sixth or so comes from
being in the top quartile. However, in venture capital only one-third of the
return of top-quartile performers comes from just being average; actually
picking the best managers in the space drives two-thirds of the 39.7%.

In more efficient markets, like public equity, where there are 16,000+
mutual funds picking through less than 4,000 listed securities, the market
return swamps the effect of skill. You should spend more of your time calculating the base rate or determining capital markets assumptions. That is

to say, it's an asset allocation decision, not really a manager selection one. In public equities and fixed-income markets, picking managers is a complete waste of time. Find the cheapest index with the tightest tracking error to the beta you have selected through your asset allocation work, and call it a day. If some managers do outperform, it will only be for short periods, and in modest amounts, and almost entirely impossible to predict ex ante. That's statistically indistinguishable from luck.

However, in less efficient markets, like private equity, with perhaps 5,000 active private equity funds and more than 500,000 private companies to choose from, skill actually matters a whole lot more. The base rate isn't as important as how you actually implement the asset class, and a great deal of research has shown this to be the case. In these markets, information asymmetry still exists. And if the persistence of returns is high and dispersion of returns is wide, there is significant value embedded in selecting specific managers, provided you can identify characteristics associated with persistent, higher-expected returns.

Due Diligence as a Source of Alpha

In perhaps the most interesting research I've seen on due diligence, A. J. Watson at startup funding platform Fundify looked at hundreds of angel investments funded via the company's platform.[4] Angel investments are very early and very small private investments made into new businesses, the earliest stage and riskiest form of venture capital. Because of information collected by Fundify, Watson was able to track these investments by the amount of time each investor had spent on due diligence as well as what the eventual return was as a multiple of invested capital.

Watson then bucketed these deals into quartiles: those where the investor had spent less than 5 hours of due diligence, those where the investor had spent between 5 and 15 hours, those where the investor had put in between 15 and 40 hours, and finally those where the investor had done more than 40 hours' worth of due diligence prior to investing. Obviously, hours spent in due diligence served as a proxy for quality of research performed, and it's certainly a fair representation.

Watson then separated these four diligence-based quartiles into performance groupings, calculating how many deals from each bucket lost money by returning less than 1x, how many fell between 1x and 5x, and how many returned greater than 5 times capital invested. So how did the various quartiles perform?

Figure 9.3 shows how they did, and the results speak for themselves: 69% of those investments that were preceded by 5 hours or less of due diligence lost money. Only 31% of angel investments in this bracket made money, and these diligence-light deals comprised by far the lowest amount of the top winners, just 8%. The deals where investors performed at least 40 hours of due diligence performed the best, with 58% of those deals generating positive returns. These heavily researched investments were more likely to be among the top deals than any of the other categories. The trend is clear. The more due diligence performed, the better the performance.

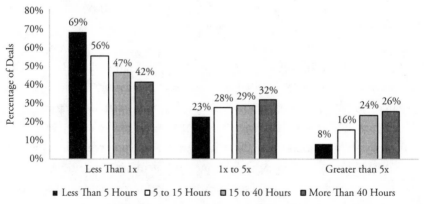

FIGURE 9.3   Angel returns and due diligence

On average, angel deals where the investor conducted 40 hours or more of due diligence returned 7.1 times the initial invested capital (see Figure 9.4). Conversely, those deals where 5 or fewer hours of research were put into validating the thesis lost money on average, returning just 80 cents on the dollar. Although this research was done on direct deals as opposed to managers, it remains a nearly perfect example of process alpha!

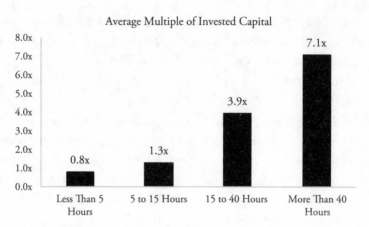

FIGURE 9.4   Average returns by due diligence

The concept of due diligence as a source of alpha is not a new one. In fact, academic research also supports the idea that in asset classes with wider dispersion of returns, and some persistence of performance, end investors can generate consistently higher returns through a disciplined approach to sourcing, vetting, and selecting managers.

One particular finance working paper from NYU investigated the effects of robust due diligence, proxied in another unique way.[5] In this piece of research, the authors tried to estimate a dollar cost of full operational due diligence (ODD), where researchers go on-site with a manager to understand back-office functions, such as how trades are executed, who approves cash transactions, and how performance is calculated and audited. Such practices are expensive and required extensive resources, and after speaking with numerous market participants, the scholars estimated that the costs for a single hedge fund ODD could run from $50,000 to $100,000. Thus, the authors reasoned that larger funds of hedge funds should have better ODD processes than smaller ones, which couldn't afford such costly research because of their smaller operating budgets. If this was the case, returns should be higher for the larger funds, which would be better able to avoid poor managers. Despite the fact that smaller hedge funds generally outperform larger ones, as we saw in Chapter 3, the author's hypothesis was borne out by the data. Larger funds of hedge funds did outperform smaller ones by 2 to 3% per annum, an effect attributable to process alpha.

Other research has tried to explicitly quantify the impact of qualitative hedge fund due diligence efforts. A recent white paper posted to the Social Science Research Network by a trio of finance professors contained some interesting proprietary data detailing the interactions of one large institutional investor and nearly 1,100 hedge funds over the course of eight years.[6] Using the unique insights from these meeting records, these researchers were able to measure the effect of soft information conveyed during due diligence. Even when controlling for strategy, fund characteristics, and past performance, the hedge funds that this investor selected outperformed by 1.5% over the subsequent 12 months. Although these results may not be repeatable across other data sets, they nevertheless clearly show once again the value of a disciplined process, particularly one that contains more subjective elements.

Similar results have been found in private equity, too. An article published in *European Financial Management* in 2016 looked at 178 buyouts from 27 Italian PE firms spanning the investment period 1999 to 2012, roughly 85% of the transactions during that time.[7] This research also measured the amount of time spent on due diligence as a rough approximation for the thoroughness of the research. The research found that multiple measures of performance improved the more work was done. Interestingly, more due diligence led to higher returns only when the due diligence was performed by in-house employees. When the work was farmed out to third-party vendors, results were more mixed, suggesting a problem of agency (which we'll touch on more in the next chapter on governance!).

Finally, even more recent research from the *Journal of Finance* attempted to measure the skill of institutional limited partners.[8] Using a data set of over 12,000 private equity funds in which 630 different limited partners had invested, this research had a very large and robust sample size. The distribution of limited partner returns showed strong persistence of returns, both above and below median, stronger than a random sample should have. Hence, the authors argued that persistence of both above- and below-average returns is strong evidence of skill, since you cannot lose a game of chance intentionally. And there were investors who demonstrated such skill, consistently picking private equity funds better than average. An increase of 1 standard deviation in manager selection skill resulted in 3% higher returns.

So picking managers in alternatives does matter, given the extremely het-erogeneous nature and dispersion of return in such asset classes. After all, they're called "alternatives," not "sames." But given the fact that managers in these asset classes are so different from one another, the act of picking a man-ager generally involves simultaneously selecting a strategy. You can't surgically separate the two acts. This makes the idea of trying to measure success by beating a benchmark a silly exercise. Investors would instead be better served by employing a cost of capital approach, requiring a specific return for each allocation. Thus, success becomes ensuring outcomes meet expectations.

Considering the adaptive and changing nature of capital markets, achiev-ing that requires smart habits, or a process that can learn. Rather than pro-vide a static checklist for due diligence, a principles-based framework called the Five P's can help focus manager selection efforts: performance, people, philosophy, process, and portfolio. I think it's important to reiterate that this process should always adapt as best practices evolve and research around specific factors changes. For example, 10 years ago few diligence processes addressed team diversity or asked questions about how claims of harassment would be handled. Now most institutional investors do.

Any effective due diligence process should assess the most important characteristics of an asset manager, combining experiential knowledge with empirical research. As we've seen, there is some persistence of performance in certain asset classes, so past performance, while certainly no guarantee of future results, is not an entirely unreasonable place to begin. We've also seen that performance can only reasonably be expected to persist if you have the same team executing the same strategy, so these things must be important to vet as well.

Performance

The manager selection process quite literally begins and ends with perfor-mance. However, it's important to realize that performance is the output; it's the dependent variable in the grand experiment that is investing. If you get the other four P's right, the independent variables, then performance should follow. While there is definitely some persistence of performance in alternatives, it's certainly no guarantee of future returns. There's a very good reason that the mantra of "Past performance is no guarantee of future results" is repeatedly ingrained in all investment professionals. However, at the very least, assessing some amount of past return data can often inform researchers that prior returns have not met the required cost of capital for a particular strategy, allowing them to efficiently discontinue diligence. But the mere presence of attractive historical returns should always be viewed as a necessary but not sufficient condition to consider an investment with a manager.

While there are many different metrics to consider depending upon the strategy, performance analysis should be focused on establishing realistic expectations for future returns and thinking about ranges of outcomes. A mentor once told me that until you can define market conditions in which it would be expected that the strategy will lose money, you don't understand it well enough to invest. This premortem tactic allows investors to contemplate ahead of time what could go wrong and plan systematic remediation steps for specific drawdown levels. Finally, even if attractive returns are present historically, researchers must turn to the other four P's for evidence of skill, or the lack thereof, and characteristics associated with persistence of returns. As we've seen, where persistence does exist, it is only possible when you have the same team running the same strategy. So team and strategy must be highly important factors.

People

Recalling the hierarchy of alpha from Chapter 5, it becomes more critical to assess the people managing an investment strategy that falls nearer to the top of the pyramid. The combination of greater potential dispersion of returns with broader investment discretion in the strategy means the skills, abilities, and experience of the individuals making investment decisions will have a commensurately greater impact on your investment outcome.

Warren Buffett once said that when hiring someone, you should look for intelligence, energy, and integrity, and if you don't have the latter, the first two will kill you. When assessing the people at an investment firm, I've isolated three clusters of personality traits that helpfully form another alliterative mnemonic device that I call the Three I's—intelligence, integrity, and intensity.

Intelligence

Research on several hundred portfolio managers equity funds with doctoral degrees has shown that investors with PhDs unequivocally outperformed those fund managers without such degrees on multiple measures of performance—gross returns, net returns, four-factor alpha, Sharpe ratio, and information ratio.[9] The evidence is clear; higher intelligence leads to better returns, and that's in an asset class with virtually no evidence of excess returns. Imagine how impactful it would be in asset classes with actual performance dispersion and persistence!

Charlie Munger, Warren Buffett's pithy straight man for over 40 years, has offered another great quote on intelligence. Munger has said he would rather have someone with an IQ of 140 who thinks it's 130 than someone with an IQ of 150 who thinks it's 170 (that Dunning-Kruger effect again!). The best managers must be smart, but humble. And this means they must be driven to continually learn. In addition to pure intelligence, experiential knowledge is highly important to investment success.

Integrity

In investing, integrity should be the cost of admission. It is a must-have, full stop. In short, don't do business with people who lack integrity. While it is common sense to not give your money to dishonest people, plenty of research has shown people with undesirable personality characteristics—such as narcissism, Machiavellianism, and antisocial personality disorder—make poor investors anyway.[10]

Finally, the potential investor should ensure that interests are aligned and the terms and fees of the potential partnership are fair, at the very least. Managers with high integrity won't have eviscerated investor governance, reduced duties of care, hidden means of extracting economics, and conflicts of interest in their contracts or business models.

Intensity

This last "I" combines several related characteristics into one broader cluster: intensity. To me, this means that managers must have a passion for the work. Investing isn't just a job for them, or worse, a paycheck. It's a vocation, a higher calling. This passion should translate into a strong work ethic. Great investors tend to be the ones who turn the office lights on in the morning and shut them off at night. While there's value in being well-rounded with outside interests, just outhustling your peers can often compensate for other shortcomings in the world of alternative investments. This intensity should also involve an element of competitive drive, an ambition to be the best, stopping just short of obsession.

Obviously, it makes sense to apply this analysis to the critical decision makers and key individuals at the firm. But most hedge funds or private equity funds are founder led and managed. It's a good assumption that such founder entrepreneurs have built a business to do what they wanted to do. Since culture starts at the top, understanding the members of the management committee or investment committee will also provide insight into the philosophy of the firm, purpose, values, strategy, and approach that will guide the investment process.

Philosophy

It's important to understand the motivations of key individuals running the firm and investing the money, which at most boutique asset managers are one and the same. However, good teams are more than just the sum of their parts, and appreciating team dynamics is where underwriting the firm philosophy comes in to play. On the other hand, some of the most underachieving teams have been those that were built around a collection of talented stars with little regard for team dynamics. But high-functioning teams put the right people in the right positions to make the right plays, and they all pull in the same direction. We'll learn more about this in Chapter 10.

To summarize some of the findings, teams that are built on a culture of collaboration tend to outperform those that are more siloed in their investment process.[11] Investment firms organized around accountability and empowerment best those with a more hierarchical structure based on blame and power.[12] And investment groups that have the right mix of sames and differences—those with shared values but complementary skill sets and experiences—generate better results than those that are more homogenous.[13]

One very important philosophical characteristic to assess is where the firm falls on the spectrum of "asset gatherer" versus "performance shop." Performance shops are firms whose primary focus is generating the best investment results possible. These organizations tend to dedicate significant resources to research, analysis, and portfolio construction, often touting an "edge"—or at least a "differentiated approach"—in these processes. Conceptually, they try to make money by making money. Asset gatherers, on the other hand, are those firms that expend greater effort toward product development, marketing, and distribution. These firms generally have great narratives around benefits of scale and have with many different product offerings for sale. Such organizations seem to make money by raising money. If a firm isn't putting as much effort into generating superior returns as it is into selling, it is probably telling you where its bread is buttered.

Finally, there is a great deal of research that suggests younger, smaller firms tend to outperform older, larger ones.[14, 15] There are a lot of plausible reasons why this may be the case. First, there is definitely survivorship bias inherent in alternative investment indexes. This means those funds that survive—and continue to report returns into the index database—are by definition those that have done pretty well. The bad ones—the ones that implode—disappear, and those returns are not captured, resulting in the database overstating returns. Estimates around the size of this effect vary, and I think it is lower today than in the past, but it is still a factor.

Smaller, younger firms also probably take more risk than larger, more established shops, and higher risk leads to higher returns. In fact, many established managers admit as much about their early careers during honest conversations. However, most of the same research cited above shows that emerging managers do outperform in risk-adjusted terms as well, so there probably is something real about the effect. There is also the fact that larger pools of capital are harder to deploy, and they often arbitrage away the very mispricings that they would otherwise access.

However, I think there is another important effect occurring, and it relates back to the point about performance shops. Smaller, newer asset managers are by default generally in the earlier phase of their professional careers. This means they are not as far along in building their own personal wealth. Putting it another way, they are still highly motivated to make their fortunes, and since their funds are small, that can only come by generating strong returns.

If this is indeed the case, we would need to see evidence of different risk decision-making from ultra-high-net-worth individuals. Essentially, their marginal utility of another dollar should be lower, and this should result in capital preservation increasing as an investment objective. This is entirely consistent with human behavior. Recall the sections on the endowment effect and loss aversion from Chapter 7? The mere act of owning an asset increases its perceived value, and losses are more painful than gains are enjoyed.

Once again, it's consistent with what the academic research shows. An article in the *Journal of Risk and Insurance* in 2001 investigated the demographic characteristics of 2,400 households with life insurance policies to estimate a coefficient of relative financial risk aversion across families.[16] While a bit complicated, this study found that risk aversion begins to increase steadily at higher and higher levels of household net worth. Wealthier families were more risk averse according to the measures the authors calculated. In another study called "Risk Aversion and Incentive Effects," other researchers conducted an experimental design using 175 MBA students as participants who were presented with a series of lottery options ranging from low-risk/ low-weighted average expected payout to high-risk/high-weighted average expected payout.[17] Subjects progressively selected the lower-risk option as the absolute level of possible payouts rose, demonstrating increasing risk aversion with increasingly larger potential gains.

Wealthier people favor reducing investment risk and protecting gains already achieved, whereas those without substantial wealth prefer to allocate more toward wealth creation activities. So it seems unlikely that the effect of smaller, younger managers outperforming older, more established ones is purely a statistical artifact or a function of bad data. The scale of the effects is fairly substantial.

The research cited previously showed that smaller hedge funds and private equity tend to outperform by 1 to 3% per year, but the age effect was shown to be even more powerful. Emerging funds, even after controlling for size as a separate variable, generate higher excess returns than small firms in general. Research from PerTrac demonstrated that new hedge funds beat more established shops by a wide margin and, importantly, had nearly twice the Sharpe ratio (see Figure 9.5).[18]

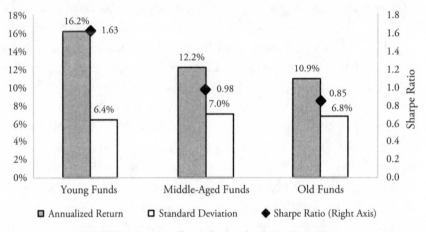

FIGURE 9.5   Age effect in hedge funds (*PerTrac, 2011*)

In private equity, first-time funds also beat their more established peers by hundreds of basis points annualized, often doubling older funds in many vintages.[19] I believe the fact that the age effect is so consistently larger than the size effect lends support to the idea of a behavioral cause. That's not to say that naïvely picking smaller, newer managers is a guarantee of excess returns. Indeed, both categories of investment organizations have far wider dispersion of returns than more established shops do, which increases the potential upside—and risk—to manager selection. However, by identifying newer, smaller managers that also have other factors shown to be positively correlated with excess returns, investors can tilt the odds in their favor. This will create a portfolio with lots of little edges, similar to the Barclays Global Investors Alpha Tilts product of old, but for asset managers. Lots of little edges often add up to one big alpha.

By embedding an analysis of the life cycle of the investment professionals and their risk profile into the understanding of the investment philosophy of the firm, an investor can identify situations where the principal risk takers are fully engaged in the task of investing in such a way that their personal desires and risk-return functions, and by extension the firm's, are truly aligned with the expectations of asset allocators. The best outcomes occur when expectations are set accurately.

Process

Process is where the investment rubber meets the road. It represents the operationalization of the investment philosophy. A great process sustaining an average philosophy is more likely to result in an acceptable investment outcome than the best investment strategy in the industry supported by a terrible process. Similar to the investment process we have discussed for allocators, it involves several discrete steps. Each step requires dedicated efforts to fully analyze and understand the strategy. The asset manager investment process generally follows the four steps listed below:

1. **Idea generation and research.** In this step, the asset manager sifts through various pieces of information in order to identify the opportunities that are most attractive. Idea generation naturally evolves from gathering data to analyzing it, as the most attractive opportunities are then more thoroughly vetted.

2. **Security selection and portfolio construction.** In the second step, individual trades or securities that are deemed to be the most appropriate for the investment objective are added to or removed from the portfolio. During this stage, rather than merely researching the stand-alone characteristics of the potential investments, the portfolio manager analyzes the impact of adding the position to the portfolio as a whole. There must be clear and transparent rules around what goes in or out of the portfolio and why. And it's important to ensure that the portfolio represents the best investment thinking of the entire organization. The best ideas need to win, not the best stories. Exactly who has ultimate investment discretion is important to understand for obvious reasons as well.

3. **Execution.** Execution is the process of how trading is handled, how securities are purchased, and how cash movements occur. While risk of this process is higher for some strategies than others, execution is where the investment ideas are actually crystallized. Ensuring the process is adequately resourced and the appropriate separations of duty are in place is critical for successful implementation of any investment strategy.

4. **Risk management.** Finally, risk management is the separate process of monitoring the portfolio at regular intervals to ensure that it remains invested according to the mandate and that all current investments are tracking appropriately. Sometimes this process may be referred to as asset management, property management, or servicing depending upon the strategy. In all cases, it should involve a dedicated team to either manage or monitor the asset and report information back to the investment committee. There should also be explicit guidelines in place about working out troubled assets or selling positions that are no longer appropriate or attractive for the specific mandate.

An effective investment process across all these steps must be disciplined and consistent to minimize the impact of the behavioral biases that we've identified. Having a predetermined and clearly defined playbook removes a lot of the room for error. Further, a consistent process is also essential to expectations of persistence of future returns. The more investment decision-making resembles a manufacturing process, the less heroic it is to assume that future returns will look similar to product fresh off the assembly line today. If the process is materially similar, one has but to look at the inputs—the raw materials, so to say—to set expectations about the future. If the quality of the inputs is the same, then persistence of returns becomes a more defensible assumption.

Portfolio

The final "P" involves analyzing and understanding the current exposures in the portfolio. Just as the process is the operationalization of the philosophy, the portfolio is the implementation of the investment process. Analyzing the current portfolio is important not only to ensure that the manager is being consistent with the stated philosophy and in compliance with the processes and risk guidelines, but also to ensure that the fund itself is appropriate given your specific portfolio context and required rate of return. Importantly, you cannot set accurate expectations for future returns without a practical understanding of the current portfolio.

For those researching alternative funds, this often requires a certain amount of flexibility. For instance, a volatility arbitrage fund with thousands of positions across both individual securities and asset classes, as well as contract months and long and short, is virtually impossible to analyze at a line item level, particularly as it may also change rapidly in real time. However, understanding ranges of exposures, the fund's positioning with respect to the Greeks,[20] and use of leverage is critical.

On the other hand, drawdown vehicles like private equity will typically not have made any investments at the time of commitment. A researcher is left with no options but to investigate prior portfolios that the investment team has deployed in a similar mandate, as well as to understand what the fund's investment limitations permit. Regardless of what strategy is being investigated, the biggest predictor of future returns will be the portfolio today—the securities owned, the prices paid, and the yields.

But this is where the Five P's take a little detour; smart habits need to learn. Like all other forms of alpha, process alpha must adapt to stay ahead of the game. To be a truly smart habit, the process must evolve, as alternative asset managers themselves must gradually improve and refine their investment processes over time, to stay ahead of competitors. Manager selection must follow suit.

The only way to do this is to be constantly taking meetings with new managers. First, you need to meet as many managers as possible in a given space before deciding to hire any single one of them. Obviously, you have higher odds of finding a better manager if you meet 100 than if you only meet 15. However, the truth is that good teams aren't always run a specific way. What works for some firms doesn't necessarily work for others. The only way to be able to truly identify the characteristics of process and team that work in a new market segment is to take a lot of meetings with managers, both good and bad. Repetition is the key to this pattern recognition.

It's important to accept that you don't have all the answers. Don't be afraid to ask as many questions as needed until you get those answers, even if it might make you look stupid. Alternatives are complex, and you can't make a good decision about complex strategies unless you dedicate the time and effort to understanding the complexity. In alternatives, this effort is often rewarded.

Finally, an investment memo is a critical step in the manager selection process. It serves the same role as the IPS does for asset allocation. Not only should this include a summary of the actual research conducted, but it should establish ex ante expectations around risk and returns. These ranges must be attributed to specific characteristics of the investment in order to appropriately vet the accuracy of the thesis ex post. Focus on the three to five critical drivers of risk and return, because getting these right will impact the outcome a lot more than the hundreds of ancillary items.

Importantly, a due diligence memo should spell out specific steps to take if things go sideways with the investment, such as departure of key individuals at the asset manager or style drift. Establishing expectations ahead of time allows you to make rules-based decisions at critical inflection points without being influenced by emotional factors (we'll soon see how much value such a disciplined methodology can add in rebalancing). By thinking about what could go wrong ahead of time, you'll be able to plot a change of course more rationally when you need it. And aside from managing change when things don't go according to the blueprint, such a postmortem can also help in identifying precisely where the plan went wrong so that manager selection can evolve and improve next time.

Portfolio Management

After the investment managers have been selected to meet the asset allocation objectives, the final step in the process is monitoring and managing the portfolio in real time. For some allocators, this may involve a more passive approach to measuring and reporting various risk metrics. On the other hand, some investors more actively manage the portfolio, removing unwanted positions or managers and rebalancing exposures back to desired levels. For the purpose of this section, we'll focus on tactical asset allocation and specifically on what I like to refer to as smart rebalancing.

Simple rebalancing is the process by which the weights of a portfolio are realigned to the target policy allocation objectives after diverging due to market movements. Let's return to our simple 60%/40% stock/bond portfolio from Chapter 8. Now, let's assume stocks returned 10% and bonds yielded 2% for one year. Well, the portfolio as a whole would have generated a total return of 6.8% (which beat our required rate of return), but at the end of the year, if we reinvested all cash distributions, the portfolio would be roughly 62% stocks and 38% bonds, because stocks appreciated more. This may not seem like a big change, but if we let it compound for a few years, our risk profile will be out of line from what our policy objectives permit. Rebalancing is the process of correcting that.

There are generally two types of triggers that investors use for determining when to rebalance. The simplest is a time-based rebalancing formula. For example, once every six months or at the end of every year, the investor would execute rebalancing trades and bring their current portfolio back in line with their target allocations. In the example above, at the end of the year, rebalancing back to target would require selling 2% of the stocks and investing those proceeds back into bonds to get back to 60%/40%. This has the benefit of removing behavioral biases from the process, but it is somewhat arbitrary.

The other approach involves the use of range triggers. Continuing with our illustration, if range triggers were set at plus or minus 5% for each asset, no rebalancing would be needed. Stocks would have to reach 65% before they could be sold back down to 60%. While still somewhat arbitrary, this has the added benefit of being more responsive to significant market dislocations. However, it's still not a truly adaptive or smart process because it is naïve with respect to capital markets assumptions. In essence, it rebalances to fixed-allocation targets that were based upon stale capital markets return assumptions, when in reality those have likely changed as well.

AlphaEngine, a tactical rebalancing firm, describes these simplistic approaches using a sailing analogy: "Naïve rebalancing is like setting the rudder in the direction of the destination without adjusting for wind direction, tides, or choppy seas."[21] It doesn't make sense to ignore important factors that are known to impact asset class returns when rebalancing. Why wouldn't an investor take capital markets assumptions into account when determining tactical allocations, particularly if they are so essential to strategic allocations? After all, rebalancing is making a decision about the relative attractiveness of the risk and return of various assets classes. So wouldn't a systematic approach to a more informed decision be superior to a methodical uninformed one? Smart rebalancing is a way to incorporate these adaptive capital markets assumptions directly into the rebalancing methodology.

Let's use our 60%/40% portfolio discussed previously to examine how smart rebalancing differs from the more standard approach. After one year, the allocation to stocks has grown to 62% and bonds have dropped to 38% of the fund. If we return to our capital markets assumptions, it follows that market valuations and yields have also changed, and then by definition, so will have return expectations as well. The valuation of equities will likely have risen as price increased, meaning both higher risk and lowered future returns. And since bonds have underperformed initial expectations, the yields on bonds have probably risen as well.

With a lower expected return to equities now and a higher yield for bonds, smart rebalancing incorporates these factors into the allocation as opposed to automatically resetting it back to the original 60%/40%. Perhaps the higher yield on bonds would result in a higher allocation target for them, for example going to 58% stocks and 42% bonds. In other approaches, perhaps a momentum factor would lean into stocks more heavily in the short run, justifying a mix of 61% and 39%. If momentum is used, and it should be for shorter time horizons, it should be calibrated specifically for the rebalancing periodicity. Short-term momentum is more effective for quarterly rebalancing, whereas longer-term momentum should be used for less frequent changes in allocations.

Of course, this is an overly simplified discussion on a complicated subject; building a smart rebalancing model that works is no trivial matter. However, it can be done,[22] and when successful, it can add significant value. Using a simple four-asset portfolio, AlphaEngine has conducted an analysis showing the impact of a smart rebalancing process.[23] Using domestic equities, international equities, bonds, and commodities as the four asset classes, the authors were able to compare the effects of three different rebalancing methodologies from 1990 to 2008, a period that included several bull and bear markets. The comparison evaluated the performance of not rebalancing at all, rebalancing back to target objectives every quarter, and quarterly rebalancing incorporating tactical asset class capital markets assumptions. The results are shown in Table 9.2.

TABLE 9.2   Smart Rebalancing, or Tactical Asset Allocation

	No Rebalancing	Quarterly Rebalancing	Smart Quarterly Rebalancing
Annualized return	6.2%	6.4%	6.9%
Standard deviation	9.3%	8.6%	8.7%
Return-risk ratio	0.67	0.75	0.79
Maximum drawdown	–31.9%	–33.1%	–31.7%

Even including conservative assumptions for transaction costs, a passive quarterly rebalancing approach outperformed the static buy-and-hold portfolio, generating modestly higher returns but more importantly reducing volatility more substantially. That's the main objective of rebalancing—keeping risk from straying outside of intended parameters. Notably, the AlphaEngine smart rebalancing model added significant excess returns while keeping risk nearly identical to the simpler technique. In some ways, smart rebalancing completely removes the distinction between strategic and tactical, using informed inputs to continually target an asset mix designed to keep the plan on track with its policy objectives. Once the rules are articulated, the plan can be implemented in a disciplined, structured manner and followed consistently.

Habits are reinforced through repetition. Much like a hiker in a forest who takes the most beaten-down trail simply because it's literally the path of least resistance, neural pathways also get stronger the more they are used. Smart habits are about systematizing as much of the investment process as possible, automating what works in order to become both more efficient and more accurate. Whether that be creating intelligent checklists to help us screen and prioritize the most attractive managers, or using informed rebalancing methods that take the emotion out of keeping the portfolio in line with long-term objectives, such smart habits limit opportunities for our cognitive shortcomings to adversely impact the portfolio. Implementing the plan consistently will drive successful outcomes.

However, process cannot be turned into a closed-end formula where we "set it and forget it." Strategic does not equal stagnant, much like tactical does not mean market timing. Investing, like good health, is simple in theory but difficult in reality. A disciplined and objective process is important, but it shouldn't be something that is entirely static. Things change, and the process, much like a fitness regime, should change over time as well. I'm certainly not 20 anymore, and I can't act like it in the gym. And our knowledge of nutrition has improved significantly in my lifetime. Similarly, we know vastly more today about the impact of certain behaviors and characteristics on returns. Behavioral alpha and smart habits are about being the rational architect of your investment behavior instead of the unwitting victim of it. We can use both System 1 and System 2 thinking more effectively, although each requires slightly different tools to best manage. Ultimately, the difference between financial success and failure will come down to those investors who do this. Next we will discuss how investment institutions as a whole can put organizational structures in place to support this.

Notes

1. See Mauboussin (2012).
2. Fama and French (1996).
3. The scale of this economic effect is so large that I doubt it becomes insignificant even if properly adjusted for the effects of market beta or differences in volatility as opposed to this dirty math.
4. Watson (2015).
5. Brown et al. (2008).
6. Brown et al. (2016).
7. Cumming and Zambelli (2016).
8. Cavagnaro et al. (2019).
9. Chaudhuri et al. (2013).
10. ten Brinke et al. (2017).
11. Ware et al. (2015).
12. Hsu and Ware (2014).
13. Jones (2013).
14. Joenväärä et al. (2012) and Aggarwal and Jorion (2010), among others, confirmed that younger funds outperform older ones. Boyson (2008) demon-

strated that persistence of returns, or skill, was much stronger for younger funds as well. An updated analysis by eVestment continues to show both size and age effects.

15. Fung et al. (2008), Ding et al. (2009), Teo (2009), Joenväärä et al. (2012), and PerTrac (2011) all show positive excess returns across measures of total return, risk-adjusted return, and alpha for small funds using different data sets and different time periods.
16. Halek and Eisenhauer (2001).
17. Holt and Laury (2002).
18. PerTrac (2011).
19. Preqin (2016).
20. The Greeks, when referenced regarding options, are various mathematical models that measure an option's sensitivity to changes in various inputs, such as the underlying asset price, volatility, time, and interest rates. The most common of these are delta, gamma, vega, and theta.
21. Muralidhar and Muralidhar (2009).
22. Whyte (July 2019).
23. Muralidhar and Muralidhar (2009).

10
Organizational Alpha—
Smart Governance

Good governance depends on the ability to take responsibility
by both administration as well as individuals.
—NARENDRA MODI

If behavioral alpha is the value we can add to investment returns by individually improving our decision-making, then organizational alpha is the institutional equivalent. It's the improvement in investment performance that comes from better organizational decision-making. However, it's impossible to truly optimize either without simultaneously optimizing both. And that's because governance simply means ensuring an institution has the right people in the right positions to make the right decisions.

There are some institutions that get this very right, with governance structures that empower the appropriate people, effectively balancing the competing needs for oversight and efficiency. In these organizations, everyone is pulling in unity in the same direction, and individual and collective performance are harmonized. Unfortunately, there are also many institutions that do not get this trade-off right, creating internal challenges, bureaucratic morasses, perverse incentives, and adverse selection bias. In many of these institutions, the greatest enemy to returns is the organization itself. And investment professionals at those entities, even if they are able to individually mitigate their decision-making biases, are subject to collective biases that drive institutional decisions. Ultimately, the difference between good and poor investment governance can be measured through the investment performance—the only metric that really matters.

In this chapter, I will attempt to more fully explain some of these challenges, describing specifically the problems they create, before finally suggesting improvements based upon a few simple principles that have been applied productively at successful institutions. If smart thinking allows us to beat back our cognitive biases and generate behavioral alpha through process, then governance is the tool by which we empower smart processes instead of static ones.

But first, as always, the effort begins with defining what governance is. If you ask 10 people what governance means, you might well get 10 separate answers. It means authority to some, policies to others, and leadership to yet others. I think the best definition is that governance is simply a body of rules, policies, and practices by which an organization is directed and controlled. In short, governance is deciding who decides.

For an investment organization, this obviously extends to those rules, policies, and practices around how investment decisions are made and executed. We've mapped out the handful of discrete steps in the investment process previously and how to improve them individually, but governance is essentially how an organization determines who does what at each point. And organization alpha is optimizing those steps collectively.

In order to discuss what effective investment governance should look like in practice, let's start with what effective governance means in general. To do that, I'll turn to a framework created by German sociologist, philosopher, and political economist Max Weber. Born in 1864, Weber was a prolific author and wrote extensively about rationalism, capitalism, and legitimate sources of authority. He ultimately went on to cofound the German Democratic Party after World War I, a party committed to restoring democracy after the collapse of the Weimar Republic, but he is perhaps best known for his book *The Protestant Ethic and the Spirit of Capitalism.*[1]

In an earlier essay titled "Politics as a Vocation" based upon a series of his lectures, Weber separates authority into three distinct types based upon the source of power behind that authority.[2] While each category of authority still defines the entities who decide, the reasons behind why they are the ones to decide vary dramatically. These reasons speak to the legitimacy, or illegitimacy as the case may be, of that authority.

Traditional Authority

The first type of authority is traditional authority. Weber defines this type of authority as that which derives from the long-established customs, traditions, and social norms of a group of people. One example that he references is the hereditary rule of monarchs, which passes from generation to generation, not through consent of the governed, but merely because that is the established rule. Tribal chieftains, kings, emperors, czars, and shahs would be considered leaders who govern through this type of authority. They have the power to lead simply because they are the named leader.

Such truly hereditary authority exists virtually nowhere in the world anymore among modern societies. However, we do have many positions of institutionalized hierarchical power, whereby leaders often get to select their own successors, regardless of the views or beliefs of various constituents, such as stakeholders or employees. For instance, oftentimes the retiring CEO of a company will promote his or her deputy, transitioning authority purely by rote to the next generation. While not hereditary per se, this authority is vested and transitioned solely through a shared collective fiction. Essentially, CEOs have authority because it is adjudicated by rule that they have authority; they are the named leader.

Furthermore, other types of authorities could fall within this broader group of hierarchical authority, as they share more in common with the classical traditional authority than they do with the other categories we'll discuss below. For instance, the premier of a nation with less than democratic processes for election clearly has the same type of hierarchical authority within the country, although again such power is typically not established via hereditary claims. Nor is there any recourse for constituents who may disagree with their leadership. I would even argue that a democratically elected president of a truly free nation would fall into this category after the election. Once in that post, an enormous amount of authority is vested in the person via the seat itself.

In other words, the source of power resides in the hierarchy: When an individual is placed in a hierarchical position of authority, regardless of how the person gets there, that person's power is virtually absolute over his or her specific domain. Absent extraordinary means, it is nearly unchallengeable, whether that is a boss, a general, a president, or a king. Thus, I believe a more helpful classification for this type of authority, while similar in spirit to Weber's initial structure, would be *hierarchical authority*. The power from this type of authority comes from the position itself, by decree, as opposed to the person who holds it.

Charismatic Authority

The second kind of authority that Weber delineates is charismatic authority. Charismatic authority is the power that flows from a person with strong inherent leadership characteristics. Charismatic people are genuine, natural leaders who motivate and inspire those around them. Individuals with such intrinsic personality characteristics naturally stimulate devotion and obedience, and people readily follow these types of leaders, even if they do not have vested traditional authority roles.

Oftentimes those with strong charismatic abilities will use those inherent talents to pursue, and obtain, seats of traditional authority, but humans naturally follow such leaders even without hierarchical power endowed behind them.

For example, regardless of one's political inclinations, it must be acknowledged that President Donald Trump is clearly an individual with strong charismatic authority who used that ability to achieve the hierarchical authority of the Office of President of the United States. Similarly, many legendary sports coaches such as Vince Lombardi and Mike Krzyzewski, or generals such as Douglas MacArthur or George Patton, also had authority legitimized by both charismatic and hierarchical sources. They were strong leaders in positions of leadership.

On the other hand, rebels, revolutionaries, missionaries, community organizers, even cult leaders, and, in today's digital world, social media influencers are all examples of people with charismatic authority able to inspire followers to action, for good or bad, without the benefit of hierarchical authority that mandates obedience. Such individuals are strong leaders without traditional positions of leadership. Thus, this type of power is legitimized by traits intrinsic to the individuals themselves.

Rational/Legal Authority

Third, and the last type of authority presented by Weber in his discourses, is rational/legal authority. I believe this construct requires the most modernizing to remain useful today. I'll first discuss Weber's definition and some objections to it; then finally I'll propose what I believe is a more useful concept that, I hope, remains true to the genius of Weber's original framework.

Weber argues that rational/legal authority stems from the collective decision-making of a society to design a set of complex rules and policies for selecting who gets to decide, ostensibly based upon a rational analysis of who is best qualified to decide; hence, the dual name. Modern societies depend upon this authority, and it is what drives governments around the world. Without explicitly endorsing the moral superiority of this type of authority, it's clear Weber believed that this source of power is the most critical for effective functioning of complex human activity. Weber thought that by creating formal rules, setting up bureaucracies tasked with deciding on behalf of the general public, and hiring technically qualified professional bureaucrats, more rational authority could be exercised.

This was of course before bureaucracy became a four-letter word. Indeed, in the early 1900s, bureaucracy was sometimes held out as a model of efficient decision-making for institutions. Hire experts, and have them decide. Or at least, that was the idea.

Today bureaucracy is nearly synonymous with inefficiency and waste. Many such bureaucratic institutions no longer have domain experts making decisions in technical areas. Rarely are important regulatory bodies run by such technocrats; instead, they are managed by lawyers, politicians, or career bureaucrats. Indeed, it's almost a rarity when the administrator or commissioner of entities such as the FTC, EPA, or SEC is a functional industry expert as opposed to a lawyer. Among such bodies, only the FDA is consistently chaired by a qualified medical professional.

Further, rarely are these directors independent of political influence. Most are hired, and fired, by the president, and their tenures are directly linked to the changing views of the electorate. As Ben Bernanke once noted in a private breakfast I attended after he had left the Federal Reserve, when your boss is a politician, your job is political (although he was much more diplomatic in his words!).

Indeed, Weber endorsed bureaucracies precisely because they were thought to eliminate political influence, conflicts of interest, and favoritism, while maximizing rational decision-making. Few familiar with the failings of today's legacy bureaucracies saddled with truly traditional methods of decision-making based upon nothing more than historical precedent or organizational inertia would argue there is anything "rational" about them. Since Weber's view of a bureaucracy was idealized based upon rational experts, let's simply remove the "legal" from the concept and idealize this source of authority even more.

I think clearly delineating a separate type of authority as *expert authority* more effectively captures a meaningful distinction in the source of power while still remaining true to the intent of Weber's concept. The legal authority instilled in the seat of decision-making moves into the hierarchical authority grouping, whereas the rational authority willingly granted to an individual with recognized experience and expertise in a certain area of knowledge would fall into the category of expert authority.

Now, the distinction between charismatic authority and my classification of expert authority may seem minor. However, it's important to note that expert authority is knowledge-based, whereas charismatic authority is character-based. For example, think of the doctor whose advice you consult for a second opinion, the executive whose mentorship you seek when considering important career decisions, or even an outside expert witness brought in to testify in a court case. People willingly seek out these individuals, not because they are necessarily magnetically drawn to follow them, but because they explicitly acknowledge the domain expertise such individuals have.

A New Framework

I believe this structure of hierarchical authority, charismatic authority, and expert authority then improves Weber's prior three-source model by more clearly differentiating among sources of authority. Even more importantly, I believe this updated version holds up better to what is essentially reverse engineering. We can reverse-engineer the identification of the separate loci of power on an applied bottom-up basis as opposed to a conceptual top-down approach by answering the hypothetical question, "Why do people follow this leader?" There are only three answers to that question; hence, there can only be three sources of authority.

- **Hierarchical authority is coercive.** People follow these leaders because they *have* to.
- **Charismatic authority is emotive.** People follow these leaders because they *want* to.
- **Expert authority is rational.** People follow these leaders because they *ought* to.

We've seen that some leaders can have combinations of these characteristics. Powerful leaders are those individuals who have both charismatic and hierarchical authority. Competent leaders are those with both hierarchical and expert authority. People who combine charismatic and expert authority are often highly successful individuals, without typical institutional power roles, such as entrepreneurs. And effective organizations are those that have charismatic experts in positions of hierarchical authority. See Figure 10.1.

When these three sources of authority are not aligned, there are several decision-making problems that occur that often result in suboptimal outcomes. Literature on corporate governance has identified such issues through the lens of problems of agency. An agency problem is the inherent conflict of

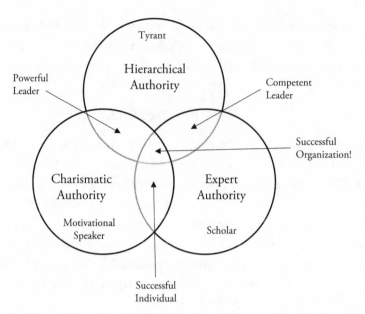

FIGURE 10.1 Effective governance as convergence of sources of authority

interest whereby one party (the agent) is expected to act in the best interest of the other party (the principal). For example, management executives—the agents—at a publicly traded company have hierarchical authority granted to them on behalf of the shareholders—the principals in this case—to make day-to-day decisions about how to run the business. These corporate executives are obligated to manage the company in order to maximize value for shareholders as opposed to maximizing their own personal wealth, and those objectives can sometimes run contrary to one another.

However, similar challenges occur in government institutions, where public officials are supposed to make decisions on behalf of the public for the overall greater good, not for their personal financial well-being. Politicians that steer government contracts to businesses where they have a personal financial interest serve as the prototypical, and illegal, example of this conflict of interest materialized.

Institutional investment organizations have the same power dynamic, where both investment professionals and trustees make fiduciary decisions on behalf of the principals, the underlying asset owners. In investment organizations, these problems of agency or governance shortcomings tend to fall into three main categories: adverse selection bias, perverse incentives, and implementation shortfall.

Adverse Selection Bias

Adverse selection occurs in a situation where the buyer or seller of a good or service is biased into making an inferior decision for various reasons. We've seen in Chapter 7 that all humans have inherent biases that result in suboptimal decisions; in this case, the bias is endemic to the governance as opposed to the individual. For example, adverse selection can occur when the decision maker does not have sufficient knowledge or experience to make an informed decision. Politically mandated decisions often also create adverse selection bias.

Perverse Incentives

Perverse incentives are unintended consequences that occur for a variety of reasons. They happen when decision makers are incentivized to make decisions that actively run contrary to the objectives of the organization. They can be a type of moral hazard, such as when an investment committee member desires to take more (or less) risk than is appropriate for the account. Or it can occur when desirable behavior is not adequately compensated, such as a salaried individual with no performance incentive potential being forced to choose either putting in more and more diligence hours to find high-performing, off-the-run managers or just hiring safe, brand name funds despite lower return expectations and calling it a day.

Implementation Shortfall

Implementation shortfall is the gap between when an investment decision is properly authorized and documented and when it is executed. The most common example of implementation shortfall is the difference between the price of a stock when the decision to buy it was made, for instance when it gets added to an index, and the actual price of the stock when it is added to a portfolio. A case in point: If a stock is added to an index when it is trading at $20 and the index replication account doesn't purchase it until it hits $21, that $1 of lost gains is the implementation shortfall.

In an institutional setting, this can arise when an asset owner decides to allocate to a new asset class, say high-yield bonds, but then does not actually deploy for several quarters. The difference between the yield on the bonds at the time of the decision and the yield when actually invested, and the subsequent returns forgone in the interim, can be considered an implementation shortfall. So while not a decision-making problem, implementation shortfall still arises from a governance failure, whereby the authority to act in a timely manner is not adequately vested with the appropriate individuals.

Again, it's worth stating that the less overlap in the Venn diagram, the worse the governance. The more, the better. Remember that governance means ensuring that an institution has the right people in the right positions to make the right decisions. How you achieve that balance requires aligning these three underlying components of governance that correspond to the separate sources of authority—hierarchy, leadership, and management.

Hierarchy

This is the component of governance relating to institutional authority, reporting lines, the organizational chart, and all bylaws, policies, and procedures around these various elements. It defines who has been selected to retain the hierarchical authority to make which specific decisions on behalf of the institution.

Leadership

This module of governance pertains to establishing the vision for the institution and mission statement, as well as to setting priorities, creating the culture, and establishing motivation and teamwork. An organization may not always have natural-born, charismatic leaders in place, but it can (and should) document and systematize these elements for more effective governance.

Management

In my opinion, this final component of governance is ultimately the most important. It is where the proverbial governance rubber hits the road. Management incorporates setting specific performance measurement and accountability metrics in place for each role; establishing a formal process for identifying and retaining talent appropriate for those roles, which also includes compensation and alignment of interests; and finally managing the execution and implementation of the decisions.

Without ensuring this element is adequately operationalized, the first two components of governance are entirely moot. Much like a coach who refuses to adapt his strategies to the strengths and weaknesses of his players, a static hierarchical structure if saddled with the wrong people in management positions is doomed to fail, no matter how rationally intentioned the rules were to begin with.

While these principles hold true across any type of organization or decision-making process, for the sake of providing concrete investment governance advice for generating organizational alpha, I'll turn to a discussion of the investment process as a means to frame these concepts.

As discussed previously, the investment process is composed of several separate basic elements. For each component, distinct decisions are required, and oftentimes these decisions are owned by different individuals with differing processes. And the success of each of these subprocesses can be measured independently from one another, although ultimate investment success requires effective decision-making at each step. These elements include:

1. **Policy and objective setting.** This decision includes establishing the risk tolerance, liquidity needs, investment time horizon, and return objectives for the portfolio. It is generally a one-time organizational decision, and the effectiveness of this decision point can be measured by the ability of the portfolio to achieve the foundational mission over time, whether that is funding monthly retirement checks, meeting the operating budget of an institution, or even paying for your children's college tuition. Setting policy objectives is the most strategic decision and requires the least technical investment knowledge.

2. **Asset allocation.** This step comprises selecting the various asset classes to invest in and determining the relative weights the portfolio will allocate to each asset bucket. It is usually separated into strategic, or long-term, asset allocation where the target policy allocations are decided, and tactical or dynamic allocation, which is shorter-term and responsive to current market conditions. The effectiveness of the strategic asset allocation (SAA) decision-making process can be measured by comparing the returns of the long-term asset allocation mix with the policy objective, while the effects of tactical asset allocation (TAA) can be measured versus the strategic allocation benchmark. Setting the SAA is both highly strategic and fairly highly technical, whereas managing the TAA process is very technical but less strategic in nature.

3. **Manager or security selection.** This portion of the investment process involves the selection of the specific external managers, or if asset classes are managed internally, it considers the individual securities within each asset class. The effectiveness of this decision point is determined by comparing the returns of each manager or asset class against a risk-matched asset class benchmark. Recalling the discussion around benchmark selection from Chapter 1, this is the decision point most commonly associated with finding alpha. Selecting managers, particularly if any given account is only 1 or 2% of plan assets, is not a strategic decision, but it does require expert knowledge.

4. **Portfolio management.** As mentioned, this is not really a discrete process but rather an ongoing, iterative management step integrating steps 2 and 3 with risk management considerations in real time. Its effects are very difficult to disentangle from steps 2 and 3. Frankly, effectiveness at step 4 is best thought of as improving the decision quality of both prior steps. Hence, it is important to have granular and timely data and processes for this step. This step not a strategic decision, as it represents day-to-day functioning of the investment process. (The word "management" in the description should be a big hint).

The final actual step in an investment process is implementation, also referred to as execution. This stage involves carrying out the investment decision once it has been appropriately authorized. This step is unambiguously a management function, not truly a governance one, but poor governance can impact it. To the extent possible, execution should never involve non-investment professionals. I've observed institutions with significant investment staffing in place where all investment execution runs through one non-investment individual, creating a single point of failure and multiple delays, which had significant impacts on costs and total net returns.

But we're getting a bit ahead of ourselves. Before we take a look at some common governance structures found at institutional investment organizations, let's lay out a systematic framework for analyzing the effectiveness of each decision above. This framework is conceptually simple, and my hope is that it will provide individuals in a position of oversight of such decisions a practical analytical tool for understanding where their institution is making effective decisions—and where it is not. If you want to generate organizational alpha, you need to first start with understanding where decisions can be improved, and only then can you figure out how to improve them.

Let's imagine that an institutional investor has a simple objective: to return 7.0% over the long term. To accomplish this objective, the investor has selected a familiar strategic asset allocation of 60% stocks and 40% bonds. How did this investor pick that asset mix? Well, the investor expects stocks to return 8.5% and bonds to make 4.5%, but wants limited volatility and so does not want more than 60% stocks. This means the strategic asset allocation should yield 6.9% (60% × 8.5% + 40% × 4.5%) based solely on market returns. To get to the objective of 7.0%, the investor needs to find 10 basis points of alpha somewhere. See Table 10.1 for an outline of plan objectives.

If the fund returned 7.0% overall, it met its objectives. If we assume that this investor only made 6.0% instead, obviously that policy objective is not met. But figuring out where the process failed requires informed oversight, a critical component of successful governance. Using the decision-making framework above, we'll build a performance analysis tool to help figure out exactly what went wrong. Let's start at the top.

The policy objective of 7.0% was not met. The portfolio only made 6.0%, so the portfolio missed the policy objective by 1%, or 100 basis points. What

TABLE 10.1   Plan Objectives

Asset	Allocation		Expected Return		Weighted Return
Stocks	60%	×	8.5%	=	5.1%
Bonds	40%	×	4.5%	=	1.8%
			Total market return assumption		6.9%
			Plus alpha goal		0.1%
			Total return objective		7.0%

did the asset allocation decision contribute to that performance? To determine that, we need to compare the strategic benchmark index returns, not the actual portfolio returns, with the policy objective.

If the stock market index returned 7.7% and the bond market index yielded 3.2%, the 60%/40% index return would be 5.9%, as shown in Table 10.2. This analysis separates the actual return of the portfolio from the return of the index, or market, which allows us to isolate the strategic asset allocation effect directly. So the excess return due to the strategic asset allocation alone was −110 basis points.

TABLE 10.2   Asset Allocation Contribution

Asset	Policy Allocation		Index Return		Weighted Return
Stocks	60%	×	7.7%	=	4.6%
Bonds	40%	×	3.2%	=	1.3%
			Strategic benchmark return		5.9%
			Minus total return objective		7.0%
			Strategic allocation excess return		−1.1%

The plan return of 6.0% beat the strategic benchmark return of 5.9%, which means somewhere active decisions added 10 basis points compared with the market returns. So the company hit its alpha goal, but was this from tactical allocation decisions or manager selection?

First, we need to ensure the target strategic allocation is actually how the portfolio is allocated. If we assume this plan was not at target, we could measure a tactical allocation contribution. So let's assume our fund had an actual weight of 65% to equities and 35% to fixed income. This could well be due to an intentional overweight driven by short-run expectations for higher returns from stocks, or possibly it could be from concerns about rising interest rates impacting bond prices. Or the plan could simply have a passive approach to rebalancing, where the allocation to equities is allowed to increase via compounding by 5% before being rebalanced back down. Regardless, the decision for actual allocations to deviate from strategic allocations should be an intentional one, as opposed to merely implementation shortfall or the unintended consequences of failing to get your actual allocations to target. For these results, see Table 10.3.

TABLE 10.3 Tactical Allocation Contribution

Asset	Actual Allocation		Index Return		Weighted Return
Stocks	65%	×	7.7%	=	5.0%
Bonds	35%	×	3.2%	=	1.1%
			Tactical benchmark return		6.1%
			Minus strategic benchmark return		5.9%
			Tactical allocation excess return		0.2%

By taking the actual asset class allocations multiplied by the index returns, we get a tactical benchmark return of 6.1%. Two things (should) become immediately apparent. First, this simple overweight to equities, which had higher returns than bonds, resulted in an additional 20 basis points of total return compared with the long-term strategic allocation benchmark, which is good.

The second point, however, is not as good. Recall that the plan actually returned 6.0%, which means we must have obtained −10 basis points from manager selection. We can confirm this by comparing the returns to each asset class with the relevant benchmark for that asset class, multiplied by the actual asset class weight, as shown in Table 10.4.

TABLE 10.4   Manager Selection Contribution

Asset	Actual Return			Index Return		Actual Allocation		Weighted Excess Return
Stocks	(7.5%	−	7.7%)		×	65%	=	−0.1%
Bonds	(3.3%	−	3.2%)		×	35%	=	0.0%
						Manager excess return		−0.1%

For our portfolio above, returns trailed the policy objective by 1.0%, returning 6.0% instead of the required 7.0%. The strategic allocation accounted for all the underperformance, and given the impact of asset allocation on long-term returns, this is where most of the mindshare around decision-making should be focused. Perhaps this plan needs a higher allocation to equities to meet its objectives, or perhaps those return objectives need to be lowered. Either way, governance here needs to be addressed.

Tactical allocation added positive excess returns, but it remains to be seen whether that was intentional or not. The organization needs to assess this contribution with intellectual honesty and self-awareness, and if it was merely a case of being right for the wrong reasons, decision-making should be improved. Once again, being lucky is not alpha. Finally, manager selection underperformed. Governance there should also be improved, but the overall impact is the smallest of the three, as shown in the performance summary in Table 10.5.

TABLE 10.5   Performance Summary

Total policy excess return	−1.0%
Strategic allocation excess return	−1.1%
Tactical allocation excess return	0.2%
Manager selection excess return	−0.1%

OK, now that we have a framework to easily measure and manage the effectiveness of the investment decision-making process across several distinct strata, let's take a look at some typical governance structures found in institutional asset owner organizations and determine where decision-making authority resides for these functions. There are usually three layers of authority found at pensions, foundations, and endowments, although the exact structure of any organization can vary. These three levels of governance are:

- The board of trustees or a board subcommittee (e.g., investment committee)
- Executive director, CEO, or president
- Chief investment officer and/or investment staff

At small endowments or pensions, there may not be any investment staff. So the board or a subcommittee thereof, along with the executive director, typically shares authority for all investment decisions and execution. However, at larger institutions, staff may be delegated a significant component of investment discretion, and oftentimes the CIO and executive director are combined in one role. Further, at private institutions, often no board members or executive director is involved in the investment process. Canadian plans or insurance portfolios sometimes have nearly all of investment discretion with investment professionals. And finally at asset management firms, such as mutual fund companies, investment decisions are made exclusively by investment professionals, whether that is through a staff investment committee or through authority delegated to portfolio managers. A few examples of these various structures are provided in Figure 10.2, but there are many other variants.

Keep in mind, different steps of the investment decision-making process can be vested by policy at any level of the organization in the sample governance models shown in Figure 10.2. For a small plan with six financial professional trustees appointed to the board and no internal investment staff, it may be perfectly appropriate for the trustees to make investment manager selection decisions. There is no one-size-fits-all.

However, designing the appropriate governance structure for any organization requires understanding the problems of agency that arise from failing

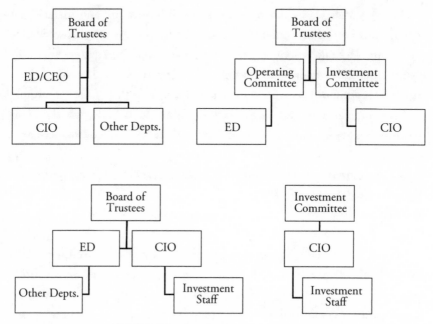

FIGURE 10.2   Sample governance structures

to align the three sources of authority within the institution. So taking into account the performance oversight and analytical framework established previously, let's look at some research that investigates the impact of different governance structures on the different steps in the investment process, starting with policy outcomes first, or the ability of the institution to meet its foundational objectives.

Policy Outcomes

In 1994, a few scholars performing research on behalf of the National Bureau of Economic Research conducted a survey of 269 US public pensions, documenting their various governance structures and measuring two policy outcomes—the total investment returns on the portfolio and the funded status of the plan.[3] The overall investment performance certainly reflects the efficacy of the total investment decision-making process, but more directly, the funded status of a pension calculates how likely the system is to meet its payment obligations,[4] measuring the policy outcome explicitly. Pensions that fail to achieve their required rate of return over time will see their funded ratio decline and will be less able to meet their payment obligations.

This research showed that boards with a higher percentage of retired trustees underperformed those with fewer. The researchers calculated that average five-year returns declined by 2% for each 10% increase in retiree board members, who are possibly less accountable and certainly less informed than investment professionals. Importantly, this effect controlled for asset allocation differences, suggesting the reduced return was solely attributable to the governance variable. Pensions with mandated in-state investments, which ostensibly are a politically motivated as opposed to a rationally motivated policy objective, experienced a 1% lower overall return for every 10% increase to in-state allocations, regardless of the asset mix.

But more directly, funded status was also statistically significantly lower for such boards as well. Plan-funded status was improved by almost 10% when pensions had an in-house actuary. Those that did not have an actuary on staff instead had these assumptions set by a nonexpert board. This finding provided additional evidence that outcomes that require technical expertise are improved when decision-making is pushed to internal experts.

It is also worth looking at the difference in funded status between US corporate and US public pensions. As discussed above, public pensions typically have at least some layer of investment decisions made by the board or non-investment staff. Corporate pensions, on the other hand, rarely have board-level involvement in the day-to-day management of the pension portfolio, with professional financial staff delegated much, and many times all, of the investment responsibility.

As of March 2019, actuarial consultant Milliman reported that the average funded ratio of the top 100 US corporate pensions was 91%.[5] On the other hand, Milliman's calculation for the funded status of the largest 100 US public plans was a mere 71% as of the same date. Of course, funding requirements for public and corporate plans vary quite widely, making the comparison not exactly fair. However, with an average discount rate of 7.5% for public plans and 3.6% for corporate plans,[6] private-sector pensions report far higher liability numbers to begin with, giving public pensions a huge advantage in reporting a smaller denominator.

However, Canadian public pensions, which have far more investment authority delegated to professional investment staff, have average funding ratios well over 100%.[7] And academic research that has compared the returns of US, Canadian, and European pension plans has found that American systems underperform their global counterparts by approximately 50 basis points per year on average, despite having more equity exposure in their asset allocations.[8]

However, such allocation differences make it critical to measure the performance effects of the asset allocation and manager selection decisions independently as well. Now let's turn to some research that does just that.

Asset Allocation Outcomes

In research published in the somewhat obscure *Journal of Public Budgeting, Accounting & Financial Management,* a trio of academics looked at 246 large state and local US pensions with a board of trustees providing oversight[9]; the authors of the study investigated the performance of these plans across multiple time periods. These authors found that pensions whose boards had authority over asset allocation decisions underperformed those systems where allocation authority did not reside with the board, and they estimated that the governance difference resulted in 300 basis points of underperformance for such plans.

In prior research, one of the same scholars along with a colleague looked at a smaller set of similar pensions over a shorter sample period.[10] Employing several different measures of performance, including a risk-adjusted metric, this earlier work found that systems whose boards had authority over asset allocation decisions earned between 136 and 192 basis points less than plans where trustees were not afforded such purview, once again showing that having non-investment professionals choose the asset mix leads to a lower return for the fund.

Then, in 2016, a pair of Swiss economists looking to extend similar research to their home market created a proprietary governance score called the G-SCORE by which they attempted to measure the effectiveness of the governance structures of 139 Swiss pensions.[11] This metric incorporated objective verifiable underlying factors, evaluating each pension's governance in terms of policy objective setting, organizational structure and design, investment objectives, investment processes, and management procedures and transparency.

Pensions with higher degrees of transparency, well-defined objectives, highly structured processes, clear separation of duties between oversight and executive functions, and robust performance measurement and accountability scored higher on this G-SCORE. And what these researchers found was that those pensions that scored in the top quartile on the governance metric outperformed those pensions in the bottom quartile by about 1% annually. More importantly, compared with their asset allocation benchmark, top-quartile plans generated excess returns 0.75% higher than bottom-quartile ones. And these plans had higher Sharpe ratios as well, accounting for any differences in risk—truly organizational alpha.

Their research also showed that in addition to lower returns, plans with weaker governance likewise demonstrated poorer policy outcomes, having lower funding ratios and longer amortization periods. Finally, these authors found a strong correlation between the governance score and plan size, with larger pensions having more professional staff, greater delegation, and more institutionalized processes in place.

Several of the studies in this area have found that, generally speaking, larger funds and those with more professional staff allocated higher amounts of their portfolios to equities and alternatives and less to bonds and cash, which undoubtedly helps to drive higher total returns. Although to be clear, many of the studies mentioned demonstrated excess returns for the better managed plans relative to the policy benchmarks as well. Such mixed findings require analysis of manager performance versus the respective benchmarks to continue examining the impact of governance on investment returns.

Manager Selection Outcomes

Thankfully, an even larger body of work has been done on the impact of various governance structures on manager selection. And the results of these studies are nearly unanimous in showing that governance that empowers accountable, aligned, and properly incentivized investment professionals to select asset managers generates higher returns than does an organizational structure that has non-investment professionals tasked with such decisions.

In 2014, CEM Benchmarking, a foremost consultant providing third-party performance and cost benchmarking to large, global institutional investors, published a research report utilizing its proprietary database of US pension funds, both corporate and public.[12] This database incorporated over 900 US institutional investors covering the period 1998 to 2011. The research presented a number of interesting findings.

First, CEM found that large funds outperformed smaller ones because of a number of effects, not the least of which was the larger allocations to private equity that the bigger pensions had. This allocation difference could be due to increased sophistication around alternatives or simply to the larger scale of the bigger plans, likely some combination of both. CEM also found that corporate pensions outperformed publics by 67 basis points per year on average, in no small part because of a large allocation shift from equities to fixed income that corporate plans had made in aggregate prior to the Global Financial Crisis, an intentional asset allocation change driven by professional investment decision-making. The combined effects of superior strategic and tactical asset allocation allowed large corporate plans, the best-performing subcategory of all, to outperform the average plan in the report by 0.9% annually, 7.5% versus 6.6%.

Turning to the effects of manager selection specifically, the report compared individual asset class returns across 12 subcategories of asset classes by investor type. By comparing managers within an asset class, any excess return can only be attributed to selecting better managers. Tellingly, corporate plans outperformed public plans in every single asset class in which both groups reported returns.[13]

Even more significantly, the excess returns for corporate plans got even larger in asset classes that were generally more complex and less efficient. For example, corporate pensions beat their public brethren in US large-cap stocks, a fairly efficient market, by just 0.07% per annum, whereas these same plans outperformed by over 1% annually in private equity where, as we've seen, manager return dispersion is much wider. This is evidence of superior decision-making, from either better processes or more informed decision makers, on behalf of corporate pensions, where manager selection is driven almost exclusively by investment professionals. Disconnecting decision-making from expertise creates suboptimal results, and the effects become more pronounced the more complex and technical the decision.

This study, shown in Figure 10.3, provides a great example of true organizational alpha. The chances of such a pattern of excess returns being due to luck is quite small. However, the research painted with a fairly broad brush: corporates versus publics. It didn't carefully examine the effects of granular differences in governance structures, which, to be fair, could be relatively minute and difficult to detect in most asset classes.

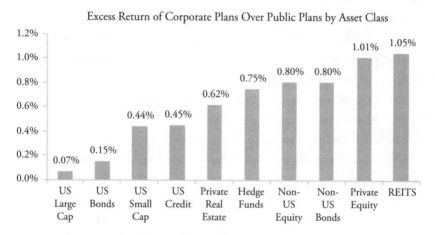

FIGURE 10.3 Organizational alpha from manager selection

However, by focusing on returns within private equity exclusively, where dispersion is the widest, later research funded by the Hoover Institution, a policy think tank at Stanford University, was able to isolate the effects of nuanced differences in the governance structures of public pensions on investment returns.[14]

Utilizing information from the audited financial statements of approximately 210 large US public pensions, the authors of this research grouped board members into three main categories: state, participant, and public. According to their classifications, state officials comprised ex officio state officers or elected state officials appointed to a pension board by virtue of their official title (hierarchical authority), such as state treasurers. This same group also included other government employees appointed to the board by the governor, mayor, or legislature, such as mid-level managers at cabinet departments or state agencies.

The participant group was made up of trustees that were members of the retirement plan, either active or retired, and could include, for example, teachers, police officers, and government workers. The final group, the public trustees, were defined as independent members of the general public who do not work for the government and who are either elected or appointed ostensibly due to their financial knowledge (expert authority). Not all plans had public appointed board members.

The authors found some significant effects when analyzing the returns of the private equity portfolios across pensions. First, public pension plans with a higher percentage of ex officio or state-appointed board trustees did notably worse in private equity, even when controlling for strategy and sector of underlying funds. Overall net IRRs declined by 0.9% with each additional 10% of the board appointed via political processes.

Additionally, such plans also typically exhibited adverse selection bias through suboptimal decision-making in private equity, picking managers for noneconomic reasons. For instance, these plans tended to use expensive funds of funds more frequently, which lowers net returns, or they invested far more with in-state managers, who subsequently underperformed. And plans where state-appointed board members had recently received campaign contributions from financial firms performed even worse.

The best-performing public pensions were those with finance professionals appointed to their boards from the general public, and this phenomenon held when looking at PE returns by either IRR or multiple of invested capital. The investment professional boards outperformed the state-appointee boards by 0.33x MOIC and by a whopping 8.55% in IRR terms.[15]

Other research has also confirmed that manager returns decline when made by less accountable and less qualified decision makers. The Rotman International Centre for Pension Management, a research institution affiliated with the University of Toronto that is globally recognized for leading-edge thought leadership in pension design and management, published research showing that pensions with a higher percentage of ex officio trustees and those with longer board terms both exhibited significantly lower excess individual manager returns.[16] Once again, disconnecting decision-making from accountability generates inferior outcomes.

A summary of the results of the majority of the research on investment governance structures (see Table 10.6) shows that the less internal experts are authorized to manage their respective areas of competence, the worse the investment outcome at all levels of decision-making.

TABLE 10.6 Summary of Governance Findings

Research	Policy Outcome	Asset Allocation Outcome	Manager Selection Outcome
Mitchell and Hsin (1994)	• Lower-funded status with more retired board members • Higher-funded status with in-house actuaries • Lower total returns with more retired board members • Lower total returns for mandated in state investments		
Milliman (2019)	• Public plans 20% less funded than corporates • Canadian public plans 25% better funded than US publics		
Amman and Ehmann (2016)	• Poorer governance led to lower funding ratios • Poorer governance led to lower total and risk-adjusted returns	• Poorer governance led to lower excess returns relative to benchmark • Tactical allocation negative for all plans	

(continued on next page)

Research	Policy Outcome	Asset Allocation Outcome	Manager Selection Outcome
Albrecht and Hingorani (2004)		• Lower returns when board selects asset allocation	
Albrecht et al. (2007)		• Lower returns when board selects asset allocation	
Beath (2014)	• Corporate plans generate higher total and risk adjusted returns • Larger plans outperform smaller plans	• Corporate plans have superior strategic and asset allocation returns	• Corporate plans outperform in every asset class
Harper (2008)	• Pensions with more elected trustees had a higher funding status	• Little to no asset allocation effects from differing board composition	• Lower manager returns for more ex officio trustees • Lower manager returns for longer board terms
Andonov et al. (2017)	• US pension performances lag those of other pensions globally		• US pension returns lowest in alternatives
Andonov et al. (2016)			• State-appointed trustee boards had lowest private equity returns • Public-appointed boards, generally financial professionals, had best private equity returns
Summary of effects	• Worse governance lowers funded status by 10 to 25% • Worse governance lowers returns by 0.25 to 1.5%	• Worse governance lowers returns by 0.25 to 2.0%	• Worse governance lowers returns by 0.15 to 3.0%

In an article titled "Information Production and Capital Allocation: Decentralized Versus Hierarchical Firms," economist Jeremy Stein may have put it best. Contrasting the nimble and effective lending decision-making of small banks versus those processes found in larger, more bureaucratic financial organizations, Stein argued that diseconomies of scale and inefficient decision-making emerge where "the authority to allocate capital is separated from expertise, which tends to dilute the incentives to become an expert."[17]

When an institution has poor governance, when there is a misalignment between technical competency and decision-making authority, the evidence shows that such investment institutions have poor outcomes. (See Figure 10.4.) And it's not merely empirical evidence from dry, academic research that shows these effects. There are numerous stories about disastrous decisions made by unqualified individuals in hierarchical positions of investment authority that demonstrate exactly how perverse incentives and adverse selection bias impact real-world investment outcomes.

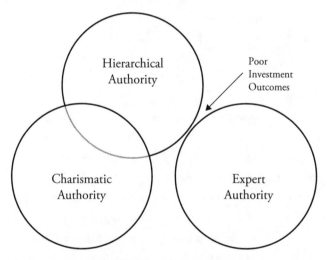

FIGURE 10.4   Poor governance

Fred Buenrostro, the former CEO of the California Public Employees Retirement System, was convicted of felony bribery for taking kickbacks from a placement agent, Alfred Villalobos, who himself had previously been on CalPERs board of trustees, for attempting to steer the pension into funds represented by Villalobos. While Buenrostro has since been sentenced to federal prison and is facing up to 30 years in prison, Villalobos committed suicide before his trial could begin. Sadly, this is not the only instance of pay-to-play in institutional investment organizations.

But even when not explicitly corrupt, perverse incentives and lack of technical competence too often combine for disastrous effects. For example, at the Dallas Fire and Police Pension, hundreds of millions of write-downs from poor real estate investments over the last several years have pushed the fund into a precarious financial position. The problem arose because these investments were directed by the fund's former chief administrator of nearly 20 years, Richard Tettamant, a man whose professional qualifications included running a Dairy Queen and whose idea of due diligence meant lavish vacations in the general vicinity of potential investments.

It's not just that professionals are more knowledgeable about investments, although that should be the case. In Chapter 8, we presented some examples around System 1 decision-making that was improved through experience. Research shows that nurses, who have to make assessments about an uncertain future based upon imperfect knowledge using both quantifiable and qualitative inputs, very similar to investment professionals, are able to improve the accuracy of their diagnoses over time through repeated trials and lots of immediate feedback. Although the feedback takes longer, manager research professionals who have seen 2,000 hedge funds should be more likely to select better ones than someone who has seen just 4 or 5.

But perhaps more importantly, they are far more likely to avoid the terrible ones! Experienced professionals also have the metacognitive ability (remember the Dunning-Kruger effect?) to understand the potential consequences of failure. They can more accurately assess and evaluate risks, particularly qualitative ones. Correspondingly, they are generally more accountable.

Fortunately, there are ways to mitigate such conflicts of interest and perverse incentives and better align the underlying components of governance toward a higher probability of better outcomes at each level of investment decision-making.

Pension governance expert Keith Ambachtsheer has spent more than three decades researching, evaluating, and consulting on governance issues for institutional investors. He founded both CEM Benchmarking and KPA

Advisory services, a governance consulting firm. Ambachtsheer is also the director emeritus at Rotman. In his career he has advised over 400 pensions on plan design, governance, benchmarking, and management issues. He's also authored four books on the subject and numerous articles. In short, he is the definitive (expert!) authority when it comes to effective institutional investment governance.

Over his career, Ambachtsheer has conducted decade-spanning research on the effectiveness of various governance and decision-making structures in public pension plans. And like the research cited above, he's also shown that better governance strongly correlates with objective measures of better long-term strategic investment decision-making. Among the most important governance recommendations made by Ambachtsheer and his colleague John McLaughlin are:

- Separating and ensuring clarity between board oversight and management responsibilities
- Creating a board skill/experience matrix to design roles and ensure a match with needs
- Creating a board evaluation protocol and establishing performance orientation throughout the firm
- Establishing formal board education and improvement requirements
- Addressing agency problems with outsourcing and compensation problems with insourcing[18]

In a nutshell, Ambachtsheer says it is important to critically evaluate what skill sets and experiences individual board members and staff bring, intentionally match roles and responsibilities with the relevant competencies (or harmonize hierarchical and expert authority) and clearly delineate between oversight and management, set up formal evaluation protocols for various responsibilities at all levels (such as the framework detailed in Tables 10.1 to 10.5), ensure ongoing training and education, and align interests through appropriate compensation structures based on these performance metrics.

Ben Carlson is an institutional investor, author of several widely read books on investing, and a blogger whose pithy posts at AWealthofCommonSense.com have helped institutional and individual investors alike make better investment decisions for years. In his 2017 book *Organizational Alpha,* Carlson endorses similar ideas, arguing that concepts such as collective effort, personal and professional respect, integrity, a focus on the client outcome, and a culture of accountability distinguish high-performing investment organizations from less effective ones.[19]

Let's take a look at a thought exercise where we can implement some of these concepts in a couple of theoretical scenarios using the decision matrix shown in Table 10.7. A matrix of skills and responsibilities for the entire organization would certainly include responsibility for oversight of budgetary, audit, and human resources functions, all critical components of managing an organization, but for the sake of discussing organizational alpha, we'll limit this analysis to investment responsibilities. An institutional investment organization can utilize a similar tool to engage in an honest, open internal dialogue around these roles and responsibilities. In some cases, marking an "X" in the relevant box on the matrix might be an easy exercise for the team; in other columns, it might reveal fundamental disagreements that must be resolved *before* beginning any actual investment activities.

First, picture a large public pension, say $35 billion, with a portfolio globally diversified across all asset classes, including alternatives. Let's assume this system has a seven-person volunteer board composed solely of participants in the pension fund. Additionally, the plan has an executive director that oversees administration, a chief investment officer that reports to the board, and a deep professional investment team of 30 dedicated individuals that work directly for the CIO.

The members of the volunteer board do not have investment experience, and cognizant of this, they should focus their efforts within the investment context to clearly defining the investment objective, creating organizational agreement around time horizons and risk thresholds, establishing the investment policy statement, setting up performance metrics and compensation structures for staff that incentivize desired behavior, and monitoring and reviewing performance relative to these metrics. They should be involved in the asset allocation discussion and at least should set permissible ranges for asset classes. They need to have an understanding of how the strategic allocation was selected even if they are not explicitly involved in approving the

TABLE 10.7 Example Investment Decision Matrix

Experience	Investment Objectives	Investment Policy	Strategic Asset Allocation	Manager Selection (by Individual Asset Class)	Portfolio Management	Execution	Performance Monitoring
Board	X						
Individual trustees							
Investment committee		X					X
Committee members							
Executive director							
Chief investment officer			X		X	X	
Investment officers				X			

251

decision. However, the board's most important responsibility is to monitor the performance of the asset allocation and CIO and decide if changes are needed.

The chief investment officer at such a system should have responsibility for implementing the strategic asset allocation, overseeing any tactical allocation or rebalancing strategy, setting all procedures for portfolio and risk management, and monitoring the performance of each asset class and asset class director. Manager selection in this context also becomes part of the day-to-day management responsibilities of the investment staff and can be overseen by the CIO or by a professional internal investment committee or even delegated to asset class directors as portfolio managers.

Now, let's imagine a fairly small nonprofit foundation, a charity with $50 million of endowed tax-exempt assets. This organization has no investment staff, just an executive director with some limited financial experience. However, this particular foundation has a 20-person board and a 6-member investment committee that is composed solely of volunteer investment professionals from the community. In this setting, the board might set objectives and policies, or it may defer such decisions to the expertise of the committee members.

The investment committee could then select a strategic allocation, perhaps a simple 65% equity and 35% bond portfolio, determine allowable ranges, establish management responsibilities, and select managers. However, with only an executive director to oversee the management functions, such as rebalancing, contracting with managers, funding investments, etc. it may not be feasible to retain those functions internally. Demonstrating the interaction between the governance structure and portfolio construction, if the investment committee and executive director believe they should retain manager selection discretion, then a simpler, more concentrated balanced portfolio of fewer managers is prudent versus a more complex and broadly diversified one.

On the other hand, good governance for a more diversified or alternatives-heavy portfolio at the same institution would require outsourcing at least some of the investment responsibilities to a third-party provider, such as a fund of funds or outsourced chief investment officer (OCIO), with competencies selecting hedge funds or private equity managers. This entity could implement the portfolio within the stated guidelines determined by the investment committee by selecting managers and tactical ranges; a slightly different arrangement might even include delegation of the strategic asset allocation range to the OCIO vendor. Regardless, the most critical element of the responsibility of the investment committee above in either case would certainly be performance monitoring and oversight of the portfolio. Selecting lots of managers across lots of asset classes, including complex ones, should not be a part-time job.

While there are certainly areas open to debate regarding who should own what decision in all the examples above, a frank conversation around governance using this framework can best address those disagreements by bringing objectivity to the discussion. Remember that the primary objective of good governance should be aligning roles and responsibilities with skill sets and abilities, measuring performance, and ensuring accountability across the organization, as outlined in Figure 10.5.

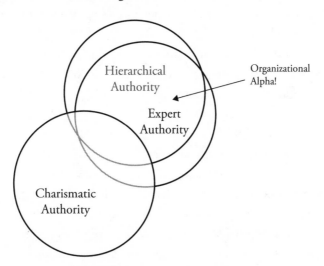

FIGURE 10.5   Good governance

In my experience, the biggest objections to this approach for determining appropriate organizational investment governance center on the concept of fiduciary duty, and they are interrelated. First, boards contend that they are the ultimate investment fiduciary, and rightfully so; but they often argue that as such, they cannot prudently delegate authority. However, it is precisely a fiduciary responsibility, when properly understood, that is the strongest argument for delegation in many cases.

Second, fiduciaries are held to a process standard as opposed to an outcome standard. That is to say, they can't be held accountable if outcomes did not achieve the desired objective when a prudent process was followed. Once again, this is an argument for precisely why the process must be designed initially with an outcome orientation in mind. A process devoid of any considerations for outcome is hardly a prudent one by any standard. And as we've seen, the evidence about the efficacy of process design is unequivocal.

For any individual in a position of investment authority (agent) over the assets of others (principals), a fiduciary duty of care quite simply means making financial decisions in the best interest of the beneficiaries as opposed to your own. What you want to do doesn't matter. What makes you comfortable doesn't matter. What you find interesting doesn't matter. Every decision made must be driven by a rational, evidence-based process focused on what's best for the beneficiaries.

The CFA Society has helpfully laid out five principles for meeting a fiduciary standard of care in its Code of Conduct for Members of a Pension Scheme Governing Body.[20] These are:

1. Act in good faith in the best interest of the plan.
2. Act with prudence and reasonable care.
3. Act with skill, competence, and diligence.
4. Maintain independence, objectivity, and adherence to all relevant laws and statutes.
5. Review on a regular basis the effectiveness of the plan's success in meeting its objectives, and the relevant processes and people in place.

This list closely aligns with Ambachtsheer's principles for good governance. It's also important to note that while prudence and reasonable care may be legal standards, skill, competence, and diligence are all professional ones. When designing the process initially, fiduciaries must consider potential outcomes and select the process that objectively provides the highest probability of achieving the best outcome for their beneficiaries.

Now, investment outcomes cannot be known with certainty, or even with much precision around the degree of uncertainty. But as we've seen, they are also not entirely unknowable either. Let's consider one last short thought exercise. Imagine a hypothetical scenario where process A has a 50% likelihood of meeting the required objective, but it is easy and fun. On the other hand, process B is more complex or requires more work, but it has a 75% probability of success. Assuming these are facts and not opinions, a prudent fiduciary should probably select option B as the one to implement, even if it makes the fiduciary uncomfortable. As all the research has shown, governance structures that push decisions to the most qualified individuals generate excess returns relative to ones that do not.

Finally, as the CFA society states with its fifth principle, governance should never be static. Just as manager due diligence continues with quarterly monitoring, and asset allocation remains ongoing through a periodic rebalancing process, governance must be continually assessed and reassessed objectively over time. If outcomes are consistently failing to meet objectives, governance may need to be changed. And importantly, if the mission of the organization, nature of the portfolio, or composition of the board or staff has changed dramatically, governance probably should, too. Otherwise, the overwhelming bureaucratic inertia of traditional, hierarchical authority pushes out expert authority, as graphically demonstrated in our Venn diagram in Figure 10.4.

Legacy governance structures implemented in an environment where many pensions were prohibited by law from investing in risky assets are not the appropriate governance framework for all portfolios. With the broad abolition of restricted lists and the widespread move to alternatives-laden portfolios, a wholesale redesign of governance is required that should be informed by industry best practices. Alternatively (pun intended), keeping the legacy governance structure may make sense if the investor is not interested in moving into hedge funds or private equity, which is entirely defensible. If you are not going to do alternatives right, you certainly should not try to do them at all.

Notwithstanding, governance does not exist in a vacuum. What objectives, constraints, resources, staffing, and risk tolerances an institution has all meaningfully impact what appropriate governance should look like. In order to drive the best possible outcomes, governance needs to be thoughtfully designed taking all these factors into consideration and in open conversation with the most experienced investors at the institution.

In the end, governance is quite simply deciding who decides. And the answer should be clear: whoever is most qualified. In a successful investment organization, the best ideas need to win. If you can't get experts into hierarchical positions, push the actual authority to the relevant experts, internally or externally, and make sure they're doing their job. By doing this, institutions can increase the chances of meeting their total policy and investment objectives relative to more hierarchical, bureaucratic structures. Inefficiency has a real cost, and eliminating it is where organizational alpha can be easily harvested.

Notes

1. Weber (1958).
2. Weber (1965).
3. Mitchell and Hsin (1994), aptly titled "Public Pension Governance and Performance."
4. Funded status is technically a net asset or net liability, but it is generally reported as a ratio in order to compare across pensions of different sizes. The ratio is very easy to calculate. For a plan with a net asset value of $150 million and present value of future pension obligations of $200 million, 150 divided by 200, or 75%, is called the funded ratio. Obviously, the higher the better.
5. Comtois (2019).
6. The discount rate is the interest rate at which future liabilities or payment obligations are discounted. It represents the plan's time value of money. Dividing the future value (FV) of the liability by (1 + interest rate r) compounded over the relevant time period n yields the discounted present value (DPV), as is shown in the formula below. The lower the interest rate, the higher the present value.

$$DPV = \frac{FV}{(1 + r)^n}$$

7. Baert (2018).
8. Andonov et al. (2017).
9. Albrecht et al. (2007).

10. Albrecht and Hingorani (2004).
11. Ammann and Ehmann (2016).
12. Beath (2014).
13. Two categories were omitted from my analysis, as they did not appear in both the public and corporate plans, only in one or the other of them. Corporate plans reported large allocations to long bonds, but public pensions had none due to corporate pension accounting and interest rate hedging. Conversely, private real assets had significant exposure in public pension systems' portfolios, but corporate plans had none, likely because of differences in the cost of capital for illiquidity.
14. Andonov et al. (2016).
15. IRR and MOIC return numbers are controlled for a number of factors, such as fund type and vintage year.
16. Harper (2008).
17. Stein (2002).
18. Ambachtsheer and McLaughlin (2015).
19. Carlson (2017).
20. Schacht and Stokes (2008).

11
The Future of Alpha

Life can only be understood backwards,
but it must be lived forwards.
—SØREN KIERKEGAARD

Perhaps the final truth about alpha is that it is a bit of a paradox. The search for alpha has been the story of the investment industry for the last century, but it has been a fruitless effort for most. We do have strong evidence that alpha may have been available across numerous asset classes for long periods of time, but it is becoming increasingly difficult to find today. Yet still it consumes the greater portion of most investors' activities, even in the benchmark-constrained world of public markets.

Public Markets Alpha

The efficient markets theorists uncovered a piece of this alpha puzzle when academics showed that certain factor tilts in public equities were predictive of excess returns. They showed that what we thought was "true alpha" was probably a mirage. First, it was value, then small capitalization, and then momentum, growth, yield, merger arbitrage, and convertible arbitrage, but time after time after time, history has taught us that these strategies were nothing more than systematic exposures to underlying factors.

These investment approaches were simply a means of accessing the underlying drivers of returns—the fundamental building blocks of return streams—in different percentages and ratios. And once these strategies became broadly known, imitated, and overcapitalized, any excess return that may have been there at one point was arbitraged away. That excess return may have looked like alpha for a while—it may have been called superior security selection—but the aggregate evidence across time and markets, from academics and practitioners alike, suggests that it was never really alpha to begin with. In hindsight, if it was systematic, durable, and repeatable, it was because of factors. If it was temporary and fleeting, it was probably luck.

Today, in public markets, I do not believe the effort of manager selection is worth it. Not only that; it's counterproductive. Pick your index, or pick your factor exposures, and get them as cheaply as you can. If some active manager comes to you with a simple, rules-based approach that looks like alpha, keep your hand firmly on your wallet.

Private Markets Alpha

With the decay of alpha occurring in liquid markets, private markets may not be too far behind. Now that's not to say that excess return potential does not exist at all. Private markets, although increasingly competitive, do still offer both dispersion and persistence of return. And the wider the dispersion of returns and the longer those returns persist, the greater the excess return potential there is for picking better managers. It's at the intersection of these two axes that alpha can still be found.

Private markets are an area where innovation is still rewarded. Unlike in public markets, where most, if not all, of Mr. Market's hidden secrets have already been uncovered, significant information asymmetry can often be found in private markets, and this can lead to that alpha edge. However, this requires a willingness to look where others are not willing to go, to accept illiquidity, and to work with smaller, newer, and nimbler managers.

As investment author and director of the CFA Research Institute Larry Siegel once said, if a manager is teaching you something new, you at least have a chance of earning excess returns.

In addition, investments in private markets regularly include the option to manufacture additional alpha alongside the returns embedded at acquisition. Directly owning the asset, whether it is financial, like a stock, or physical, like property, allows the investor to make changes that can create higher returns. Hiring more sales professionals to grow revenue faster, retrofitting an old office building to attract new economy inhabitants, or even mining cryptocurrencies—all these actions are value-accretive strategies that cannot accrue to the diffuse passive holders of public securities. You can build factors in private markets.

However, such strategies by their very nature will be difficult to benchmark. Heterogeneous assets, particularly those with small investable opportunity sets, don't particularly lend themselves well to a benchmark comparison.

A New Alpha?

This all necessitates a new approach to thinking about excess return, and frankly, that's a good thing. The amount of time and effort spent on the incessant search for alpha relative to benchmarks has yielded very little in return, pun intended.

There is of course a role that benchmarks must play in large, liquid markets; they help us evaluate returns after the fact. Alpha is only knowable with certainty in the rearview mirror, which means benchmarks help determine whether or not we got what we paid for. If we paid for alpha, but all we got was beta—or worse, less than beta—well, we were overcharged.

As a forward-looking tool, this version of alpha has failed the vast majority of investors. In the end, beating a benchmark is an entirely pointless exercise. Really, who cares?

Similarly, within private markets, a better approach to assessing excess returns is to use a straightforward cost of capital approach. By assessing the drivers of return, investors can establish a nominal return threshold required in order to make the allocation. You certainly won't get them all right, but by focusing on giving yourself a margin of safety to this required rate of return, investors will have a higher probability of excess returns.

You see, investors don't "eat" alpha; they "eat" total return. That is, retirement checks don't get paid solely from alpha, nor are university operating budgets funded by alpha alone. Investors don't get a gold star for higher Sharpe ratios or extra credit for having alpha versus their benchmark. Total net returns are what matter, and they can only exceed, meet, or fall below our required return. There is no other end state. If you generated classic alpha but failed to hit your return target, you failed, even if you beat your benchmark. Period.

However, those investors that met their investment objectives by taking a little more leverage or volatility or illiquidity to get there—even if it wasn't classical alpha per se—were successful. That's all that matters!

Once we accept this view of success, the amorphous concept of investment risk becomes much easier to understand. Failure is the opposite of success; it's not meeting the return objective. And since risk is the proxy for failure, true investment risk is 100% minus the probability of success. It's certainly more intuitive to debate the risks of an investment portfolio with a 75% chance of meeting your objectives versus one with a 50% chance than it is to compare asset allocations with 11% volatility versus 9%.

Clearly, investors should thus focus on activities that explicitly increase the ex ante odds of meeting our objectives. We can't simply rely on our gut to know how to do this either, because intuitive, heuristic thinking often leads us astray. We overvalue information that confirms our current views and undervalue that which challenges preexisting beliefs. We predictably overreact to prominent but low-probability events and underreact to more important—but less noticeable—occurrences. We typically underestimate risks and overestimate returns.

It's because of this negative alpha that most institutional investors fail to achieve their required rate of return. By incorporating rational, empirical research into every step of the investment process through behavioral alpha, process alpha, and organizational alpha, investors can tilt the odds in their favor.

Instead of doing what everyone else is doing, investors should start with focusing on a deeper understanding of their specific investment objectives, cash flow needs, and time horizons. The concept of risk has different real-world implications for different institutions. For some asset owners, such as large endowments where spending represents but a small percentage of their respective university's operating budget, perhaps modest underperformance is no big deal. On the other hand, for an underfunded pension system with a high spending rate, incapable of increasing contributions, investments have to pull every lever possible in order to do their part. If you need to make 7%, and you only generate 6% instead, that is a far worse outcome than targeting an asset mix that actually returns 8%. The latter is a margin of safety.

By managing our decision-making with rational rules-based processes, as opposed to searching for superior trading rules and putting the right people in the right positions to make the right decisions, we can improve portfolio outcomes. In fact, some of the best institutions already are.

Alpha in Practice

For example, the State of Wisconsin Investment Board (SWIB) is one institutional investor that has successfully implemented many of these strategies. First, the investment board is itself a separate agency, independent from the administration of the overall retirement system, tasked with only the investment management of the assets. This allows best investment practices to dictate governance and processes. As a result, there are clear separations of duty between the board, who sets policy and provides oversight, and the investment staff, who executes and implements. A highly experienced chief investment officer leads the organization, serving as chair of the investment committee. Reporting to the CIO is a well-resourced team of 203 investment professionals who manage over $100 billion in assets.[1]

The CIO and staff have been delegated responsibility for asset class implementation and execution, managing approximately 57% of the assets in-house for public securities, far cheaper than using expensive external managers in a vain search for old-fashioned alpha. And for asset classes where external managers are still required, like private equity, staff applies disciplined and robust processes to select and terminate these investment firms as necessary, based solely on the expected contribution to excess returns. Further aligning incentives, the investment team is compensated on the plan's five-year investment performance, which also serves as a retention tool.

As a result, SWIB has outperformed both its policy benchmark and its required rate of return over long periods of time. SWIB's policy benchmark has returned 8.2% over the 10 years ended 2018,[2] and this exceeds the assumed actuarial rate of return of 7.2%, about 100 basis points of alpha from intelligent policy setting. However, the portfolio itself achieved 8.8% over that same time, another 60 basis points of alpha on top of the policy from solid investment processes and decision-making.

And most importantly, all these behavioral, process, and organizational alphas add up to a funded ratio of around 102%, the best in the country! SWIB is in a better position to meet its obligations—to make beneficiary payments—than most other public pensions because every decision it has made has tilted the odds in its favor.

Better Than Alpha

By improving all the little decisions along the way where costs leak out, biases creep in, and underperformance results, other investors can accomplish the same thing. In the old benchmark-linked, security selection paradigm, alpha was a zero-sum game. For every investor who found alpha, there had to be someone who gave it up.

In the new paradigm of alpha, meaning improving the odds of investment success, there is not a fixed pool of collective odds, where market participants must take from the probability distribution of others to improve their own outcomes.

Excess returns can still be found relative to our required returns, but those excess returns must come from predictable drivers of income and capital appreciation. But in truth, that's all it's ever been. There probably never was any investor with the Midas touch, any true superior ability to select securities absent other factor tilts. It's always been about intelligently accessing factors in various quantities to hit return targets. Outperforming your underwriting should be the goal of the exercise. That's a margin of safety; that's alpha.

The truth is that the final chapter of alpha has certainly yet to be written. The research around precisely how to best meet our investment objectives will undoubtedly change going forward, but that's what makes investing such an intellectually stimulating endeavor. Keeping a completely open mind, implementing a scientific approach that couples fundamental theories with empirical research, all the while acknowledging investing is a probabilistic, not deterministic, activity will allow us to make better decisions in the future.

Learning requires that we remain open to change, and change brings the potential for mistakes. But the reality is, no one bats a thousand in investing. Perfect is not attainable, but better always is. Now more than ever, institutional investors must be willing to embrace change and be open to mistakes, as long as they are not fatal ones. Small mistakes are the best source of learning. In fact, I can't wait to find out what works next, and unlearn that which no longer does! Perhaps that's real alpha.

Come to think of it, maybe that's not alpha at all, but it's better than alpha.

Notes

1. According to information available in the most recent (as of this writing) audited financial report (State of Wisconsin Investment Board, 2018), p. 5.
2. Ibid., p. 4.

References and Suggested Reading

Agarwal, Vikas, Naveen D. Daniel, and Narayan Y. Naik, "Role of Managerial Incentives and Discretion in Hedge Fund Performance," The Journal of Finance, Vol. 64, No. 5, pp. 2221-2256, October 2009.

Aggarwal, Rajesh K., and Philippe Jorion, "The Performance of Emerging Hedge Fund Managers," *Journal of Financial Economics*, Vol. 96, No. 2, pp. 238–256, 2010.

Aigner, Philipp, Stefan Albrecht, Georg Beyschlag, Tim Friederich, Markus Kalepky, and Rudi Zagst, "What Drives PE? Analyses of Success Factors for Private Equity Funds," *Journal of Private Equity*, Vol. 11, No. 4, Fall 2008.

Aiken, Adam L., Christopher P. Clifford, and Jesse Ellis, "Out of the Dark: Hedge Fund Reporting Biases and Commercial Databases," *Review of Financial Studies*, Vol. 26, No. 1, pp. 208–243, January 2013.

Albrecht, William G., and Vineeta Lokhande Hingorani, "Effects of Governance Practices and Investment Strategies on State and Local Government Pension Fund Financial Performance," *International Journal of Public Administration*, Vol. 27, No. 8-9, pp. 673–700, 2004.

Albrecht, William G., Hannarong Shamsub, and Nicholas A. Giannatasio, "Public Pension Governance Practices and Financial Performance," *Journal of Public Budgeting, Accounting & Financial Management*, Vol. 19, No. 2, pp. 245–267, Summer 2007.

Ambachtsheer, Keith, and John McLaughlin, "How Effective Is Pension Fund Governance Today? And Do Pensions Invest for the Long-Term?," KPA Advisory Services White Paper, January 2015.

Amenc, Noel, Felix Goltz, Ashish Lodh, and Lionel Martinelli, "Towards Smart Equity Factor Indices: Harvesting Risk Premia Without Taking Unrewarded Risks," *Journal of Portfolio Management,* Vol. 40, No. 4, Summer 2014.

Ammann, Manuel, and Christian Ehmann, "Is Governance Related to Investment Performance and Asset Allocation? Empirical Evidence from Swiss Pension Funds," Swiss Institute of Banking and Finance, Working Paper on Finance No. 2016/23, September 2016.

Ammann, Manuel, Otto Huber, and Markus Schmid, "Hedge Fund Characteristics and Performance Persistence," *European Financial Management,* Vol. 19, No. 2, pp. 209–250, March 2013.

Andonov, Aleksander, Rob M. M. J. Bauer, and K. J. Martijn Cremers, "Pension Fund Asset Allocation and Liability Discount Rates," *Review of Financial Studies,* Vol. 30, No. 8, pp. 2555–2595, August 2017.

Andonov, Aleksander, Yael V. Hochberg, and Joshua D. Rauh, "Pension Fund Board Composition and Investment Performance: Evidence from Private Equity," Hoover Institution Economics Working Paper, No. 16104, draft, March 2016.

Ang, Andrew, Robert J. Hodrick, Yuhang Xing, and Xiaoyang Zhang, "High Idiosyncratic Volatility and Low Returns: International and Further U.S. Evidence," *Journal of Financial Economics,* Vol. 91, No. 1, pp. 1–23, January 2009.

Anson, Mark, "Performance Measurement in Private Equity: Another Look," *Journal of Private Equity,* Vol. 10, No. 3, pp. 7–22, January 2007.

Antweiler, Werner, and Murray Z. Frank, "Internet Stock Message Boards and Stock Returns," Working Paper, draft, November 7, 2002.

Applebaum, Eileen, and Rosemary Batt, "Are Lower Private Equity Returns the New Normal?," Center for Economic Policy and Research, White Paper, June 2016.

Aral, Sinan, Erik Brynjolfsson, and Marshall Van Alstyne, "Information, Technology, and Information Worker Productivity," *Information Systems Research,* Vol. 23, No. 3, pp. 849–1085, September 2012.

Aubry, Jean-Pierre, Anqi Chen, Alicia H. Munnell, and Kevin Wandre, "What Explains Differences in Public Pensions Returns Since 2001?," Center for Retirement Research at Boston College, Working Paper No. 60, July 2018.

Baert, R., "Canadian Pension Funds Reach Median Full Funding to End Quarter—2 Reports," *Pensions & Investments,* October 2, 2018, https:/www.pionline.com/article/20181002/ONLINE/181009939/canadian-pension-funds-reach-median-full-funding-to-end-quarter-2-reports.

Baltussen, Guido, Laurens Swinkels, and Pim Van Vliet, "Global Factor Premiums," SSRN White Paper, No. 3325720, January 2019.

Banz, Rolf W, "The Relationship Between Return and Market Value of Common Stocks," *Journal of Financial Economics,* Vol. 9, No. 1, pp. 3–18, March 1981.

Barber, Brad, and Terrance Odean, "Boys Will Be Boys: Gender, Overconfidence and Common Stock Investment, *Quarterly Journal of Economics,* Vol. 116, No. 1, pp. 261–292, February 2001.

Barber, Brad, and Terrance Odean, "All That Glitters: The Effect of Attention and News on the Buying Behavior of Individual and Institutional Investors," *Review of Financial Studies,* Vol. 21, No. 2, pp. 785–818, 2008.

Bates, Timothy, William D. Bradford, and Robert Seamans, "Minority Entrepreneurship in Twenty-First Century America," *Small Business Economics*, Vol. 50, No. 3, pp. 415–427, March 2018.

Baumeister, Roy F., Kathleen D. Vohs, and Dianne M. Tice, "The Strength Model of Self-Control," *Current Directions in Psychological Science,* Vol. 16, No. 6, pp. 351–355, 2007.

Beath, Alexander D., "Asset Allocation and Fund Performance of Defined Benefit Pension Funds in the United States Between 1998–2011," CEM Benchmarking, White Paper, 2014.

Bechara, Antione, Hanna Damasio, Daniel Tranel, and Antonio R. Damasio, "Deciding Advantageously Before Knowing the Advantageous Strategy," *Science,* Vol. 275, No. 5304, pp. 1293–1295, February 28, 1997.

Becker, Stan, and Greg Vaughan, "Small Is Beautiful," *Journal of Portfolio Management,* Vol. 27, No. 4, pp. 9–18, 2001.

Betzer, Andre, Peter Limbach, P. Raghavendra Rau, and Henrik Schürmann, "Till Death (or Divorce) Do Us Part: Early-Life Family Disruption and Fund Manager Behavior," White Paper, draft, April 2019.

Bhardwaj, Anurag, Ermanno Dal Pont, Anthony Maniscalco, and Davis Walmsley, "Built to Last: Sustaining and Transitioning Franchise Value at Hedge Funds," Barclays Capital Prime Services, White Paper, October 2012.

Bogle, John C., *Stay the Course,* Hoboken, NJ, Wiley, 2019.

Boyson, Nicole, "Hedge Fund Performance Persistence: A New Approach," *Financial Analysts Journal,* Vol. 64, No.6, pp. 27–44, 2008.

Brainard, Keith, and Alex Brown, "Public Pension Plan Investment Return Assumptions," *NASRA Issue Brief,* February 2020.

Braun, Reiner, Nils Dorau, Tim Jenkinson, and Daniel Urban, "Whom to Follow: Individual Manager Performance and Persistence in Private Equity Investments," Working Paper, October 29, 2019.

Brooks, Jordan, and Tobias J. Moskowitz, "Yield Curve Premia," SSRN White Paper, No. 2956411, July 1, 2017.

Brown, Gregory W., Oleg Gredil, and Preetesh Kantak, "Finding Fortune: How Do Institutional Investors Pick Asset Managers?" SSRN White Paper, No. 2797874, draft, March 15, 2016.

Brown, Gregory W., and Steven Kaplan, "Have Private Equity Returns Really Declined?," *Frank Hawkins Kenan Institute of Private Enterprise Report*, April 2019.

Brown, Stephen, Yan Lu, Sugata Ray, and Melvyn Teo, "Sensation Seeking and Hedge Funds," *Journal of Finance*, Vol. 73, No. 6, pp. 2871–2914, December 2018.

Brown, Stephen J., Thomas L. Fraser, and Bing Liang, "Hedge Fund Due Diligence: A Source of Alpha in a Hedge Fund Portfolio Strategy," NYU Working Paper, No. FIN-07-032, November 13, 2008.

Bryan, Alex, and James Li, "Performance Persistence Among U.S. Mutual Funds," *Morningstar Manager Research*, White Paper, January 2016.

Burrough, Bryan, and John Helyar, *Barbarians at the Gate: The Fall of RJR Nabisco*, New York, HarperCollins, 1990.

Carhart, Mark M., "On Persistence in Mutual Fund Performance," *Journal of Finance*, Vol. 52, No. 1, pp. 57–82, March 1997.

Carlson, Ben, *Organizational Alpha: How to Add Value in Institutional Asset Management*, Amazon Digital Services LLC, 2017.

Carmon, Ziv, and Dan Ariely, "Focusing on the Forgone: How Value Can Appear So Different to Buyers and Sellers," *Journal of Consumer Research*, Vol. 27, No. 3, pp. 360–370, December 2000.

Cattell, Raymond B., "Theory of Fluid and Crystallized Intelligence: A Critical Experiment," *Journal of Educational Psychology*, Vol. 54, No. 1, pp. 1–22, 1963.

Cavagnaro, Daniel R., Berk A. Sensoy, Yingdi Wang, and Michael S. Weisbach, "Measuring Institutional Investors' Skill from Their Investments in Private Equity," *Journal of Finance*, Vol. 74, No. 2, May 6, 2019.

Chapman, Scott A, *Empower Your Investing: Adopting Best Practices from John Templeton, Peter Lynch, and Warren Buffett.* New York, Post Hill Press, 2019.

Chaudhuri, Ranadeb, Zoran Ivkovic, Joshua Pollet, and Charles Trzcinka, "What a Difference a Ph.D. Makes: More Than Three Little Letters," SSRN White Paper, No. 2344938, October 15, 2013.

Chen, James, "Alpha," reviewed by Peter Westfall , Investopedia, February 3, 2020, https://www.investopedia.com/terms/a/alpha.asp.

Chen, Joseph, Harrison Hong, Ming Huang, and Jeffrey D. Kubik, "Does Fund Size Erode Mutual Fund Performance? The Role of Liquidity and Organization," *American Economic Review*, Vol. 94, No. 5, pp. 1, 276–302, 2004.

Chhabra, Ashvin, "Beyond Markowitz: A Comprehensive Wealth Allocation Framework for Individual Investors," *Journal of Wealth Management*, Vol. 7, No. 4, pp. 8–34, 2005.

Chooi, Weng-Tink, and Lee A. Thompson, "Working Memory Training Does Not Improve Intelligence in Healthy Young Adults," *Intelligence,* Vol. 40, No. 6, pp. 531–542, 2012.

Chuprinin, Oleg, and Denis Sosyura, "Family Descent as a Signal of Managerial Quality: Evidence from Mutual Funds," *Review of Financial Studies,* Vol. 31, No. 10, pp. 3756–3820, October 2018.

Cimpian, Andrei, and Erika Salomon, "The Inherence Heuristic: An Intuitive Means of Making Sense of the World, and a Potential Precursor to Psychological Essentialism," *Behavioral and Brain Sciences,* Vol. 37, No. 5, pp. 461–480, May 15, 2014.

Comtois, James, "U.S. Public Pension Plans See Funded Status Rise in First Quarter—Milliman," *Pensions & Investments,* May 28, 2019.

Connolly, Rebecca, Matt HoganBruen, Derek Jones, David Weissman, Charles Willis, and Patricia Miller Zollar, "The Financial Returns of NAIC Firms: Minority and Diverse Private Equity Managers and Funds Focused on the U.S. Emerging Domestic Market," *NAIC: Recognizing the Results,* White Paper, September 2012.

Coval, Joshua D., and Tobias J. Moskowitz, "Home Bias at Home: Local Equity Preference in Domestic Portfolios," *Journal of Finance,* Vol. 54, No. 6, December 1999.

Cumming, Chris, "Pennsylvania Pensions Asked to Switch to Index Investing, Cut Illiquid Funds," *Wall Street Journal,* December 20, 2018.

Cumming, Douglas, and Simona Zambelli, "Due Diligence and Investee Performance," *European Financial Management,* Vol. 23, No. 2, pp. 211–253, October 5, 2016.

Cunha, Flavio, James J. Heckman, Lance Lochner, and Dimitriy V. Masterov, "Interpreting the Evidence on Life Cycle Skill Formation," *Handbook of Economics Education,* Vol. 1, Chap 12, pp. 697–812, 2006.

Damodaran, Aswath, *Investment Valuation,* New York, John Wiley & Sons, 2002.

Danziger, Shai, Jonathan Levav, and Liora Avnaim-Pesso, "Extraneous Factors in Judicial Decisions," *Proceedings of the National Academy of Sciences of the United States of America,* Vol. 108, No. 17, pp. 6889–6892, April 26, 2011.

Detzel, F. Larry, and Robert A. Weingard, "Explaining Persistence in Mutual Fund Performance," *Financial Services Review,* Vol. 7, No. 1, pp. 45–55, 1998.

Dewey, Richard, and Aaron Brown, "Bill Gross' Alpha: The King Versus the Oracle," SSRN White Paper, No. 3345604, March 2, 2019.

Ding, Bill, Hany A. Shawky, and Jianbo Tian, "Liquidity Shocks, Size and the Relative Performance of Hedge Fund Strategies," *Journal of Banking & Finance,* Vol. 33, No. 5, pp. 883–891, May 2009.

Ellis, Charles D., *Capital: The Story of Long-Term Investment Excellence*, Hoboken, NJ, Wiley, 2011.

Engert, Herb, Michael Lee, and Jeffrey Hecht, "Operational Excellence: One Path or Many?," *Ernst & Young, Global Private Equity Survey,* 2018.

Erb, Claude B., and Campbell R. Harvey, "The Tactical and Strategical Value of Commodity Futures," SSRN White Paper, No. 650923, January 12, 2006.

Evans, Rachel, "There Were 438,000 New Indexes Created over the Last Year," *Bloomberg Markets,* November 14, 2018.

Ewens, Michael, and Matthew Rhodes-Kropf, "Is a VC Partnership Greater Than the Sum of Its Partners?," Harvard Business School, Working Paper 12-097, June 21, 2013.

Fama, Eugene F., "Random Walks in Stock Market Prices," *Financial Analysts Journal,* Vol. 21, No. 5, pp. 55–59, September–October 1965.

Fama, Eugene F., and Kenneth R. French, "The Cross-Section of Expected Stock Returns," *Journal of Finance,* Vol. 47, No. 1, pp. 427–465, June 1992.

Fama, Eugene F., and Kenneth R. French, "Common Risk Factors in the Returns on Stocks and Bonds," *Journal of Financial Economics,* Vol. 33, No. 1, pp. 3–56, February 1993.

Fama, Eugene F., and Kenneth R. French, "Multifactor Explanations of Asset Pricing Anomalies," *Journal of Finance,* Vol. 51, No. 1, pp. 55–84, March 1996.

Fama, Eugene F., and Kenneth R. French, "Luck Versus Skill in the Cross-Section of Mutual Fund Returns," *Journal of Finance*, Vol. 65, No. 5, pp. 1915–1947, October 2010.

Feffer, Stuart, and Christopher Kundro, "Understanding and Mitigating Operational Risk in Hedge Fund Investments," Capco White Paper, March 2003.

Fitzpatrick, Dan, "CalPERs to Exit Hedge Funds," *Wall Street Journal,* September 15, 2014.

Fox, Justin, "The Best Investors You've Never Heard of—Here's How Barclays Global Beats the Market—and Why You Can't," *Fortune* magazine, Vol. 161, No. 24, June 16, 2003.

Fung, William, and David A. Hsieh, "Measurement Biases in Hedge Fund Performance Data: An Update," *Financial Analysts Journal,* Vol. 65, No. 3, pp. 36–38, May/June 2009.

Fung, William, David A. Hsieh, Narayan Y. Naik, and Tarun Ramadorai, "Hedge Funds: Performance, Risk, and Capital Formation," *Journal of Finance,* Vol. 63, No. 4, pp. 1777–1803, 2008.

Gerhart, Barry, Sara L. Rynes, and Ingrid Smithey Fulmer, "Pay and Performance: Individuals, Groups, and Executives," *Academy of Management Annals,* Vol. 3, No. 1, pp. 251–315, 2009.

Gervais, Simon, J. B. Heaton, and Terrance Odean, "The Positive Role of Overconfidence and Optimism in Investment Policy," Working Paper, draft, September 2002.

Gompers, Paul, Steven N. Kaplan, and Vladimir Mukharlyamov, "What Do Private Equity Firms Say They Do?," Harvard Business School, Working Paper 15-081, April 2015.

Gompers, Paul, Anna Kovner, Josh Lerner, and David Scharfstein, "Performance Persistence in Entrepreneurship," *Journal of Financial Economics,* Vol. 96, No. 1, pp. 18–32, 2010.

Gorton, Gary, and K. Geert Rouwenhorst, "Facts and Fantasies About Commodity Futures," NBER Working Paper, No. 10595, March 2006.

Goyal, Amit, and Sunil Wahal, "The Selection and Termination of Investment Management Firms by Plan Sponsors," *Journal of Finance,* Vol. 63, No. 4, pp 1805–1847, August 2008.

Graham, Benjamin, *The Intelligent Investor,* New York, Harper, 1973.

Gredil, Oleg, Barry E. Griffiths, and Rüdiger Stucke, "Benchmarking Private Equity: The Direct Alpha Method," SSRN White Paper, No. 2403521, February 28, 2014.

Greer, Robert J., "Conservative Commodities," *Journal of Portfolio Management,* Vol. 4, No. 4, pp. 26–29, Summer 1978.

Greer, Robert J., Nic Johnson, and Mihir P. Worah, *Intelligent Commodity Indexing: A Practical Guide to Investing in Commodities,* New York, McGraw-Hill, 2013.

Gross, William H., "Consistent Alpha Generation Through Structure," *Financial Analysts Journal*, Vol. 61, No. 5, pp. 40–43, October 2005.

Halek, Martin, and Joseph G. Eisenhauer, "Demography of Risk Aversion," *Journal of Risk and Insurance*, Vol. 68, No. 1, pp. 1–24, March 2001.

Harper, Joel T., "Board of Trustee Composition and Investment Performance of US Public Pension Plans," Rotman International Centre for Pension Management, Working Paper, draft, February 2008.

Harris, Robert S., Tim Jenkinson, Steven N. Kaplan, and Rüdiger Stucke, "Has Persistence Persisted in Private Equity? Evidence from Buyout and Venture Capital Funds," Darden Business School Working Paper, No. 2304808, draft, August 30, 2014.

Harrison, Andre, James Summers, and Brian Mennecke, "The Effects of the Dark Triad on Unethical Behavior," *Journal of Business Ethics*, Vol. 153, No. 1, pp. 53–77, November 2018.

Harvey, Campbell, and Yan Liu, "A Census of the Factor Zoo," SSRN White Paper, No. 3341728, draft, February 25, 2019.

Holt, Charles A., and Susan K. Laury, "Risk Aversion and Incentive Effects," *American Economic Review*, Vol. 92, No. 5, pp. 1644–1655, December 2002.

Horowitz, Joel L., Tim Loughran, and N. E. Savin, "The Disappearing Size Effect," *Research in Economics*, Vol. 54, No. 1, March 2000, pp. 83–100.

Hsu, Jason, and James Ware, "Does a Culture of Blame Predict Performance for Asset Managers?," SSRN White Paper, No. 2438392, January, 2014

Ibbotson, Roger G., Peng Chen, and Kevin X. Zhu, "The A,B,Cs of Hedge Funds: Alphas, Betas, and Costs," *Financial Analysts Journal*, Vol. 67, No. 1, pp. 15–25, 2011.

Ilmanen, Antti, *Expected Returns: An Investor's Guide to Harvesting Market Rewards*, New York, John Wiley & Sons, 2011.

Jagannathan, Ravi, Alexey Malakhov, and Dmitry Novikov, "Do Hot Hands Exist Among Hedge Fund Managers? An Empirical Evaluation," *Journal of Finance*, Vol. 65, No.1, pp 23–39, January 13, 2010.

Jegadeesh, Narasimhan, and Sheridan Titman, "Returns to Buying Winners and Selling Losers: Implications for Stock Market Efficiency," *Journal of Finance*, Vol. 48, No. 1, pp. 65–91, March 1993.

Jenkinson, Tim, Howard Jones, and Jose Vicente Martinez, "Picking Winners? Investment Consultants' Recommendations of Fund Managers," *Journal of Finance*, Vol. 71, No. 5, pp. 2333–2370, October 2016.

Joenväärä, Juha, Robert Kosowski, and Pekka Tolonen, "Revisiting 'Stylized Facts' About Hedge Funds," Imperial College of London Business School, Working Paper, February 2012.

Jones, Edward E., and Victor A. Harris, "The Attribution of Attitudes," *Journal of Experimental Social Psychology*, Vol. 3, No. 1, pp. 1–24, 1967.

Jones, Meredith, "Women in Alternative Investments: A Marathon, Not a Sprint," Rothstein Kass Institute, Third Annual Study, December 2013.

Kahneman, Daniel, *Thinking, Fast and Slow*, New York, Farrar. Straus and Giroux, 2011.

Kahneman, Daniel, and Amos Tversky, "Prospect Theory: An Analysis of Decision Under Risk," *Econometrica*, Vol. 47, No. 2, pp. 263–292, March 1979.

Kaku, Michio, *The Future of Humanity*, reprint edition, New York, Anchor Books, April 2019.

Kaplan, Steven N., and Antoinette Schoar, "Private Equity Performance: Returns, Persistence, and Capital Flows," *Journal of Finance*, Vol. 60, No.4, August 12, 2005.

Kaplan, Steven N., Berk A. Sensoy, and Per Strömberg, "How Well Do Venture Capital Databases Reflect Actual Investments?," SSRN White Paper, No. 939073, September 2002.

Korniotis, George, and Alok Kumar, "Does Investment Skill Decline Due to Cognitive Aging or Improve with Experience?," SSRN White Paper, No. 880460, July 20, 2007.

Kozlowksi, Rob, "Seattle City Employees Hikes 3 Target Allocations While Dropping Diversifying Strategies," *Pensions & Investments*, January 14, 2020.

Kruger, Justin, and David Dunning, "Unskilled and Unaware of It: How Difficulties in Recognizing One's Own Incompetence Lead to Inflated Self-Assessments," *Journal of Personality and Social Psychology*, Vol. 77, No. 6, pp. 1121–1134, 1999.

Kumar, Pavrita, "Hedge Fund Characteristics and Performance Persistence: Evidence from 1996–2006," *Quarterly Journal of Finance*, Vol. 5, No. 2, pp. 1–43, 2015.

L'Her, Jean-Francois, Rossita Stoyanova, Kathryn Shaw, William Scott, and Charissa Lai, "A Bottom-Up Approach to the Risk-Adjusted Performance of the Buyout Fund Market," *Financial Analysts Journal*, Vol. 72, No. 4, pp. 36–48, 2016.

Liang, Bing, "On the Performance of Hedge Funds," Financial Analysts Journal, Vol. 55, No. 4, pp. 72-85, July/August 1999

Litt, Ab, Taly Reich, Senia Maymin, and Baba Shiv, "Pressure and Perverse Flights to Familiarity," *Journal of Psychological Science*, Vol. 22, No. 4, pp. 523–531, March 3, 2011.

Litterman, Robert, and Jose Scheinkman, "Common Factors Affecting Bond Returns," *Journal of Fixed Income*, Vol. 1, No. 1, pp. 54–61, Summer 1991.

Ljungqvist, Alexander, and Matthew Richardson, "The Cash Flow, Return and Risk Characteristics of Private Equity," National Bureau of Economic Research, NBER Working Paper No. 9454, January 9, 2003.

Lo, Andrew W., *Adaptive Markets: Financial Evolution at the Speed of Thought*, Princeton, NJ, Princeton University Press, 2017.

Loeys, Jan, and Laurent Fransolet, "Have Hedge Funds Eroded Market Opportunities?," JP Morgan, Market Strategy, October 1, 2004.

Lohr, Steve, "Slow Down, Brave Multitasker, and Don't Read This in Traffic," *New York Times*, March 25, 2007, https://www.nytimes.com/2007/03/25/business/25multi.html.

Loomis, Carol, "The Jones Nobody Keeps Up With," *Fortune* magazine, 1966; reprinted December 29, 2015.

Lopez-de-Silanes, Florencio, Ludovic Phalippou, and Oliver Gottschalg, "Giants at the Gate: Investment Returns and Diseconomies of Scale in Private Equity," Working Paper, draft, August 2, 2013.

MacArthur, Hugh, Brenda Rainey, and Johanne Dessard, "Global Private Equity Report 2019," Bain & Company, February 2019.

Malkiel, Burton, *A Random Walk Down Wall Street*, New York, W. W. Norton & Company, 1973.

Malmendier, Ulrike, and Geoffrey Tate, "Behavioral CEOs: The Role of Managerial Overconfidence," *Journal of Economic Perspectives,"* Vol. 29, No. 4, pp. 37–60, Fall 2015.

Markowitz, Harry, "Portfolio Selection," *Journal of Finance*, Vol. 7, No. 1, pp. 77–91, March 1952(a).

Markowitz, Harry, "The Utility of Wealth," *Journal of Political Economy*, Vol. 60, No. 2, pp. 151–158, 1952(b).

Marr, Bernard, "How Much Data Do We Create Every Day? The Mind-Blowing Stats Everyone Should Read," *Forbes*, May 21, 2018.

Maslow, Abraham, "A Theory of Human Motivation," *Psychological Review*, Vol. 50, No. 4, pp. 370–396, 1943.

Mauboussin, Michael, *The Success Equation*, Boston, Harvard Business Press, 2012.

McConnell, John J., Steven E. Sibley, and Wei Xu, "The Stock Price Performance of Spin-Off Subsidiaries, Their Parents, and the Spin-Off ETF, 2001–2013," *Journal of Portfolio Management,* Vol. 42, No. 1, pp. 143–452, Fall 2015.

McDevitt, Kevin, and Michael Schramm, "2018 U.S. Fund Flows Trends in 5 Charts: Investors Shunned Most of Wall Street Last Year," *Morningstar,* January 28, 2019.

Merton, Robert K., "The Self-Fulfilling Prophecy," *Antioch Review,* Vol. 8, No. 2, pp. 193–210, Summer 1948.

Michaels, Dave, "SEC Chairman Wants to Let More Main Street Investors in on Private Deals," *Wall Street Journal,* August 30, 2018.

Middleton, Timothy, *The Bond King: Investment Secrets from PIMCO's Bill Gross,* Hoboken, NJ, John Wiley & Sons, 2004.

Mills, C. Wright, *The Power Elite,* New York, Oxford University Press, 1956.

Mitchell, Olivia, and Ping Lung Hsin, "Public Pension Governance and Performance," National Bureau of Economic Research, NBER Working Paper No. 4632, draft, January 1994.

Montier, James, Albert Edwards, Philip Isherwood, and Karen Olney, "Global Equity Strategy: Behaving Badly," DrKW Macro Research, February 2, 2006.

Moore, Gordon E., "Cramming More Components onto Integrated Circuits," *Electronics,* Vol. 38, No. 19, April 19, 1965.

Muralidhar, Arun, and Sanjay Muralidhar, "The Case for SMART Rebalancing," in *QFinance: The Ultimate Resource,* London, Bloomsbury Publishing, 2009, pp. 297–300.

Muralidhar, Sid, and Emerson Berlik, "What's Your Risk Appetite? Helping Financial Advisors Better Serve Clients (by Quantifying Kahneman-Tversky's Value Function)," *Journal of Personal Finance,* Vol. 16, No. 2, pp. 20–36, Fall 2017.

Murphy, Kevin R., "Is the Relationship Between Cognitive Ability and Job Performance Stable over Time?" *Human Performance,* Vol. 2, No. 3, pp. 183–200, 1989.

Nesbitt, Stephen, "An Examination of State Pension Performance, 2000 to 2017," Cliffwater White Paper, September 12, 2018.

O'Boyle, Ernest H., Jr,, Donelson R. Forsyth, George C. Banks, and Michael A. McDaniel, "A Meta-Analysis of the Dark Triad and Work Behavior: A Social Exchange Perspective," *Journal of Applied Psychology,* Vol. 97, No.3, pp. 557–579, October 2011.

Pearson, Helen, "Science and Intuition: Do Both Have a Place in Clinical Decision Making?," *British Journal of Nursing*, Vol. 22, No. 4, pp. 212–215, February/March 2013.

PerTrac, "Impact of Fund Size and Age on Hedge Fund Performance," White Paper, September 2011.

Phalippou, Ludovic, "The Performance of Private Equity Funds," *Review of Financial Studies*, Vol. 22, No. 4, pp. 1747–1776, April 2009.

Pink, Daniel H., *Drive: The Surprising Truth About What Motivates Us*, New York, Riverhead Books, 2011.

Pojarliev, Momtchil, and Richard Levich, "Do Professional Currency Managers Beat the Benchmark?," *Financial Analysts Journal*, Vol. 64, No. 5, December 2008, pp. 18–32.

Pojarliev, Momtchil, and Richard Levich, "Trades of the Living Dead: Style Differences, Style Persistence and Performance of Currency Fund Managers," *Journal of International Money and Finance*, Vol. 29, No. 8, pp. 1752–1775, December 2010.

Pojarliev, Momtchil, and Richard Levich, *The Role of Currency in Institutional Portfolios*, London, Riskbooks, pp. 355–399, 2014.

Preqin, "Hedge Funds with Highest Performance Fees Deliver Best Net Returns," press release, August 29, 2013.

Preqin, "The $1bn Club: Largest Hedge Fund Managers," *Hedge Fund Spotlight*, Vol. 7, No. 4, pp. 2–4, May 2015.

Preqin, "Making the Case for First-Time Funds," *Preqin Special Report*, November 2016.

Promberger, Marianne, and Theresa Marteau, "When Do Financial Incentives Reduce Intrinsic Motivation? Comparing Behaviors Studied in Psychological and Economic Literatures," *Health Psychology*, Vol. 32, No. 9, pp. 950–957, September 2013.

Redick, Thomas S., Zach L. Shipstead, Tyler Harrison, Kenny L. Hicks, David E. Fried, David Z. Hambrick, Michael J. Kane, and Randall W. Engle, "No Evidence of Intelligence Improvement After Working Memory Training: A Randomized, Placebo-Controlled Study," *Journal of Experimental Psychology*, Vol. 142, No. 2, pp. 359–379, 2013.

Reinsel, David, John Gantz, and John Rydning, "The Digitization of the World: From Edge to Core," IDC White Paper, No. US44413318, November 2018.

Rogers, Robert D., and Stephen Monsell, "Costs of Predictable Switch Between Simple Cognitive Tasks," *Journal of Experimental Psychology: General*, Vol. 124, No. 2, pp. 207–231, 1995.

Rose-Smith, Imogen, "New Fee Structure Offers Hope to Besieged Hedge Funds," *Institutional Investor*, January 24, 2017.

Ross, Lee, "The Intuitive Psychologist and His Shortcomings: Distortions in the Attribution Process," *Advances in Experimental Social Psychology*, Vol. 10, pp. 173–220, 1977.

Rouwenhorst, K. Geert, "The Origins of Mutual Funds," Yale ICF Working Paper, No. 04-48, December 12, 2004.

Rubinstein, Joshua, Jeffrey Evans, and David Meyer, "Executive Control of Cognitive Processes in Task Switching," *Journal of Experimental Psychology, Human Perception and Performance*, Vol. 27, No. 4, pp. 763–797, 2001.

Schacht, Kurt, and Jonathan Stokes, "Code of Conduct for Members of a Pension Scheme Governing Body," CFA Institute, 2008.

Schelling, Christopher, "The Hierarchy of Alpha," *Alternative Investment Analyst Review*, Vol. 4, No. 2, pp. 29–32, Summer 2015.

Schelling, Christopher, "High 3i: Personality Metrics of Strong Asset Managers," *aiCIO*, April 26, 2016.

Schelling, Christopher, "Getting Rich Off the Management Fee," *Institutional Investor*, February 23, 2017.

Schelling, Christopher, "The 'No Jerks' Rule of Investing," *Institutional Investor*, September 13, 2018.

Schelling, Christopher, "Manager Research Matters Even More Than You Think," *Institutional Investor*, July 24, 2019.

Schelling, Christopher M., "The Focus on Fees: A Guide to Preparing Your Funds," *Hedge Fund Journal*, No. 89, pp. 1–2, September 2013.

Schelling, Christopher M., "Guest Column: A Better Tactic for Hedge Funds Analysis," *Chief Investment Officer Magazine*, August 13, 2014.

Schmidt, Frank L., John E. Hunter, and Alice N. Outerbridge, "Impact of Job Experience and Ability on Job Knowledge, Work Sample Performance, and Supervisory Ratings of Job Performance," *Journal of Applied Psychology*, Vol. 71, No. 3, pp. 432–439, 1986.

Schneeweis, Thomas, and Richard Spurgin, "Hedge Funds: Portfolio Risk Diversifiers, Return Enhancers or Both?," University of Massachusetts, 2000.

Securities and Exchange Commission, "Investment Trusts and Investment Companies," US Government Printing Office, 1939.

Securities and Exchange Commission, "SEC Proposes to Update Accredited Investor Definition to Increase Access to Investments," press release, December 18, 2019, https://www.sec.gov/news/press-release/2019-265.

Seddiq, Oma, "How the World's Billionaires Got So Rich" *Forbes,* March 10, 2018.

Smith, Anita, "Exploring the Legitimacy of Intuition as a Form of Nursing Knowledge," *Nursing Standard,* Vol. 23, No. 40, pp. 35–40, June 2009.

Sorkin, Andrew Ross, *Too Big to Fail,* New York, Penguin Group, 2009.

State of Wisconsin Investment Board, *2018 Retirement Funds Annual Report,* https://7ffb9e60-f2dc-4359-b148-1db6b9d76c71.filesusr.com/ugd/69fc6d_e0c664dc85964d78953e358163b6a534.pdf.Retr.

Stattman, Dennis, "Book Values and Stock Returns," *Chicago MBA: A Journal of Selected Papers,* No. 4, pp. 25–45, 1980.

Stein, Jeremy C., "Information Production and Capital Allocation: Decentralized Versus Hierarchical Firms," *Journal of Finance,* Vol. 57, No. 5, pp. 1891–1921, October 2002.

Stewart, James B., *Den of Thieves,* New York, Touchstone, 1992.

Steyer, Robert, "NYCERS Pulls the Plug on Hedge Funds," *Pensions & Investments,* April 18, 2016, https://www.pionline.com/article/20160418/PRINT/304189975/nycers-pulls-the-plug-on-hedge-funds.

Svenson, Ola, "Are We All Less Risky and More Skillful Than Our Fellow Drivers?" *Acta Psychologica,* Vol. 47, No. 2, pp. 143–148, February 1981.

Swensen, David, *Pioneering Portfolio Management: An Unconventional Approach to Institutional Investment,* New York, Free Press, 2009.

ten Brinke, Leanne, Aimee Kish, and Dacher Keltner, "Hedge Fund Managers with Psychopathic Tendencies Make for Worse Investors," *Personality and Social Psychology Bulletin,* Vol. 44, No. 2, pp. 214–223, October 2017.

ten Brinke, Leanne, Christopher C. Liu, Dacher Keltner, and Sameer B. Srivastava, "Virtues, Vices, and Political Influence in the U.S. Senate," *Psychological Science,* Vol. 27, No. 1, pp. 85–93, November 2015.

Teo, Melvyn, "Does Size Matter in the Hedge Fund Industry?," SSRN Working Paper, No. 1331754, January 23, 2009.

Tett, Gillian, *Fool's Gold: How the Bold Dream of a Small Tribe at J.P. Morgan Was Corrupted by Wall Street Greed and Unleashed a Catastrophe,* New York, Free Press, 2009.

Till, Hilary, "Structural Sources of Return & Risk in Commodity Futures Investments," *Commodities Now*, Vol. 10, No. 2, pp. 57–65, 2006.

Tipple, Brian, "Avoiding the Pitfalls: Best Practices in Manager Research and Due Diligence," *CFA Institute Conference Proceedings Quarterly*, Vol. 27, No. 2, pp. 46–51, June 2010.

Toner, Ian, "Conscious Currency: A New Approach to Understanding Currency Exposure," *Russell Research*, Russell Investments White Paper, November 2010.

Van Gelderen, Joop Huli, and Georgi Kyosev, "Factor Investing from Concept T Implementation," SSRN White Paper, No. 3313364, January, 2019.

Ware, Jim, Keith Robinson, Michael Falk, and Liz Severyns, "Linking Strong Culture to Success: Findings from FCG's Elite Culture Firms," *Focus Consulting Group*, White Paper, 2015, http://www.focuscgroup.com/wp-content/uploads/2015/11/Linking_Strong_Culture_to_Success.pdf.

Watson, A. J., "One Factor That Improves Angel Investment Returns by 7x," Fundify, August 11, 2015, https://medium.com/a-startup-blog/one-factor-that-improves-angel-investment-returns-by-7x-e2367240f1f6.

Weber, Maximilian, *The Protestant Ethic and the Spirit of Capitalism*, New York, Scribner, 1958.

Weber, Maximilian, *Politics as a Vocation*, Philadelphia, Fortress Press, 1965.

Weidig, Tom, and Pierre-Yves Mathonet, "The Risk Profiles of Private Equity," SSRN White Paper, No. 495482, January 2004.

Welsh, Ian D., and Carolyn M. Lyons, "Evidence-Based Care and the Case for Intuition and Tacit Knowledge in Clinical Assessment and Decision Making in Mental Health Nursing Practice: An Empirical Contribution to the Debate," *Journal of Psychiatric and Mental Health Nursing*, Vol. 8, No. 4, pp. 299–305, August 2001.

Westen, Drew, Pavel S. Blagov, Keith Harenski, Clint Kilts, and Stephan Hamann, "Neural Bases of Motivated Reasoning: An fMRI Study of Emotional Constraints on Partisan Political Judgment in the 2004 U.S. Presidential Election," *Journal of Cognitive Neuroscience*, Vol. 18, No. 11, pp. 1947–1958, 2006.

Whitson, Jennifer A., and Adam D. Galinsky, "Lacking Control Increases Illusory Pattern Perception," *Science*, Vol. 322, No. 5898, pp. 115–117, October 2008.

Whyte, Amy, "How One Small Pension Fund Added $1 Billion in Value," *Institutional Investor*, April 18, 2019.

Whyte, Amy, "Sports Cars, Psychopaths, and Testosterone: Inside the New Frontier of Fund Manager Research," *Institutional Investor*, July 30, 2019.

Yermack, David, "Higher Market Valuation of Companies with a Small Board of Directors," *Journal of Financial Economics,* Vol. 40, No. 2, pp. 185–211, February 1996.

Zhu, Ning, "The Local Bias of Individual Investors," Yale ICF Working Paper, No. 02-30, October 2002.

Index

About the Author

Christopher M. Schelling is a highly experienced institutional investor, author, and columnist. Over nearly 20 years, Chris has invested roughly $5 billion and met with over 3,000 managers across hedge funds, real assets, private credit, and private equity funds, and he currently is a Managing Director at Windmuehle Funds, a boutique alternatives investment firm headquartered in Austin, Texas. Previously, he was Director of Private Equity investing for the $30 billion Texas Municipal Retirement System. He also worked as Deputy CIO and Director of Absolute Returns at the Kentucky Retirement Systems and as an adjunct Professor of Finance at the University of Kentucky, lecturing on alternatives. Schelling's work has appeared in the *Journal of Private Equity* and *Alternative Investment Analyst Review*, and he's routinely cited for his expertise in *Institutional Investor*, where he is a contributing columnist, as well as the *Wall Street Journal*, the *Hedge Fund Journal*, *Dow Jones News*, and many other investing publications.